There i
Season

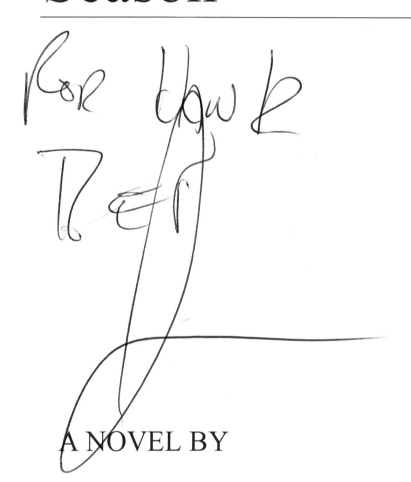

A NOVEL BY

J. HARDING MONTGOMERY

For my children:

Shawn Thomas, Emma Lee,
Sara Maureen and James Eric;
May peace always be with You,
May you never Know
The ravages of War,
And may you always Do
Your Homework,
No matter what Kind.

To order more copies go to: Amazon Books.Com
There is a Season: An Odyssey into Family
J. Harding Montgomery
http://www.amazon.com/dp/1469999021/ref=c
m_sw_su_dp

Contact the author at: jhardingmontgomery@gmail.com

The Author wishes to express his gratitude to:

Woody Carmack, President, Vietnam Vets in Canada;
For his understanding of the issues facing Canada's
Vietnam Vets and his untiring work for them; his patience in
answering the authors' endless questions; and the various
members of Vietnam Vets in Canada, for their comments,
criticisms and strongly worded suggestions.
*Thank you, Woody. Always a beer in my fridge with your
name on it.*

Istvan (Steve) Lazlo Bekessy, Master Sergeant, People's
Army of Hungary;
Participant in the revolt of 1956, who remained
underground in Hungary until May of 1957, at great risk to
himself, to care for his mother and sister until he could safely
flee to Canada.
Steve commented that the sections in the novel, dealing
with the Hungarian Secret Police, the AVO, were "too soft". I
told him that the novel was not about the AVO, but about
those that fell into their hands and survived to tell about it.
Steve knew more than he wanted to about the AVO.
*Rest in Peace, Dear Friend; Your place in Heaven is
assured.*

The Canada Council for the Arts (Explorations), for their
generous support for the research portion of 'There is a
Season'.

From the Author:

I wrote this novel because I lived it. In 1970, like a couple of my characters, I abandoned my family's tradition of military service and became a miner in the Yukon. In the mining camps I taught Basic English to refugees from Eastern Europe, many of them veterans of the Second War and the revolts in Warsaw, Berlin, Budapest and Prague. Some, then in their late forties and early fifties, were child slave miners and survived the death camps of Hitler and Stalin. Others were low-grade war criminals, and among them, unrepentant Nazis. Feuds were common and suspicious deaths not uncommon. The other common thing among them was their hatred of communists.

Helping me teach the European refugees were members of the latest generation of refugees to Canada: draft dodgers and deserters from the U.S.A. As they refused to participate in the war in Vietnam, this made them, in the eyes of some of the European refugees, communist sympathizers, and targets for their hostility.

As my own ancestry is American (my father left California to serve in the Canadian First Division during WW 2), many of the Europeans' looked well upon him, but poorly upon myself. I was not in Vietnam where "I belonged". I explained to them that I was Canadian and not subject to the draft. To them, this was meaningless. My father was American and served in the Canadian Army, therefore I, as a Canadian, should serve in the American Army.

We never settled that.

VANCOUVER, CANADA
FEBRUARY 23, 1972

SUNDAY NIGHT

Stephan Kovacs paced the living room. He was at his parents for mandatory Sunday dinner but he wasn't hungry. The familiar and comforting aromas of paprika stew, dumplings, and walnut filled pancakes didn't comfort him. He'd been keeping up a false front for them, but he couldn't do it any longer. His knotted stomach and migraine headaches told him that. Tonight, he had to tell them the truth. He wasn't lying, but he wasn't being truthful either.

One of his first moral memories was when he lied to his mother Tara, about the last cookie in the cookie jar. As she washed out his mouth with soap she said, "Before all others, be true to yourself."

"There's a special room in hell," his father Janos often said, "reserved for liars."

That was the last time he told an outright lie. He couldn't remember if it was the mouthful of soap or not understanding what being true to yourself meant that stuck so deeply. He did know what a room in hell meant, and he felt he was there.

"You got your exam marks," Janos said.

"Yup,"

"And,"

"All 'A's. Okay, I'm bullshitting you, one B plus,"

Janos grinned. "You don't get shot for one B plus,"

"Glad to hear that," Stephan said.

"But you do for two,"

"Oh, be quiet, both of you," Tara said. She stood by the mantle over the fireplace, gazing into the family photos. She took down the photo of when they first arrived in Canada, the three of them, smiling in front of Canadian Immigration headquarters in Ottawa.

"Who would have thought back in Hungary," she dusted it when it didn't need dusting, "that our Little Stephan would become an engineer?"

Janos joined her at the mantle, gazing into the photo. "Think I was better looking back then,"

Tara raised her eyebrows and smiled, "Yes,"

"And after he graduates," Janos said, "he designs 'em, and I build 'em."

Stephan felt he was betraying his parents and Janos said he was betrayed during the revolution in Budapest, but that's all he said. The revolution gave him nightmares; he'd wake up screaming, soaked in sweat and Tara said he made the sheets drip. Stephan worried that this time; he would be the cause of his fathers' nightmares. Telling his father the truth wasn't going to be good for his heart either, and something happened to his heart in the revolution. Stephan wondered that if he could get his father to talk about it, then maybe there was something he could do about it. He sure talked about Hungary and the Russian occupation, but he didn't talk about his part the revolution. Today it was Stephen's turn to talk and all his parents wanted to talk about was him being an engineer.

The phone rang. "Yes", Janos said. "Ah, Georgi, how are you?"

Janos turned to Tara, "It's Georgi. He's head of the Hungarian Cultural Society now,"

"You tell him 'hello' for me," Tara said.

"Tara says 'hello' Georgi. What's that... yes, he's here... it's another three years before he graduates... yes, he's doing fine, all 'A's he says... okay, I'll tell him that... and I'll see you Saturday at the Cultural Center... good bye, Georgi."

Stephan knew what his father and Georgi were talking about and the thought of another three years made him shudder. What about what I want to do?

Janos smiled. "Stephan that was Georgi; we were together at the Kilian Barracks during the revolt in Budapest, we came to Canada together. He runs an engineering firm right here in Vancouver and he says there's always a job for the son of Janos Kovacs."

Stephan thought about being the son of Janos Kovacs. When would he become Stephan Kovacs, known by his own name, and not by his relations?

I should wait until after dinner, he thought, when they're both settled down, full stomachs can do that. But after dinner his parents never stopped talking about how well university was going, how high his grades were, what a bright future he had, how proud they were of him. He couldn't break their hearts by telling them the truth.

So he kept up the falseness that all was well, and his stomach stayed knotted and his migraines got worse. They had done so much for him; fought a revolution and lost it, fled their home for a new and unknown one, and now he couldn't even pay them back.

MONDAY MORNING

Stephan lay in bed, wide-awake. He couldn't take it any longer. It was a hard battle these past few weeks and now each day ground by, hour by hour, just getting through the day.

Every morning was the same, drag himself out of bed, then decide on breakfast; bacon and eggs, or cereal with milk, or French toast in maple syrup, or toast with strawberry or raspberry jam; some kind of marmalade? And then the dishes.

Sheila always complained about the dishes, and Stephan was getting real tired of her. She'd been his girlfriend since forever and everybody assumed they would marry. She always made sure he made it to school on time, borrowed her Moms' car on days when Stephan had early hockey practice, waited for him when he had extra classes in algebra. Sheila had always been good to him, but Stephan wondered if she was his girlfriend or his mother. She didn't wonder, not anymore, and nobody ever asked Stephan what he thought. She came over and complained about his clothes on the floor. She'd take his clothes home, wash them, bring them back, put them in the correct drawer in his dresser. Stephan took them out of the dresser and threw them back on the floor so he could find the ones he wanted.

Sheila never cared about things that mattered. She cared about her hair and her clothes and she cared way too much about Stephen's hair and clothes. His jeans were dirty, tee shirt had holes, hair was too long, and why did he have to have a beard? She never cared about what Stephan cared about.

When he talked about the war in Vietnam, something he cared deeply about, her eyes glazed over. When he wanted to watch the news, she wanted to watch sit-coms. When he wanted to talk politics, she wanted to talk TV shows.

First thing every morning, Stephan thought, his shit stream was in full flow. A day crowded with petty challenges was doomed.

It was boredom that was killing Stephan. Every single day he had to live the life of a university student. There was nothing to sink his teeth into, nothing that got his heart pumping or his blood flowing. Class by class, text book by text book, he felt his life slipping away and there no way to tell his father and mother that he hated university, and that he would give anything to get out of it. He had already spent thirteen years sitting down in classrooms reading textbooks, with three more years and another mountain of textbooks still waiting. If only he could only find a way out, something his parents would understand, something they would agree to; then he could really start living.

For Stephan, the only thing on his mind was adventure, a challenge, some real living where things really mattered. He spent his spare time going over maps of the world, following the routes of the ancient explorers. From Marco Polo to the Pilgrims, he wanted to join them all. As child he read Moby Dick, Lord Jim, Treasure Island, Huck Finn and Tom Sawyer, Robinson Crusoe and Twenty Thousand Leagues Under the Sea; and every mystery the Hardy Boys ever solved. He could see himself in every one of them. He read all the war comics, but was bored with super-hero comics. They were too unreal, those stories didn't matter; he couldn't see himself in them. But his all time favorites were the adventure stories of Jack London and the rugged poems of Robert Service. Tales from the gold rush in Dawson City in the Yukon Territory; where immigrants, just like him, battled the freezing cold and the wild rivers, the bears and the wolves, all to get rich in gold.

Now that was an adventure worth having, but it two thousand miles to the north, and for a university student; a world away. No matter how much he hated where he was, dreamed of all the places he wanted to go, he could never forget all those evenings his father came home late from work.

"More overtime," he always said, "only way to pay for your university."

His mother worked as a waitress, saved her tips in a jar on her bedside dresser.

She always smiled proudly, saying, "I don't mind waiting on people, text books cost a lot. You're in engineering school, first university graduate in the family."

Stephan considered flunking out. He could go on strike; stop reading textbooks, stop writing exams. Other straight 'A' students bombed out their first year, why couldn't he? But he knew that wasn't the way. If he was going to get out, and he knew he had to get out, he was going out the front door. There was no way he was going to sneak out the back, there was just no way he could do that. Not a chance. Whatever way he got out, he had to be able to look his parents straight in the eye and give them one hell of a good reason. That much he was sure of.

All this was on his mind when he worked up enough energy to survive another lecture by a professor who regularly pissed him off.

He squirmed in his seat in the overcrowded lecture hall. He knew he was lucky to get a seat, but that was only because he wasn't as late as usual. He didn't feel lucky; he only felt that burning need to be somewhere else. No matter which way he twisted or turned, he couldn't get comfortable. The seat in front of him was too close, he couldn't stretch his legs so his calf muscles cramped. The seat behind him was too close; he always got somebody's knees jammed in his back. The sliding, folding desk with the up-and-drop style trapped him in a tight wood and steel box.

The air was dry and stale, and everybody's breathe stunk. He always sucked for a lungful of air and never got it. The walls pushed in and the ceiling pressed down. The lights were too bright; the glare forced him to squint. He didn't listen to the professor. He couldn't stop thinking about all the posters he saw every day in the hallways.

They all called for an end to the war in Vietnam. He thought about the nightly news on television: helicopters landing in deep grass, soldiers jumping out and piling in the wounded and dead, jet planes raining napalm on grass huts.

An irritated whisper opened his eyes. "Stephan, pay attention, the Professor is staring at you,"

He turned and looked quietly at Sheila. The same face with the same expression.

"Did you write that down, it'll be on the exam? Stop chewing your pen, stop daydreaming, Stephan, pay attention!"

Stephan hated lectures; they put him to sleep and strangers woke him up.

Sheila tapped the end of her nose; "I've had it to here with your don't-give-a-shit attitude,"

"So, what's your point?"

"I just don't know what you want anymore,"

"Well, I know what I want, and this sure as hell ain't it."

Stephan tried once again to lean back, to get comfortable in his cramped chair. He squinted into the glaring lights as the nightly news on Vietnam did a rerun in his head. He thought about the American soldiers, just a few years older than himself. Why do they have peace signs on their helmets when they're fighting a war? If they had a draft in Canada for Vietnam, what would he do? If he went, would he put a peace sign on his helmet? And if not, what country could he escape to? When he saw the choppers filling with body bags, he broke into a sweat.

Janos told him that it was so bad living under communism in Hungary that they had to revolt, almost a civil war, but they lost to the Russians. Was it the same in Vietnam? He tried to discuss it with the other students, tell them what his father told him, but they wouldn't listen. The war was wrong, they said, and that's all there was to it. Their answer was too simple.

How can they be so sure, he thought, when they know nothing of how communism really works?

He couldn't separate Hungary from Vietnam; he felt like he was on a seesaw, going back and forth, from one country to the other, one piece of history to the other; one migraine headache to the next.

Stephan knew students and professors on campus who fled
the United States because of the war. On the nightly news the
veterans, men who fought the war, not talked about it, were
marching in the streets. It was the veterans, like his father, that
convinced Stephan that something was terribly wrong in
Vietnam, beyond the nightly news, beyond the history of
Hungary. What was it?

Different countries, different languages and customs, even
different races. What made them the same? They both fought
the Russian supported communists; Hungary lost, and now it
looked like Vietnam, even with American support, was going
to lose.
What would happen then?

Stephan considered dropping out of engineering, switching
to history. Maybe there would be answers there. Hungarian
history was made and there were lessons to be learned;
American history was being made, and nobody was learning
anything. It just didn't make any sense.

Sometimes he couldn't even read his textbooks; no matter
how hard he tried to study engineering, it was history that
wouldn't leave him alone. When he tried to push history out of
his head, the nightly news on Vietnam would take over.

He kept reading the same page, over and over again, and
remembered nothing. There wasn't any more room in his head;
it was over crowded with everything he didn't want to think
about. He didn't ponder these questions, they plagued him.
And what really bothered him was why these questions
bothered him at all. Why couldn't he just accept that some
questions simply didn't have answers; then leave it at that.

Stephan felt a form of kinship with the American refugees.
Like them, his parents fled their home for Canada, a
welcoming country that wasn't at war with anyone.

But he had difficulty feeling any sympathy for them; they
still had choices.

Janos told him if they stayed in Hungary, he'd be a baby without a family. The communists would shoot his parents. The Americans could stay home and they wouldn't be shot. He didn't like it when the Americans got sympathy from other Canadians; he felt they hadn't earned it.

They weren't refugees from their own war in their own home; they were refugees from someone else's war in someone else's home. He wondered if they should even be called 'refugees'.

He also didn't like it when the Americans got abuse from other Canadians; he thought they should be left alone. It maybe someone else's war, but they still had to leave their homes. ` His father talked about Hungary before the revolution, but he either couldn't or wouldn't talk about the revolution itself.

Why doesn't anyone at the Hungarian Cultural Center explain things to him? Why did they always say, "Ask your father?"

His father wouldn't answer his questions, only talk about how bad life was before the revolution and why they had to fight, then why they had to leave.

Stephan barely remembered Hungary; Canada was home, and he knew he didn't have to worry about being sent to war, or being shot, or being abandoned. But that didn't stop his migraines. Just like Vietnam, something was missing.

Nobody would tell him what really happened in the revolution and nobody could tell him what was really happening in Vietnam. He felt that if he met a Vietnam vet, someone who'd fought in the jungles and marched in the streets, he'd explain Vietnam to him. Then he'd understand what was going on over there, so that he could understand what was going on back here. He felt as though he was on a see-saw that kept him going back and forth, and the only thing he understood was that neither war was really his; but it wouldn't leave him alone; there were too many questions that didn't have answers; and his migraines kept getting worse.

The professor interrupted the dull roar in Stephan's head. "Mr. Kovacs! May I have your attention, please?"

Stephan opened his eyes to the professor's glare.

"In case you haven't been paying attention, the review I am now giving is worth thirty percent of your final course grade. Think of that Mr. Kovacs! Thirty percent!"

Stephan nodded. Thirty percent of what? Any of those soldiers with the peace signs on their helmets give a shit about my thirty percent? Why won't my father talk about the revolution?

He looked at the Professor, "I don't give a shit about your thirty percent."

The professor's glasses fell off the end of his nose and clattered across the floor, making the only sound in the lecture hall. All the other students, in one quick move, sucked in all the dry, stale air, then held it in. Stephan stood up.

Sheila took his attention for the last time, looked up and said, "It's all over, you and I are finished. I don't love you anymore."

He knocked his notebook to the floor as he untrapped himself from his desk. He stepped on his notebook as he edged his way down the narrow aisle, trying not to step on anybody's toes.

He turned to look at Sheila. Her face went narrow, sharp and hard while her thick make-up cracked and her eyes darkened.

"Over," she said. "Done."

The professor didn't pick up his glasses. His eyes glazed over, his eyebrows closed together, his mouth ground shut.

Stephan stopped when he got clear of the seats and turned to face the professor, who blinked, waiting for Stephan to speak. The quiet in the hall was louder than the nightly news.

"Do you have anything to say for yourself," the professor said.

"No," Stephan said. He turned his back to the professor and started walking towards the door.

"Mr. Kovacs, you may consider yourself removed from the class."

Stephan stopped, kept his back to the professor, then shrugged as the nightly news repeated itself. He sighed and walked out the door.

In the hallway he looked at the posters again; pictures that jumped out and slapped him in the face, crying villagers, crying soldiers; bold black headlines screaming out at him:

Stop the War! End Canadian Complicity!

In the courtyard, he pulled in a deep breath of fresh air, sat on the lawn, thought things over. Cross-legged on the grass, he took his pen and doodled elaborate designs on his jeans.

Then he threw the pen away. Where to go from here? He went back in to the hallway, took a short cut to the pub, through the Student Job Center. Get a job?

On the far wall was a map of the world. His eyes stopped at Vietnam, then Hungary, then to the billboards where the job-cards were tacked. Car washers, dishwashers, hamburger flippers, lawn mowers; all boring. Then he saw a faded and yellowed card, half-buried under newer cards. He pulled it off for a closer look.

Laborers needed: Gold Mining in the Yukon Territory

Stephan jumped, and when he landed he knew exactly what to do. This was it, his ticket out, right to where he always wanted to go. Every gold miner was rich, everybody knew that.

Wasn't university all about a high paying job and getting rich? He'd get rich mining gold, pay back Mom and Dad, go to Europe, Asia, Africa, buy a sailboat and sail the oceans, buy a camel and cross the deserts. When you're rich you can do anything.

His heart pounded, his blood charged, he stretched taller. He had to move quickly, barged his way to the front desk. "Still got any jobs in the Yukon,"

The receptionist didn't look up. "Wait your turn in line,"

"Fuck my turn in line. Got any jobs in the Yukon,"

She looked up and sneered. "Nothing but trappers and miners in the Yukon,"

"That's where I'm going."

He ran across the hallway to the university travel agency. "Can you get me to Dawson City?"

"Only Whitehorse,"

"Get me there,"

"I can book you a flight to Prince George. You can transfer there to Whitehorse. It leaves in two hours."

He glanced at his watch, wrote a check for a one-way ticket to Whitehorse, grabbed a taxi, packed his bag as the meter ran, beat his check to the bank, emptied out his last two hundred bucks, then sped off for the airport.

With eyes squeezed shut he remembered Jack London and Robert Service. These guys knew what adventure was.

So it wouldn't be Asia or Africa, Europe or the Mediterranean, or even South America or Australia, it would be the Yukon Territory, where he always wanted to go. A land of legends and myths; where men were men and it was always cold; ice and snow, husky dogs and howling wolves. Where he knew no one and no one knew him. He liked the sound of that, and the gold that would make him rich.

Stephan didn't eat on the two-hour flight to Prince George. He stared into the clouds, rubbed his knotted stomach, slouched down in his seat and groaned while his thoughts ran in tightening circles. What have I done? What's everybody going to say?

They'd say come home and get back to class. I can always go back to University after I get rich. I can pay my own way, I won't owe anybody anything, maybe send Mom and Dad to, that's it, and I'll buy them a holiday someplace.

Then they won't be so mad at me for wasting all that overtime Dad put in and all the nights mom worked, and a new car for Dad because he has to drive that jalopy.

All because my tuition was... they did all that for me? What have I done? I have to get rich; I have to pay them back for, well, everything.

I can have fun being a gold miner. Everybody gets rich mining gold, everybody knows that. I'll pay them back and they won't be mad at me.

At the Prince George airport he had twenty-five minutes before his flight left for Whitehorse. He wasn't hungry; he knew he had to eat, but his stomach was still too knotted. "I'll have a lettuce and tomato sandwich, milk and coffee," he said to a bored waitress.

She scribbled in her pad and wandered off. When she came back with his order, he picked up the sandwich and took a bite. He chewed on it, tried to swallow it, but it wouldn't go down. He chewed some more and it still wouldn't go down.

He put a napkin to his mouth and spit out a clump of half chewed sandwich. The waitress wandered by again and he ordered a beer. When it came he drank it in two gulps.

The call came to board the flight to Whitehorse. Stephan took a deep breath, held it in, then alone, he quietly walked down a long dark hallway. He wondered why it was dark, and then looked up to see that most of the light bulbs were broken.

When he looked back down, the hallway turned sharply and he was suddenly out on the tarmac.

The wind blew hard and drove cold wet snow into his face. He peered into the white blowing haze and saw a rusted old pick-up truck slowly pull a plane into view.

The plane had a two-tone blue and black paint job; most of the paint flaked off, long deep scratches across the entire body.

It pulled to a stop and Steve looked closely at small circular dents, about the size of his fist, scattered across the body and wing of the plane

Looking even closer, the dents swept in arcs and in some places the dents were patched over with duct tape. The tape was loose at the edges and now flapped noisily in the sharp wind.

The truck driver jumped down from his cab, and jumped into the truck box. He lifted up a folding set of metal stairs and dumped them out; they landed with a loud metallic crash.

He jumped out of the truck box, stepped around the stairs, unhooked the plane from his truck, and drove off into the snowstorm.

Steve stood behind a small group of passengers huddled together in a tight knot. There was an Eskimo couple, wearing brightly beaded rawhide parkas and each carried a small baby on their backs. They nodded and smiled at each other with shiny white teeth.

Two grizzled old guys wearing heavy black toques, knee high leather boots and patched green canvas coats with fur-trimmed hoods. They did a lot of chuckling and beard scratching.

Behind Stephan, a door slammed shut and a man marched out from behind the group. He was wearing a two-tone blue and black snowsuit. The suit was patched, and at the edges of the patches the stuffing stuck out. His face was hidden in a hood secured to the back of his coat with strips of duct tape.

He wrestled the folding stairs to a standing position, kicked each of the four legs, and then jammed them up against the planes' door. The stairs rattled as he ran up and struggled with the door. It opened a crack; the wind immediately blew it out of his hand.

He fell backwards, landed head first on the top stair, quickly grabbed a step and didn't fall any further. Pulling himself into a standing position, he wrestled the door open and leaning against it, yelled out,

"God damn it! What are y'all waiting for? This is a D.C.3. Best damn cargo plane ever built. Get in before she freezes up."

The Eskimo couple took turns running up the stairs and never stopped smiling. The stairs swayed in the wind, sounding like there were about to break, then they rolled away from the plane and stopped.

One of the two grizzled old guys patted the other on the back, grabbed the stairs and pushed them back up to the plane, they both cracked up laughing, and then he sprinted up the stairs.

The other grizzled old guy went up to the stairs, kicked them hard on the bottom step, jumped heavily onto it, then bouncing and crashing as much as he could, ran up the wobbly stairs.

At the top he turned and gave Stephan a mischievous grin.

"Hey kid! You gonna stand there with your thumb up your butt, you coming or what?"

Stephan carefully climbed up the first step. He was sure the bouncing and crashing the grizzled old guy had done was enough to finish them off.

They didn't look so tall from down on the ground, but now that he was on them, they seemed a whole lot higher.

They creaked and groaned in the wind, and started to sag. He looked down and the wheels were rolling away from the plane.

"Shit," he said, took a step, then "shit-shit-shit-shit-shit-shit," sprinted up the steps and jumped the last step into to the plane.

A stewardess met him at the doorway. She wore a wrinkled uniform; her dress didn't match her coat. Her make-up was pancake thick and she stank of cheap perfume.

"Welcome to Great Northern Airways, on our non-stop trip to the Yukon."

Her speech was slurred; Stephan caught a strong whiff of whiskey and peanuts. She leaned on him as she ushered him into a seat.

He looked at the seat cushions. They were faded from blue and black to gray and white. In some places patches were stitched together, with small tears opening at the stitches. There were no pockets on the back of the seats, just a rusted coat hanger bent into a hook to hold the plastic airsickness bag.

The plastic airsickness bag was wrinkled and worn, like it had been used before and washed out. The rug running down the aisle was worn through in the middle, showing bare metal. Stephan slouched in his seat and felt broken springs stabbing his back.

The pilot walked up the aisle to the cockpit. He was unshaven and had blood shot eyes. He wore thick glasses and was tall and skinny with a large beaked nose, narrow pointed forehead, and his buckteeth were criss-crossed. He seemed quite nervous.

Steve slouched deeper into his seat, beneath the broken springs.

The plane's engines fired, the whole plane shuddered from front to back, the engines coughed out. The engines fired again, the plane shuddered from front to back again, they coughed out again. Then there was a loud crack and huge flashes of bright orange flames shot out of the engines.

Clouds of thick black smoke followed and poured down onto the tarmac. The engines started rumbling unevenly and the misfiring made the plane vibrate to an offbeat shaking.

There was a clanking and grinding as the plane rumbled away from the terminal, and as the plane's engines started to rev-up they slowed their misfiring and started to purr.

The plane began to twist and bend as it headed down the runway picking up speed and the offbeat vibration returned. The plane left the ground, returned with a bone crunching thump, then bounced back into the air and Stephan's stomach went to his knees.

The stewardess held tightly to the seats as she struggled her way down the aisle to Stephan. With a free hand she pushed an old beer cooler rolling on a small baggage rack.

"You wanna beer?" she said.

"Yes please." Stephan said.

She sat down in the middle of the aisle, hiked up her skirt and kept the baggage rack from rolling away by clamping it between her knees. Stephan noticed she was wearing panty hose.

She rolled up her sleeves and reached into the cooler. It was full of ice and water that sloshed around and spilt on the floor. She grabbed a can of beer and opened it.

The can exploded foam on her face; she wiped the foam off by lowering her face into her dress and rubbing. She pulled her face out of her dress and smiled. Now her makeup was runny and smeared. She stretched out awkwardly to hand the beer to Stephan. He reached over, she pulled it back. "You can't have this one," she said, "its pilots' favorite brand."

She reached back into the cooler, grabbed another beer for Stephan, struggled to stand up, leaned against the rack so it wouldn't roll away, then straightened her skirt and her hair and rolled down her sleeves. She took her beer cooler baggage rack and slowly pushed it down the aisle.

The two grizzled old guys filled up on beer. One of them looked up at Stephan. "First time to the Yukon, kid?"

"Yes,"

"How old are you, kid?"

"Eighteen,"

"Eight-fucking-teen? You're too young for the Yukon, kid; it's going to eat you alive,"

The other grizzled old guy spoke to his friend, "And how old was you when you first come to the Yukon?"

"Eighteen,"

"You was never eighteen, you was born old and ugly,"

"Fuck you, I was so eighteen. Just before I was nineteen,"

"I didn't know you could count,"

"Fucken, eh? One, two, three and there's a bunch more I forgot and I was rich before I was twenty,"

"And you was flat broke by twenty-one,"

"Ya, but I had one hell of a good time."

"Good luck, kid. That's all I got to say,"

"Ya, don't spend it all in one place."

"Look out the window, kid,"

"At what,"

"See them dents on the wing,"

"Ya,"

"Fifty caliber, them,"

"What do you mean, 'fifty caliber',"

"This plane was in the Korean war. Them dents is from fifty caliber bullets bouncing off. Pilot kept the plane high enough so's they wouldn't go right through,"

Stephan slightly shook. "So none got through then, right?"

"Some probably did, but them holes they patched."

It was a wild and bumpy ride north and Stephan's stomach felt every pitch and bow the plane made as it struggled its way north. He kept staring out the window, looking for something he'd never seen before. When the clouds finally cleared, all he could see was mountain after mountain, all covered in ice and snow.

He tried not to think, to worry about what he'd done, but all he got were images of his mother's jar of tips by her dresser, his tired father slowly walking up the sidewalk, and a small cloth bag filled with gold.

His stomach threatened him as the sign flashed out its warning, Fasten-Your-Seat-Belt. It was lit with red and white light bulbs, some of them broken.

The plane was about to land and Stephan was about to puke. He struggled with the airsickness bag, but it wouldn't open. When it did open, he was ready. He retched and choked, gagged and coughed, then spat out one mouthful of stale beer. He wondered why he felt ashamed of himself, that for all the noise he made, all he could produce was one mouthful.

The plane landed four times.

First a bone crunching thump and back in the air; then down again, a skid to the right and back in the air; down again, a skid to the left and back in the air; then down hard, as it skid and slid it's way to the end of the tarmac.

Stephan was sure he could feel the pilot pumping the brakes. The plane finally stopped, lurched forward, and the engines quit.

He got up on wobbly legs, walked up the aisle and down the steps, then turned his collar from the stiff cold wind.

It was overcast and cloudy, with drifts of snow blowing back and forth across the tarmac. There were no mountains visible in the distance; there was no distance, just the blowing snow and the clouds. He couldn't tell where snow left off and the clouds began.

At the bottom of the southern horizon, the sun was a dull yellow glow.

Inside the airport, with the few other passengers, he got his bag and went outside to an old school bus. Its faded yellow paint job was poorly painted over with the blue and black logo of Great Northern Airways.

A rusted Airways pick-up truck was parked, front bumper to front bumper, next to the bus and two men in Airways snowsuits were trying to charge the bus battery with jumper cables.

Steve shivered in the cold and watched as the D.C.3. was towed away by another rusted old pick-up truck.

He listened to the bus engine slowly grinding over, and as the engine finally started, he jumped as one of the grizzled old guys yelled in his ear, "Welcome to the Yukon, kid."

Then he leaned into Stephan and looked him straight in the eye. "Watch out for the thieves and liars. They'll clean you out and they're just waiting for you. Now you be sure you enjoy God's country."

The bus drove along the Alaska Highway, then down a steep hill towards the Yukon River and downtown Whitehorse. When they got to the bottom of the hill, the driver started calling out hotel names, and stopped at each one as the passengers got off. Steve went to the end of the line and got out at the Miner's Inn.

He stood on the snow-covered board sidewalk and looked around. Whitehorse was an odd blend of old and new buildings.

There were wood framed buildings with white washed signs, one story high with false fronts that made them look two stories high.

Next to them were buildings of cement and glass. Behind one of the new buildings was a three-story log cabin. It looked more like three small cabins; one stacked one on top of another. Main Street was six blocks long; it started at the Yukon River and ended at the foot of a cliff. It was two lanes wide and covered in packed snow and frozen mud. The sidewalks were narrow and made of planks, ice covered and slippery.

From the eaves of the buildings, over the storefront windows, icicles hung down threatening the few people who hurried by.

They were bundled up in parkas, wrapped in scarves, their heads covered with toques, and their ears covered with muffs. Each trailed a wispy white haze of exhaled breath.

A few beat-up pick-up trucks lumbered up and down the street, billowing out huge white clouds of exhaust that steamed into the cold night air. Steve shivered in his light sweater and jeans and looked at his watch. It was four-thirty.

Seven hours ago he was sitting in class trying to stay awake. Now he was fifteen hundred miles north.

"Hey! Hey you!" the bus driver yelled to Stephan. "Give this to Larry the bartender, will you?" He handed Stephan a letter.

"Larry the bartender," Stephan repeated, then looked at the letter. It had a Richmond, California postmark. "I'll give it to him."

Stephan scrambled up the few steps into the hotel and struggled to get his bag through the doorway. When he got in the lobby he smelled ammonia cleaner trying to mask diesel fuel.

He stood on a rug that used to be bright red, now it was mud brown. It had some kind of pattern long faded out, and was frayed around each corner where it had come apart from the wall.

There was a threadbare path from the door to a small front desk wedged under the stairs. To the left the path led to a swinging door into the bar.

There is a Season   J. Harding Montgomery

The door had a window made of stained glass picturing a young maiden carrying a bucket. The glass was chipped, and in some places the lead had fallen out. Above the picture, in more cracked glass and missing lead, was the name of the bar – The Fuel Pit.

To the right, over the front desk, the stairs went up to the rooms. On the stairs were pieces of rug tacked at the corners of each step; the centers worn through, showing floorboards polished to the grain. By the door to the bar there was a ragged old couch thrown up against the wall, sagging in the middle.

On the wall behind the couch was a painting on black velvet of a pack of wolves attacking a bull moose.

The moose was fighting off the wolves, but was bleeding from his hindquarter and his blood had stained the snow.

The wolves had shreds of flesh hanging from their bared teeth and they looked like they were dancing as much as attacking. The picture hung crooked.

On the couch a man was sleeping spread-eagled on his back, one muddy boot on the floor, the other boot up on the back of the couch where a puddle of mud and snow ran down to the arm rest.

A mongrel dog, as big as a wolf, stretched out between the man's legs, sleeping on his side. The dogs' hind legs had slipped off the couch to the floor, his forepaws curled up to his rib cage.

His shoulders were tucked into the man's crotch, which he used as a pillow, and his head leaned back with his nose tucked into the man's coat. The man's hands were neatly folded, one on top of the other on his stomach, inches from the dog's nose.

Both the man's and the dog's mouths were wide open, and both snored loudly. Standing between the man's fingers, tall and straight, was a single plastic red rose.

The man's nose looked like it had been broken and never set straight. His hair was dark, shoulder-length and fuzzy, tied at the back, the tail having slid to the side.

He had a scruffy beard, long and lop-sided with what looked like large chunks of pizza in it. He had a black toque on the back of his head that he used as a pillow.

His faded jeans were dirty with grease and mud and showed graying long underwear through holes in both knees. He had felt-lined calf-high black rubber boots laced to the tops, both laces undone and hanging loose. He wore an old army jacket, with Sergeants' stripes on the arms.

The right breast pocket had the name, McGarret; and on the left breast pocket, U. S. Marines. On the left shoulder, a peace sign.

Steve watched him open one eye, use it to look him up and down, and then look at a clock on the front desk. He yawned, rolled over, squashed the plastic red rose, woke the dog who let out an indignant yelp, then curled up and went back to sleep. The man mumbled, "Fuck it," closed the one eye, and started snoring into his toque.

There was nobody at the front desk so Stephan picked up his bag and headed towards the bar, looking for the desk clerk. He pushed the swinging door open and stepped in.

"Put your bag in the lobby," said a voice from inside the dark bar.

Steve turned and squinted into the darkness. He couldn't focus his eyes to where the voice came from.

"Got your eyes working yet," It was a male voice, and Steve heard a gentle, amused side to it.

"Can't see in the dark," Stephan said.

"Only Indians can see in the dark, and you don't look Indian to me. Want me to hold your hand to the bar,"

"I'll make it," Stephan's eyes focused in on a large bartender, but he still couldn't make out any details.

"Can you see now," the bartender asked.

Stephan blinked a few more times, "Now I can,"

"Good, then put your bag in the lobby. Don't want nobody messing up my nice clean bar with their dirty bag,"

"There's nobody at the desk. Who's going to watch it?"

"Watch it? What's it gonna do? Song and dance maybe? No sweat, Rolly'll watch it,"

"Who's Rolly?"

"The guy on the couch,"

"He's asleep,"

"How do you know?"

"He's snoring,"

"So what? Rolly snores when he's awake."

Stephan shrugged his shoulders and packed his bag back into the lobby. He propped it up against the desk, listened to Rolly and the dog snoring, then went back into the bar.

Now that his eyes were beginning to focus in the dark he could make out the bartender. He had a big forehead, six feet plus tall, broad-shouldered with a thick neck and solid jaw.

Black curly hair that stuck straight up and out over his ears, and a closely trimmed beard. A dirty blue sweatshirt had a picture on it of two vultures sitting in a tree. His ear-to-ear grin had a split between his front teeth big enough to fit another tooth.

Weight lifter arms folded across his barrel chest, and his left forearm had a wrist-to-elbow rosebush tattoo. The thing that struck Steve as odd and out of place was his granny-style glasses.

They had long thin handles reaching down to small wire rimmed lenses that straddled the end of his large broken nose. They seemed far too small and frail for such a big man.

"Who are you?" said the bartender.

Stephan thought about that question and decided that now would be a good time to change his name.

Instead of "Stephan' his name since forever, he would be called 'Steve', which was his close friends called him, but never his family or Sheila.

"Name's Steve, who're you,"

"Me? I'm Larry-The-Bartender, but you can call me Larry,"

"Got a letter for you, Larry, bus driver gave it to me,"

"Lemme see," Larry grabbed the letter from Steve's hand and read the postmark. "Out-fucking-standing."

He stuck the letter in his pocket. "Well, Steve, you are most definitely in my good books, and that gets you one free beer. You just got off the plane from where?"

"Vancouver,"

"Before that,"

"Hungary,"

"Hungary? You're not from the states,"

"No,"

"Thought maybe you was,"

"No, why,"

"No reason, just asking. You want a room; cash, no checks,"

"I got cash,"

"Okay, ten bucks, out by noon,"

Steve walked up to the bar and put down a ten-dollar bill.

He used the brass foot-rail running along the bottom as a step to climb up onto an old three-legged stool and took a look around. The bar had ten stools, and ten or twelve tables unevenly arranged on the floor. Half of them had customers. In the back of the lounge was an old pool table, with four small tables crammed around it. The rack for the pool cues was missing half the cues. There was a fluorescent light hanging over the pool table, with two tubes, but only one worked. The walls were covered with faded and yellowed pictures of miners. Some were operating heavy equipment, driving trucks or bulldozers; some were underground, leaning on rock drills or driving the electric trams used for hauling ore. Others were surveying on mountaintops, or taking soil samples in the valleys. Some were digging or panning for gold while still others were sitting or lying down, looking tired enough to die. In the center of all the pictures was a famous one Steve recognized. It was the Chilcoot Pass, on the Alaska-Yukon border, and showed a long string of miners climbing the steep hill into the Yukon. At the bottom of the picture was the caption:

Each miner of 1898 had to pack his own weight
in supplies before he was allowed into the Yukon.

Steve stared into that picture, thought of his one bag in the lobby, and knew that he had to find a job, quickly.

Larry handed him his room key."Seven, up the stairs, fourth on the left. No visitors, but if you can get them up without me seeing and they're quiet, you're okay. If I see them, I gotta throw them out. Other than that, have fun,"

"Sound's fair enough to me."

An old man walked into the bar. He was very small and thin, with a short, wide fuzzy gray beard and a mustache that grew down over his mouth. He wore an old green parka, a weathered black cowboy hat, pink fake fur ear muffs, what looked like a torn piece of bed-sheet for a scarf.

His blue jeans were baggy with the crotch halfway to his knees, and black cowboy boots that dragged on the floor sounding like they were two sizes too big. He was clutching something in his hands.

"Got something for you, Larry," he said.

"You here to pay your bill, Sammy?" Larry said.

He came over to Larry and put his closed hands on the bar, then opened them very slowly. Larry peeked in.

"Looks real," Larry took it and bit it. "Where'd you get the nugget?"

"Rolly give it to me," Sammy said.

"Did he get you that moose meat he was talking about?"

"Plus a bunch of veggies and some cheese and some tobacco he got from the warehouse,"

"Probably got himself in a pile of shit for that. Weren't you after him for a new wood stove?"

"Got it last week, he brought it out to my cabin, got his truck stuck in the snow,"

"God damn it, where'd you be without Rolly looking out for you?"

"Hungry and cold,"

"How much you want?" asked Larry.

"How much is my bill?" asked Sammy.

Larry reached under the bar and pulled out a shoebox full of receipts and an old balance beam set of weigh scales.

He dug through the box, pulled out a receipt and put the nugget on the scales.

"Sixty-five buck bar bill. Trade you for the nugget,"

"No, a hundred dollars,"

"Now what did this thing weigh?"

"One ounce," said Sammy.

"No, three quarters. Okay, your bar bill and ten bucks,"

"Newspaper says gold's sixty-five dollars,"

"When did you learn to read? Newspaper says gold's fifty-five dollars,"

"Rolly told me, he can read,"

Larry sighed and grinned at Sammy, "Yes, Rolly can read. Tell you what, I'll clear your bill and give you a bottle of whiskey,"

"Two bottles or I tell Rosie you cheat on your girlfriend,"

"Like hell I do,"

"I tell her and she belicves me. She never believes you,"

"That's some pretty bullshit blackmail,"

Sammy shrugged, "Works."

"Fucken' crook," Larry sighed. "Okay, and I clear your bar bill. And don't tell Rosie nothing,"

"Thank you very much," Sammy said, "and a hot dog,"

"And a hot dog," Larry turned around and put a hot dog in an old rusted heater, then handed Sammy a bottle of whiskey. Sammy spun the cap off and put the bottle to his lips.

"You're not supposed to do that, Sammy! You can't buy a bottle, then drink it in here. It's against the law."

"Didn't buy it, you gave it to me,"

Larry reached across the bar and grabbed at the bottle. "Give it to me,"

Sammy jumped back. "Mine, I'll tell Rosie,"

"You made a deal," Larry pleaded.

"Different deal," Sammy shrugged.

Larry poured a drink of bar whiskey, and put it in front of Sammy. "Put the bottle away and drink this," he said.

"Okay," said Sammy.

Larry made another grab for the bottle and Sammy jumped back again. "I tell Rosie, my bottle,"

"Shit. Well put the damn thing in your pocket and leave it there."

Sammy smiled, settled comfortably back on his stool, took the shot Larry gave him and drank it. When Larry turned his back, Sammy took out the bottle, filled his glass, winked at Steve, downed his drink and poured himself another.

The bar door swung open, and Rolly walked in yawning, one hand scratching his beard, the other scratching his stomach. The dog walked in behind him, sat down, lifted his hind leg and started scratching his jaw. He yawned, showing teeth the size of fingers, a tongue the length and width of a large hand. He slumped down in the corner, stretched out his massive forepaws, yawned, rested his head on his forepaws and watched.

"Rosie stabbed me with a rose," Rolly said. "Got a smoke,"

"She said she'll be back later," Larry said. "Smokes on the table,"

"Damn thing stabbed me," Rolly sucked on his finger, then lit one of Larry's' cigarettes. "Pour me a beer, will you."

Rolly took the corner stool at the bar, next to Steve, and put his back against the wall.

"Hey, Sammy, you get that wood stove hooked up right,"

"Yup, works good,"

"What about that moose meat? You gonna get me some smoked jerky,"

"Next week,"

"Good. You get those veggies in the stew pot,"

"Yup. Come up tomorrow and you can eat some,"

"Can't, gotta take Rosie out tonight and I'm back to work tomorrow,"

Sammy smiled a toothless grin and seeing Larry's back turned,

poured himself another drink.

Larry handed Rolly his beer and Rolly headed back to the couch.

"Dog," ordered Rolly. The dog lifted his head, looked around, yawned again, then got up and followed Rolly back to the couch.

Larry turned to Steve, "So what brings you to this frozen hell-hole?"

"Time for a change, don't really know, need a job,"

Larry chuckled. "Heard that a thousand times before,"

"How's that?"

"I tell ya," Larry went on, "this territory is safe ground for all the misfits, castoffs, fuck-ups, black sheep, and every other kind of poor soul who can't or won't fit in somewhere else."

Larry poured himself a beer, took a long slow drink, and then squinted his eyes in thought. "The Yukon is home for the run-aways and refugees of the world, and a lot of people are here because it's important that they not be some other place. The Yukon's a good place to hide out,"

"'Hide out'? What from?"

"Some folks are wanted someplace, ran out on a marriage, skipped their bail, lot of different reasons. Everybody's running from something,"

"Sounds weird to me," said Steve.

"It is. The rest of the world don't know we're up here, and for most folks that suits them just fine. It's okay with me. What are you running from?"

Steve shrugged, "Nothing particular, quit school this morning and just got on the plane,"

"Why the Yukon,"

"I wanna go gold mining."

"Stupid reason, should have gone to the Amazon,"

"Why,"

"More gold and it's warmer. Too damn cold here. Why'd you quit school?"

"Ever been to university before,"

"Back in California, what made you quit,"

Steve took a long slow drink. "Too boring,"

Larry sat on a stool and propped his feet up on the bar. "Boredom is a man's worst enemy. Good reason to leave."

"Sure enough. Why'd you leave California if it's too cold up here?"

As soon as the question left Steve's mouth he remembered the posters back in the university hallway; the pictures of the battle in the rice paddy and the ones calling for an end to the war.

Larry stared into the emptiness of the bar, thought for a bit, and had another long slow drink of his beer. "I had scholarship to play football, and that got me a deferment from the draft board. I had an 'in' with a philosophy professor. Anyone who was draft eligible signed up for his course. He guaranteed us a passing grade. He didn't think we should go to Vietnam for flunking out."

"That's how I became philosophy major. But some redneck hawk professor figured it out and turned us all in.

That's when me and Rolly came to Canada, "My professor got canned; the rest of us got drafted.

"No shit," Steve said. "That's how you ended up in the Yukon,"

"No, that's how I ended up in Canada. I ended up in the Yukon because me and Rolly ran out of car before we ran out of road;

We crossed the border and just kept driving. Car broke down about twenty miles out of town. Mechanic said it would be a week to ten days before they could fly in the parts, so I got a room in this hotel. Rolly took off to work in the bush. The week to ten days turned into two months. By the time the parts got here, I already sold the car, and was working here. I got no place to go,"

"Is that why you asked me if I was from the states?"

"Thought maybe you had problems with the draft board, too,"

"Nope. You have any problems at the border?"

"Crossing the border was easy, getting to the border was the problem. Rolly was wanted by the marines, my draft card was burned up, every state bordering Canada was full of cops and troopers on the watch for young guys headed to Canada."

"Rolly's got no hair and I got hair half way to my ass, so I cut it. We couldn't have anything on us that would tip them off. If they got their hands on us, we'd be in real deep shit,"

"What kind of stuff would tip them off?"

"You know, family pictures, extra clothes or food, anything looks like you plan on being gone for more than a day or two,"

"What kind of deep shit would you be in?"

"Well, to start with they lock you up and accuse you of being disloyal to the state, then they beat the shit out of you for as long as they got you, then they send you to boot camp where they beat the shit out of you some more, then they send you to 'Nam, where you get to go right to the war." Larry paused to sip on his beer. "Then the sergeant there knows you tried to dodge out of the country and he hates you so he puts you on point where you get shot right quick.

Leastways, that's what Rolly told me happened to some guys he knew in the 'Nam, so we were wired pretty tight headed to the border,"

"But the border was fine,"

"American border says, where you going, for how long, we says the weekend, gonna get some Canadian women, he laughs. We got an empty car, change of socks, and a hundred bucks between us. Canadian border we got papers to fill out for political asylum so they don't throw us out, now Rolly's turning colors from fear.   I'm scratching my head 'cause it's itchy from the haircut I just gave myself. Canadian guy says, now get this Steve, "not everyone agrees with American foreign policy", and I about shit myself and Rolly's almost crying, and this guy is in a uniform and I never seen anybody in a uniform in my life that questioned the government."

"How long you gonna stay in Canada," Steve said.

Larry finished his beer. "Maybe someday this war will end and we can all go home,"

"Well, Larry," Steve stuck out his hand "Until that day comes, Welcome to Canada,"

Larry stood back, eyed Steve and looked puzzled, then stepped forward to shake his hand. "Nobody ever said that to me before,"

"I just did." Steve said.

The bar door swung open and Rolly walked back in, followed by Dog. "That jalopy was a piece of junk," Rolly said, as he took his corner seat at the bar, back to the wall.
""Fill 'er up, will you,"
"No it wasn't," Larry said. "that car was a beauty,"
"We're lucky it made it this far," Rolly said.
"No, we're not. If we was lucky it would've broke down in Vancouver where the sun always shines and it's never cold, and we'd never got to this place,"
Rolly shrugged, "That's true,"
"So why are you still here if you don't like it?"
Steve said. "Why not goes some other place,"
Rolly smiled and leaned his chin into his hands. "What? Leave here and go back to civilization? The Yukon may be the biggest lunatic asylum on the planet, but it sure as hell beats all that other stuff." He kept on grinning and nodded knowingly, "More beer, and make it stronger," he laughed out, "Who's this guy? Never seen you before,"
"Just got here, name's Steve Kovacs," Steve reached out his hand. Rolly looked Steve straight in the eye, then shook his hand. His handshake was firm and steady.
"Name's Rolly McGarret,"
Larry kept chuckling, "Quit university this morning in Vancouver and just got on the plane. That right, Steve,"
Rolly leaned over to look Steve straight in the eye again as his eyes narrowed. "Lemme ask you a question; did you quit proper or just walk out? Did you fill out any course drop forms? Did you say good-bye to anyone? Who knows you're gone and where you're gone to,"
"Just packed and left," Steve said. "Didn't say goodbye to anyone. Nobody knows I'm gone."
The realization was beginning to sink in deeper and he didn't want to think about it anymore. He stared at Rolly's jacket. There was a strange ribbon on it.
"What's that," Steve said
"Vietnam Service Medal."

Steve thought again of the posters in the university hallway of crying soldiers. Now, they were more than just posters in a university hallway. He felt like he had ten thousand dumb questions, but he didn't know where to start.

"Were you in any battles," Steve stuttered out.

Rolly squinted one eye. "What do you think war is?"

"Sorry, I didn't mean to,"

"Sure you meant to; if you didn't 'mean to' you wouldn't have asked. Worst question is the one you don't ask,"

Steve stopped. He folded his hands on the table; he was stumped for the next question. Rolly sat and smiled back at him, didn't stop smiling, seemed to be patiently waiting for Steve to ask the next question.

Then Rolly went on, "You asked if I was opposed to the war,"

"No, I didn't,"

"Yes, you did. You just didn't use those words. Being opposed to the war makes about as much sense as being opposed to an earthquake; don't mean shit if you're in the middle of it. All you want to do is survive and go home,"

Steve went back to the nightly news "Did you have a peace sign on your our helmet?"

"What's that got to do with anything? Peace signs don't stop bullets. Draftees were the ones that started with the peace signs. I volunteered; we didn't do that shit, leastways not when I was in-country,"

"Did you think the war is right?"

Rolly leaned his head from right to left, thinking things over. "When I went over in '67 I did, just like my Dad did in '42. He thought his war was right and I thought my war was right. He got the Japs and I got the Cong. Turned out he was right and I wasn't. Welcome to war,"

"'Welcome to war', what's that supposed to mean?"

"Every generation gets a war, that's what history is,"

"My Dad fought the Nazis in Hungary, then the Russians,"

"What was he doing in Hungary?"

"Lived there, that was home,"

There is a Season   J. Harding Montgomery

"Your Dad with the Partisans?"

"They called themselves the Mokan, the Independent Army,"

"'Independent Army'? No government meddling, I like the sound of that,"

"I don't know much about it. He never talked about it,"

Rolly straightened up again, got that narrow look in his eyes again. "Did you ever ask?"

Steve folded his hands on the bar, twiddled his thumbs.

Rolly reached over and firmly covered Steve's twiddling thumbs. "I said, 'Did you ever ask him about the war he was in'?"

"No,"

"Why not?"

"He never talked about it,"

"Maybe he never talked about it 'cause you never asked,"

"You think so?"

"How the hell am I supposed to know that? You should know

this shit. It's important to you and your family."

Rolly took another drink. "So, you ran away from your family and you're up here to make it rich in the gold mines?"

"Well, I guess so, that was my idea this morning,"

"That was this morning, now it's this evening, two different times, two different places. Fat chance with the mines you know how to run a chain saw?"

"Not yet,"

Rolly cracked up laughing. "'Not yet,' he says. That's a good one. Know how to work hard? I mean real hard?"

"Ya, I can out work anybody,"

Rolly cracked up one more time. "'Outwork anybody.' That's even better than the last line of shit. I got a job for you. Money's good, work's harder,"

"Doing what?"

Larry came back from talking with Sammy. "What happened to those two Frenchies you had,"

"Lazy buggers, had to fire them,"

"What for?"

"All they wanted to do was smoke dope and meditate in the mud,"

"Isn't that what you do?"

"No, that is not what I do. What I do is work my ass off all day, then I smoke dope and meditate in my nice warm cabin,"

Larry turned to Steve, "Don't listen to Rolly, Steve. He'll work your ass off and then ask for more,"

Then Rolly joined in, "Don't listen to Larry, Steve. He's a lazy shit, ain't done a real day's work his entire life,"

"What's the job?" Steve asked.

Rolly finished his beer and put it down hard on the bar. "Work, work and more work; cutting wood. Cut and stack, cut and stack, and after that we cut and stack. Sell firewood and building logs. Got a cut zone on Ethel Lake, built a cabin there, and this part is important Steve, you got to remember this, you got a warm bunk and all you can eat and we eat good, lots of fish and moose meat. You interested,"

"Where's Ethel Lake,"

"Deep, deep boonies, 'bout two hundred miles north."

Steve didn't want to get sidetracked to a wood cutting job. It didn't sound exciting, and like Rolly said, work, work and more work. He didn't want to work; he wanted to get rich.

Going two hundred miles into the bush, and working for this guy from Vietnam, who just fired two guys for smoking dope, no, didn't sound too good at all.

Besides, how could he go home and tell everyone he went to the Yukon and got rich cutting wood?

"Well thanks for the offer, but I still want to go gold mining,"

"Good luck, nobody's hiring till spring thaw,"

"What?" Steve hadn't thought about that.

He was considering his next move when into the bar came one man, heading straight to him and Rolly. He was tall and lean, both hands in his pockets, and he walked with a skip. His head nodded as he walked, as though he was listening to a song only he could hear.

Bright blue independent eyes, each aimed its own way, a nose bent like a coat hanger, half a mouthful of yellow teeth, top two missing, and he grinned with a cigarette at the edge of his thin lips.

Flapping ears partially buried under scraggly brown shoulder length hair that tangled into a long, thin beard. His voice sounded like the mix of a chain saw and a gravel crusher.

"Hey Rolly, wanna shoot a game,"

Rolly threw him a silent glare, "No, Hank, I do not want to shoot a game,"

"How about you," he said to Steve.

Steve didn't notice Rolly's glare. "Don't see why not," he said.

Rolly whispered to Steve, "Shark,"

Steve winked at Rolly, same wink as Sammy, when tricked Larry. "Played a few games, myself."

Walking over to the pool table Hank said, "You play eight ball,"

"Any game you want, anyway you want," Steve took the stick, chalked it like a pro, and watched Hank flip a coin.

He looked closer at Hank. He was missing his left arm; his coat sleeve was pinned to his pocket.

Hank saw Steve looking at his missing arm, "No problem," he said, "Forestry chopper cut it off, your break,"

"You can shoot with one arm,"

"Like I said, no problem, your break."

Steve took his shots easy and relaxed, one after the other, until he got hooked on the eight ball. Hank took over, lined up the stick on the stick rack, shot, pushed down on the butt-end of the stick and rack and they both flipped up into his hand. He sunk three balls. Steve finished the table, Hank handed him a ten-dollar bill.

"Didn't know we were playing for money," Steve said.

"Oh ya, every game in this bar is for ten or more,"

"Don't want to break the rules," Steve pocketed the ten dollars.

"Double-up," Hank said.

"Twenty it is." Steve said.

Hank took the break, sunk four. Steve got up, ran the table, and pocketed twenty more dollars.

"Double again," Hank said.

"Your money," Steve ran the table, Hank handed him forty dollars.

"Play this one for thirty bucks,"

"Still your money,"

Same game, same result. Steve pocketed the thirty dollars.

"That's a hundred bucks you got off me," Hank said with a chuckle, "I don't care, I still got a lot of pool in me, let's up the stakes,"

Steve fingered the hundred dollars he won from Hank in one pocket, his two hundred in the other pocket. This money, he thought, will have to last until I got a job. Would be nice to hang onto this extra hundred, could take it easy for awhile, maybe travel around the Yukon and do the tourist thing. I can beat this guy again.

"What kind of stakes you want to play for," he said.

Hank leaned his head to one side, then the other, thinking things over. "How much you got to spend,"

"How much you got to spend," Steve said.

Now Steve thought some more. He knew he was the new kid in town and that sooner or later he would have to prove himself. It was the same as playing hockey; he always had to prove himself with every new team, whether he played for them or against them. Why not prove himself in Whitehorse by beating the town pool shark?

"I want my hundred bucks back," Hank said.

"Okay,"

Hank won the toss, got one off the break, missed the next. Steve played one shot, sewered the eight, automatic loss, handed Hank his hundred dollars back.

"Let's play for another hundred," Hank said.

Steve was angrily shaking his head; why didn't I see the possible sewer? Rookie mistake, no excuse for it.

Never tried a shot if it was a possible sewer, why'd I try such a stupid shot? I won't do that again.

"You're on," he said.

Steve won the toss, got one, dropped two more, sunk the cue ball, automatic shot loss. Hank got up, ran the table. Steve handed him one of his two hundred dollars.

"Another for a hundred,"

It can't happen again, Steve thought. Two stupid plays, Hanks' hundred dollars gone, now one of mine. The eight was a stupid shot; but the cue going down, now that was just plain bad luck. Take enough shots, it's bound to happen, and now that it's happened, it won't happen again.

"You're on." Steve said.

He yawned, trying to hide his nervousness. What would happen if he lost? Broke, in a town where he barely knew anyone. Hadn't phoned to say goodbye, how to phone for help? Hey folks, I bounced a check for a flight to a town I've never been to, looking for a job at a mine that's closed for the winter, and I lost all my money playing pool to a guy with one arm.

Steve won the toss. Chalked his cue, broke the table, one down, two down, three down, then he was hooked.

One possible shot, has to be a long bank: made it, two to go. Dangerous shot, eight ball sitting over the hole, don't sink it again. Cluster of balls around the eight, got to be a soft shot, don't breathe the wrong way. Just push the shot; it'll go in, no sweat. One more shot, piece of cake, almost there; two more shots, another piece of cake; all done then, enough is enough, too close for comfort, just get these last two shots, get back to your seat and quit pissing around with this shark.

Eight ball just sitting and waiting for Steve; might just as well have his name written on it. "This eight-ball is waiting for Steve to tap it in."

He softly shot, barely touched; it rolled just the way he wanted it to, couldn't have been any better. It connected and sat, wavered at the edge, sat some more, wavered some more; then sat and sat and sat.

Hank took his cue, ran the table, put out his hand; Steve put out his hand, Hank emptied it.

"Another," Hank said.

"No," Steve said.

"Fine," Hank said, and walked off counting what used to be all of Steve's money.

Steve's knees went weak and his stomach churned. How did I let that happen? He reached in his pocket and counted the change. Maybe enough for breakfast. Phone home for money? Room's paid for, gotta be out by noon. This was his big move, stand on his own, be a gold miner, go home rich. How long did it take? And to top it off, the guy only had one arm.

Rolly knew exactly what happened. "How'd you do with the one-armed bandit?"

He wasn't surprised when Steve said, "Cleaned me out,"

"Told you he was a shark, how much he get you for?"

"Everything,"

"That bad? I'm leaving first thing in the morning, you coming or what?"

Rolly had a warm cabin and food, and like he said, that was important; and now Steve knew just how important that was. Never in his life did he consider eating and sleeping as something he had to go out and get, or as something he could lose. It was always there for him, his parents made sure of that. Now he was getting hungry and it was damn cold outside. He could work with Rolly till spring thaw, then go gold mining, then go home rich. Things weren't that bad.

"Ya, I'm coming," Steve said.

"We leave first thing in the morning; I got all the gear you need. You got enough for breakfast,"

"Umm,"

"Don't sweat it, you'll get fed. Paid your bar tab, yet,"

"Umm,"

"Shit, Steve, quit your god damn pissing and moaning. Think you're the first to get sharked by the one-armed bandit? How'd you think he got so good?"

"He had to, that's how he feeds himself, he got shit for a pension for that missing arm, so he's a pool shark."

Rolly sighed and had a drink, "There it is."

Steve sighed along with Rolly. "Anybody else on this job?"

"Anybody else? The last crew I had was so bad they couldn't get wrong right. You're it buddy, you, me and the great outdoors."

Rolly turned his head and smiled at a young native woman walking in, then turned back to Steve, "And my cook, Rosie, here. Hey, sweets, how you doin'," he said.

"Don't you 'sweets' me. Where've you been all day,"

"Sleeping on the couch. Where've you been all day,"

"None of your damn business, that's where I've been,"

"Hope you enjoyed yourself." smiled Rolly.

Steve turned around to have a good look at her. She had jet-black hair halfway down her back, braided into a ponytail.

Her nose was curled up at the end, like a little ski-ramp, and her cheekbones stood out, solid and high, graceful.

Her eyes were bright blue, and her skin had a clear complexion, lightly freckled, but dirty. She wore no make-up. She was just over five feet and one hundred pounds, but it was easy to see that she carried herself larger. She wore no coat, but a heavy wool sweater, thick scarf and toque. Her blue jeans were tucked into the same kind of army-issue cold weather boots that Rolly wore, though her boots weren't torn, or dirty. They were clean and her laces were tied.

Steve couldn't take his eyes away from hers. She ignored him as she took off her gloves, toque and scarf, threw them on a chair, then pulled her sweater over her head. Steve stared through her tight tee shirt at her breasts. He blinked, lost his breath, then blinked again. Rolly watched Steve stare and grinned.

She snapped at Steve, "What are you gawking at,"

"Nothing," he stammered.

"Bullshit!" She pointed her finger at him, "You a friend of this guy," she said to Rolly.

"Yes," Rolly laughed.

"Should've known, bull-shitters run together."

Rolly couldn't stop smiling. "Careful, Steve, good-natured Rosie here is the best cook this side of the Rockies; worst boss this side of anywhere. Be nice to her and she won't bite you,"

"Okay," Steve stammered.

"Rosie, this is Steve. Steve, this is Rosie,"

"You better remember this Steve, her ancestors were hunting and fishing the Yukon when ours were hairy and hanging in trees; don't matter if you forget, she'll remind you,"

"Fuck both of you," Rosie said.

"You the boss," Steve said.

"I'm the boss," Rosie said. "I push the plow and set the pace. Nothing is beneath me, and nothing, you listening to me Rolly McGarret, nothing is above me. And once in a blue moon Rolly actually listens to me,"

Rosie glared at Steve, "Stare at my tits one more time and I'll break your nose,"

Rolly grinned again, "Told you so,"

Rosie sat down next to Steve and stared at Rolly with a deep, penetrating intensity. Her nose twitched and she pursed her lips. "What's with the plastic flower? You playing some sick Yankee game with my name,"

"Now Rosie," Rolly said. "Would I buy you a flower that's already dead? I know how much you like roses, so I bought you one that would last forever,"

"Oh, Rolly," smiled Rosie. "You are so full of shit. That's why I gave it back,"

"I know, I was awake," Rolly said.

"You do that one-eyed thing on me,"

"Rosie, you're so damn pretty, I can only handle one eye-full at a time,"

"Oh, Rolly, I wish I could bottle your charm, then I'd have something to scrub the outhouse with,"

Rosie sat back, let out a deep sigh, gave Rolly another smile, then shook her fist at him. "Rolly McGarret, what am I going to do with you,"

"I have a few ideas,"

"I'll bet you do, and they're all sick,"

Rolly shrugged and yawned. "Steve here is coming back to Ethel Lake with us. He's my FNG,"

Rosie faked a look of surprise. "But, Rolly, you said he was a friend of yours. Why would you treat him like that,"

"He needs a job,"

"Well, Steve, welcome to Ethel Lake Logging," Rosie said.

Rolly stood up, scratched his belly, "Piss break," he said, and walked off.

Rosie tilted her head slightly sideways and rested her chin in her hand, "You got any idea what you're in for,"

"No. What's a FNG?"

"Fucken' New Guy. You're a rookie, everybody got to start someplace, that's what Rolly says,"

"What am I 'in for',"

Rosie stretched out and plopped her feet in Rolly's chair. "Rolly's the finest man you could ever meet. He was in Vietnam, and that makes him a mirror,"

"What do you mean 'mirror',"

"Whatever you give him, you get back ten times as much. You treat him straight, you can bet your life on him; you cross him, that's another thing. It's a Vietnam thing. He was a squad leader, a sergeant. I don't understand it, but Larry can explain it all to you,"

"What's Larry got to explain?"

"You fuck Rolly in any way, and unless it's an honest mistake, he'll eat you alive. He's a marine, that's how they do it. Like it or not, you're now part of Ethel Lake Logging. You've been drafted. Don't let Rolly down."

Steve didn't like the sound of that. He wasn't sure what he should do. Stay with Rolly after being warned, or maybe tell him he had changed his mind and was going to stick to his original plan of being a gold miner.

But if he quit on him, would that be letting him down, and Rolly would eat him alive?

Rolly was in Vietnam, he could do all kinds of things to him. He'd heard stories about Vietnam vets going crazy, but he never believed them.

Rolly sure could get intense; it was obvious there were some things that he felt very strongly about. Steve felt he should watch himself, but he wasn't sure how.

They were going two hundred miles into the bush with no one else there, except Rosie, and she just warned him about Rolly. What if he wanted to leave after they got way out in the bush? He did have a cabin with a warm bunk and all he could eat, and like Rolly said, that was important. Besides, he was broke and hungry, and working way out in the bush could be some kind of adventure.

Rolly seemed like a nice enough guy; besides, what could go wrong once they were two hundred miles into the bush?

Larry walked by with another tray of beer. "How you doing, Rosie,"

"Don't you 'how you doing' me! You're on my shit list. I've been talking to Sammy,"

"He was supposed to keep his mouth shut,"

"Well, he didn't. Next time you give him a better deal for his nuggets. He's an old man and needs the money more than you do,"

"I gave him a good deal,"

"You better have."

"Got something better than that," Larry yanked Rosie out of her seat and dragged her into a corner. "Came in on today's plane," whispered Larry. "Steve brought it,"

"Are you sure its' from Peter," Rosie whispered back.

"Check out the post mark,"

Rosie stared at the letter and read the Richmond, California, postmark. "This is going to blow Rolly's mind,"

"I hope so," Larry said. "I hope so. When you gonna give it to Rolly,"

"When we get back to Ethel Lake."

Larry looked over Rosie's shoulder. "Well, what have we got here? If it isn't my good friends, Sergeant Yo Yo and Constable Boo Boo. Out fighting crime are we, boys,"

Steve turned around to see two very large Yukon Security officers walk in. Both were over six feet tall and wide shouldered, and carried long-handled flashlights like they were small clubs and they both carried 357's in loose fitting holsters.

The sergeant had his hat pulled down to cover his eyes. The fat beneath his chin hung down to cover the knot in his tie and spread out across his collarbone beneath his ears. Fat arms hung off the sides of his body like broken tree boughs, his hands turned so the backs of them were in front. He had a potbelly that hung out over his belt and was barely held in by his coat.

A faded white shirt spread open between the buttons, showed an equally faded white undershirt.

His pure white hair matched the color of his skin and was greased straight back. No facial growth at all. Bright blue eyes bulged out of his face like marbles in a bowl of cream of wheat.

He pushed the peak of his hat out of his eyes with the butt-end of his flashlight and surveyed the bar like he knew what he was looking for.

The corporal looked like a reject from a third-rate football team. His eyes were sunk deep into his skull, hiding under dark bushy eyebrows. Uncontrolled tufts of wiry hair stuck out from under his hat. He had a flat forehead that seemed too large for his small jaw, giving his face a distinctly triangular look. His lips were pulled tight across brown teeth, which were evenly spaced with gaps and his hat refused to sit squarely on his head.

He leaned against the wall behind the sergeant, and like an apprentice learning his trade, followed the sergeant's eyes as they searched through the customers.

The sergeant slipped his flashlight into its holster like a sword into a scabbard, pulled the peak of his hat back down to cover his eyes, then folded his arms across his chest and leaned back on his heels. "You know what I like about being with the Yukon Security Police," he said to the corporal.

"No," the constable didn't know. "I don't."

"It's the undying respect and admiration we get from the community,"

"Well this here ain't the community," Larry said. "It's the Fuel Pit."

He placed his hands squarely on his hips, trying not to chuckle. "If you don't want a beer, get out of my bar. You're scaring my customers,"

"Only if they have something to be scared of,"

"Now be nice, Larry," said the corporal, "or next time we get a riot call to this place, we won't come,"

"You never come anyways,"

The sergeant leaned his elbow on the bar next to Steve, pulled his flashlight from its holster. He tapped it in the palm of his gloved hand. "Listen, Larry, if you call us in advance of your next riot, we'll be here on time. All you ever do is call us after it's started. That breaks up our crib game,"

Larry leaned forward to go eye to eye with the sergeant, "Well, golly gosh and gee whiz. Shucks, I'm sorry."

Steve sat motionless, not knowing what to do. The last thing he wanted to do was get tangled up in this, so he looked straight into his beer, afraid to sip, to move, or even breathe.

Larry's eyes hardened, and his voice steadied, "A question, Sergeant,"

"What's that?" The sergeant's expression changed from mean to meaner.

Larry leaned closer and closer until their noses almost met, "How 'bout a kiss?"

"Get away from me," The sergeant spat out as he jumped back.

Larry's face opened up into an ear-to-ear grin, his eyes turned up, and he started to howl like a wolf. Steve let out the lungful of air that was starting to turn him purple.

Rosie walked by the Sergeant and sneered at him.

He turned to Rosie. "You still hanging out with that no-good deserter?"

Rosie turned back, walked straight up to the sergeant, placed her hands on her hips, looked up and said, "Yo Yo, if you find it necessary to piss on Rolly, could you at least have the common courtesy to do it while he's present?"

"Well, aren't you the prissy little Indian bitch tonight,"

Rosie swung. SLAPP

Caught him clean from ear to chin. The bar went dead; like somebody unplugged the jukebox. The sergeant stumbled back; more surprised that hurt. The constable looked to the sergeant for guidance. Both of the sergeants' hands automatically went to his flashlight-club and his holster as Larry vaulted the bar to land right between Rosie and the sergeant, stretched out his arms to keep Rosie behind him.

Rosie looked at the sergeants' hand on his holster, leaned around Larry and yelled out, "Hey Yo Yo, you gonna take out your dick-on-your-hip and shoot me,"

Larry rolled his eyes to the ceiling, then stared directly at the corporal. He spoke quietly and forcefully. "'Bout time you guys got on with your rounds, don't you think,"

"Ahh, Sergeant," the corporal lightly touched the sergeant's arm, "I think we should go on our rounds now."

The sergeant slapped the corporals' hand off his arm, then shook his finger at Rosie. "You'll get yours, little lady. You'll get yours,"

"Not from you, that's for sure."

Rolly walked back from the washroom, holding his beer in one hand and pulling up his fly with the other. He walked past Larry, still glaring at the corporal; past the sergeant, still glaring at Rosie; then winked at Steve.

Finishing his beer, he put the empty on the bar and helped himself to another from Larry's tray. He turned, leaned his back against the bar, pointed his finger at the stripes on the sergeants' arm, and said, "Get them in a box of corn flakes,"

"Earned them,"

"Ate the whole box in one sitting, did you?" Rolly drank his beer and smiled at everyone in the bar, except the sergeant and his corporal, then said to the sergeant, "I miss something here?"

"Nothing, not a damn thing. I'd watch myself pretty close if I was you,"

"And why is that?"

"I could have a little talk with the folks down at Immigration about you,"

"Really? And what are you going to say? I got slapped by Rolly McGarrets tiny little girlfriend,"

The Sergeant knew his threat had just evaporated. "Anytime, McGarret, anytime,"

"Jesus, Yo Yo, I'd eat you for breakfast and have you shit out by lunch. Better you get on with your crime fighting boys, and leave us no-good deserters to our beers."

The sergeant stomped out of the bar with the constable stumbling behind him.

"God damn it," Rolly said, wiping his sleeve across his mouth.

"I love teasing that guy." He looked around the bar, slightly shook his head and rolled his eyes to the ceiling. Everybody chuckled, went back to their beers and the jukebox blared again.

"I don't mean to get you in trouble with immigration," Rosie said. "but he bad-mouthed you,"

"I don't give a shit what Yo Yo says about me," Rolly said. "But if he ever talks down about your family again,"

"He didn't say anything about my family,"

"Yes, he did. If he wants to call you a bitch, that's one thing, that's about you; when he calls you an Indian bitch, that's about your family. Then he's gone too far."

Rosie nodded while Rolly drank his beer in one mouthful, then he said, "How you think Steve here is going to work out,"

"The tit-watcher," Rosie said.

Steve shuddered and stared deep into his beer.

"Steve," Rolly said. "Get your face outta your beer glass and come up for air. Rosie won't bite you,"

Rosie laid her head on the table, and stared through the beer filled glass to smile at Steve and in a warm, soothing manner, said, "Steve, do like Rolly says, get your face out of your beer glass and come up for air. I won't bite,"

"Promise," said Steve.

"No, but you can still come up for air,"

"Okay," said Steve.

Rolly stood up, grabbed Rosie's beer and drained it down. "Come on Rosie, I'll buy you dinner,"

"Better be good. You owe me,"

"Anything you want, anytime you want it,"

Rosie had another deep sigh and rolled her eyes to the ceiling.

"Steve, what room number you got," Rolly said.

"Seven,"

"See you at zero six hundred in the Ice Box Cafe, Fourth and Main. We leave right after breakfast. Get some sleep. Say good-night Rosie,"

"Nice to meet you, Steve, hope I didn't scare you too bad,"

"Not too bad."

Rolly stared at Steve. "So tell me," he said, "how's your first day in the Yukon shaping up?"

"It's not what I thought it would be,"

"Well, what did you think it was going to be?"

"I dunno,"

"Great fucken answer, see you at zero six hundred. Good night."

Steve was afraid to ask what the hell 'zero six hundred' was.

ROSIE AND ROLLY'S HOTEL ROOM

After dinner, Rosie half-carried Rolly up the hotel stairs. He wasn't any drunker than usual, but he did seem more tired than usual. She knew that most nights he drank until sun-up, slept for a few hours, then got up to work all day. He'd sweat out all the beer and whiskey from the night before and nothing seemed to stop him or even slow him down. She knew he was driven, but he had no direction; he just worked and drank.

Tonight Rosie was scared. Nothing she could explain or ask about, but that 'far-away' look was back in Rolly's eyes. It gave her the feeling that when Rolly was looking at her, he wasn't actually looking at her, but to some place far behind her. She used to look over her shoulder, thinking she was missing something, but she'd look and there'd be nothing there.

Every time Rolly had that 'far-away' look, something would happen and it wasn't ever nice. The first time she saw it, Rolly and her were sitting in a bar, quietly talking when he just slipped off to some other place. His body was there, but he was a long ways away, his eyes focused into the distance. This irritated her because he didn't pay any attention to what she was saying. He was only gone for a few seconds when some guy turned on the television news. Rolly blinked, came back from wherever he went, told the guy to turn off the news. The guy snapped back at Rolly to mind his own business.

Rolly was out of his chair and on the guy so quick that Rosie had to look back in Rolly's chair to make sure it was him punching the man.

It was, and Rosie had to hustle Rolly out of the bar before the cops could get him. After that she learned to pay very close attention when Rolly got his 'far-away' look.

She also learned that Rolly did not like the television news, or any other news from any other place.

Climbing up the stairs that night, Rosie was glad that they were out of the bar, and that Rolly looked like he was going to sleep.

He rarely slept well and always looked tired, though Rosie knew that occasionally Rolly would stretch out anywhere, and look like he was fast asleep. But he rarely was.

One eye would open and roam about, looking over wherever he was, then close again. Rolly's 'far-away' look always scared her and tonight he had it for a while; though nothing - so far- had happened.

She laid him down on the bed, he mumbled, "Good night," and started snoring. She shrugged, thought nothing of it, had a shower. When she got out, he was still snoring. She quietly climbed into bed next to him, leaned over to kiss him and instantly that her lips touched his, he sprang up screaming,

INCOMING

He wrapped his arms around her, flipped them both onto the floor, pushed her under the bed tight up against the wall, covered her mouth with his hand, and whispered,

"Don't move, Charlie's through the wire,"

She felt the drips of sweat as they ran off his face and down her cheeks. His heart beat too fast, too irregular. Neither moved for an infinite minute, then Rolly's breathing slowly returned to normal.

He picked up the bed and flung it off them, then collapsed back in the corner. He looked up at Rosie, swung his head from side to side, and mumbled, "I thought you were in trouble".

There was a banging at the door. Rolly sprang up, aimed at the door, ready to pounce.

"Hey," a voice said. "What the hell is going on in there? I'm gonna call the cops."

Rosie went to the door and slowly opened it. "It's okay now. We'll be quiet." She turned to Rolly; he was scared and confused. Rosie tiptoed over to Rolly, put her hand on his, and they sat down. He curled up beside her, shook from his cold sweat.

Rosie took her towel, still wet from her shower, wiped it across Rolly's forehead, down his back. The towel came away even more soaked. "You're in the Yukon now," she whispered smoothly. "Remember that, Rolly. You're in the Yukon, now."

She took the blanket from the floor, put it over Rolly, tucked him in, put his head on her lap and waited for sunrise.

"Thank you for being here," he said.

"I'm with you, wherever you are,"

"Ya," he nodded, "the Yukon. Got a smoke?"

He smoked the cigarette, ground it out on his boot, then crawled into the bed Rosie made on the floor. He went back to sleep, but one eye kept opening, just to make sure everything was okay.

STEVE'S HOTEL ROOM

Steve let out a deep breath, shook his head one more time, left the bar and headed up to his room. It was a long day and he'd covered a lot more ground than he thought he'd cover when he got up and went to class that morning. He was too tired to be upset by the pool game, too tired to consider what lay in store for him.

Larry caught up to him at his door. "I didn't want to say this in the bar, but I gotta warn you about Rolly,"
Oh shit, Steve thought, "Now what is it?"
"Rosie fill you in,"
"She said he was a mirror,"
"That's true. Did Rosie tell you about his flashbacks?"
"What's a flashback?"
"Rolly thinks he's back in the jungle, sees things that aren't there. It's a Vietnam thing. Rosie can handle it. If she ain't around, just keep telling Rolly, 'you're in the Yukon; you're in the Yukon'. Remember that,"
"Okay, 'he's in the Yukon'. Got it."

Steve closed the door slowly and quietly, then lay on his bed. "You're in the Yukon; you're in the Yukon", ran circles in his mind, he couldn't figure out what it was and it wouldn't let him go.
There's got to be more to it than just that, he thought. Some deep memory was trying to push its way to the surface... then, he sat up straight.
He remembered when he was a child, back home in Vancouver, his Dad came home drunk, passed out, then woke up screaming, "Tanks, tanks, tanks."
His mother took him in her arms, rocked him back and forth like a baby, quietly repeated over and over again, 'You're in Canada, you're in Canada.'

Now Steve understood. It wasn't a Vietnam thing; it was a war thing. He felt as though a fear had left him, a fear he didn't know, but somehow he could recognize, and now that fear was gone, and that felt better.

If Rolly had a problem, a Vietnam thing, he knew he could handle it, and that knowledge was comforting. He dug around in his bag. Somehow, in the rush to the airport, he'd forgotten to pack his aspirin. He always kept his aspirin handy; he never knew when a migraine might flare up. He sat still, shook his head back and forth. No headache, no need for aspirin.

More memories were pushing their way to the surface. He remembered a cellar; it was cold and dark and there was a picnic.

BUDAPEST, HUNGARY
NOVEMBER, 1956

Little Stephan Kovacs sat on the bottom stair cuddling his brown and white and patched teddy bear. He was in the cellar of their tenement and it was cold, wet, poorly lit by one cracked window and smelled badly of mould and backed up sewage. He watched his mother, Tara, get prepared.

She leaned on her cane with her left hand, put her hip next to a heavy oak table and push-by-push worked it into the corner under the window. She climbed up on the table, closed and locked the window, then pulled down the shades. She lit a small candle, then tacked up a torn piece of blanket over the shades. She climbed back down off the table, limped over to the other corner of the basement, dug through a pile of planks and boards, picking out the best ones, then dragged them over to the table.

Dumping a small tin can of rusted and bent nails next to the planks on the table, she separated the straight ones from the bent ones. She had a small hammer with a cracked wooden handle so she tied the crack together with pieces of string, hammered out the bent nails, put them all in her apron pocket, put the hammer in her teeth and climbed back up on the table.

She picked up one of the planks, held it up against the window frame with her left shoulder, dug in her apron pocket with her right hand, pulled out a nail and passed it to her left hand, and held it in place with her thumb and ring finger. She pulled the hammer out of her teeth and hammered in the nail. A few minutes later she had planked over the entire window frame. She climbed back down from the table, pushed the few remaining planks under the table, spread them out and covered them with an old mattress.

She went to the bottom of the stairs, picked up a small duffel bag, put it under the table, then pushed some chairs against the table. She sat on the step next to Little Stephan, wrapped him snugly in her one woolen blanket, got the candle and crawled under the table.

She pulled Little Stephan in behind her and tucked him up into the corner.

Tara pulled a piece of cotton stuffing from the old mattress, rolled it into little balls and stuffed them into Little Stephan's ears, then her own.

She rearranged the woolen blanket around his head, making sure it was wrapped well around his ears, then placed her grandfathers' army helmet on his head.

Little Stephan struggled under the heavy helmet, "Mommy,"

"Now don't you worry sweetheart, even though grandpa is long gone, he's still here to help you. See, he left his helmet for you and it fits just fine."

She reached into the duffel bag, pulled out two bottles of water, one can of condensed milk, a loaf of bread, then said to Little Stephan, "We're going to have a picnic and I have a surprise for you,"

"What's that, Mommy?"

She opened her hands, and Little Stephan let out a happy howl as she showed him two chocolate cookies.

"One for you, Mommy, and one for me,"

"That's okay, sweetheart, I have some bread, you can have them both,"

"No, Mommy I want you to have one, too,"

Tara smiled and said, "The chocolates' a little sweet for me. You can have one now and save one for later,"

"Mommy, when can we go back upstairs?"

"When this is over,"

"When will that be,"

"I promise you this, Little Stephan, if it isn't over soon, we'll leave and go to a country where we will be safe all the time, where there are no tanks, where we won't be hungry and cold, where..."

"Where's that, Mommy,"

"Your Daddy told me about a country called Canada. He says they have big farms full of cows and pigs and chickens and fruit trees and chocolate factories that make chocolate all day long,"

"Where's Canada,"

"It's by the United States,"

"My kindergarten teacher told me that the United States is a capitalist country and they don't feed their people,"

"Not in Canada, nobody goes hungry in Canada,"

"Mommy, I want to go to Canada. When Daddy and Uncle Stephan come home can they take us to Canada?"

Tara smiled for Little Stephan, gave herself the cross of Jesus, and said, "I pray for it my Little Stephan, I pray for it."

Tara heard the gunfire in the distance; the single cracks of the rifles, the rapid cracks of the automatics, the booming of the bombs.

She felt them as they got closer. They didn't bother her anymore, she'd heard and felt them all before; when the Russians last invaded.

She knew how to sit and wait them out, wait for them to go away. She didn't worry about her own death anymore, she was ready to die since she was a child; it was nothing new.

It wasn't her own death that scared her; it was Little Stephan's life. Who would be his mother? Some Russian who didn't love him? Some Russian who hated all Hungarians? What kind of a mother would that be? What kind of life would Little Stephan have without his own mother to love him, without his own father to teach him the things he needed to know; that's what had her so scared. She had to stay alive to keep him away from the Russians, to let him know that no matter how hard life got; it was still worth living. She had to make sure they both survived the next tank attack.

She listened to the clanking, grinding sounds of the tank treads as they ground up the bricks in the road just outside their boarded up window. She checked the helmet on Little Stephan's head, watched a family of rats run up the stairs, then blew out the candle.

ZERO SIX HUNDRED! DROP YOUR COCKS AND GRAB YOUR SOCKS, THE GRAVEYARD'S THE PLACE TO SLEEP

Steve jumped awake. Who was yelling at the door, what the hell was zero six hundred and what was that about your cocks and socks and sleeping in graveyards?

"UP, UP." He heard again He shivered in the darkness, reached to the back of his neck, dipped his fingers deep in sweat. A black shape stood in the open door, a shadowy silhouette against a dim red hallway. Rolly. The door was kicked hard as a cold breeze circled the room. He heard boots clomping down the stairs. The sheets were soaked, his fingers dripped, he couldn't stop shaking. The cold breeze circled back.

Steve staggered to the shower, turned it on hot, stepped in, slumped against the wall. He slid down into the tub, steaming hot water pouring over him. He shaved the peach fuzz from his upper cheeks, dressed warmly, packed his bag, walked the three blocks to the Ice Box Cafe.

Morning had struck, cold and crisp, still black with a sharp wind from the north. His face, the only skin exposed to the cold, prickled and burned. His eyes were raw, his stomach hard. He elbowed his way into the packed and noisy cafe', worked his way into the middle of the crowd before he saw Rolly. He had the last two seats at the end of long table, and in front of him was a breakfast of four pieces of toast, four eggs, half a plate of hash-browns, eight sausages, an eight ounce steak, a plate of pancakes followed by three large glasses of milk.

Steve though it was for both of them.

"What took you so long? Hurry up and order, eat lots, we gotta long road ahead of us,"

"That's not for both of us?"

"Nope, I'm hungry. You order, I pay."

Rolly used a fork and spoon alternately to shovel food into his mouth. Both doubled as knifes and as he cut with one he shoveled with the other.

His hands were in perfect motion; one after the other, cutting and feeding, back and forth, never once missing the target mouth.

When either fork or spoon was put down he picked up his milk, and head bent back, sucked it down. He could swallow in one mouthful what the average man would in three, and he did it twice as fast. He also got his napkin up to his face at regular intervals without changing speed or losing coordination; a ballet of bad manners.

Steve watched the show. "Anybody ever teach you table manners?"

"I got more table manners than you can shake a stick at. When I was a kid if I didn't use my manners Mom would yank my ear,"

"So why don't you use them?"

"Save 'em for when I need 'em."

Rolly ate his meal without a spill. Steve ordered his breakfast, and by the time it arrived, Rolly was finished.

"Listen to this," Rolly said. He slyly looked all around the cafe, put both hands to the sides of his stomach, massaged a little, opened his mouth wide, pushed his hands hard, and let out an ear-cracking long-winded burp that rattled the windows.

The waitress dropped her order pad. The cook leaned out through his order window. Everyone turned and stretched to stare at Rolly. Silence took over like a quick wind from the town dump.

Rolly nodded and smiled. The quiet was so thick you could float in it. Applause started in one corner then spread through the cafe like an ovation for a symphony performance. There were cheers and whistles. Some stood and clapped. Rolly acknowledged the applause by standing up and taking a formal bow.

"No need for the applause, folks, just throw money."

He stretched out his arms and bowed again. Nickels and dimes flew over to the table like rice at a wedding and Rolly made a grand stand show of bending over to pick up the scattered change.

"Thank-you, thank- you, thank-you. All donations gratefully accepted."

Steve didn't know if he was proud or ashamed to be sitting with Rolly. "How much did you get,"

"It's impolite to count your makings at the table," Rolly whispered, then inhaled his last glass of milk as he pocketed the loose change. "Cheap pricks, all that work and no quarters.'

Rolly grabbed a piece of steak off Steve's plate, stuck it in his mouth and started chewing.

"God damn it, get your hands off my food," Steve shouted.

"Okay, fine," Rolly said. He took the half chewed piece of steak out of his mouth and put it on the edge of Steve's plate.

Steve put his hands up in the air and shook his head.

Rolly said, "Okay, fine," then took the half chewed piece of steak, put it back in his mouth and started chewing again. "Now this is what we gotta do before we leave town,"

Steve started back at his breakfast and Rolly picked up his fork. "Not again," Steve said.

"Okay, fine. First we stop at the Yukon General Warehouse. They sell everything 'cept fresh meat and truck parts. All of it wholesale so I save a lot. I got an old friend there. He salts my order,"

"What's 'salt your order' mean?"

"I put my order in two days ago, pick it up this morning. It's half of what we need; all our food, smokes, shit like that. I met my old friend in the bar and told him the other half. He runs the night shift so he makes sure that he, and this is important, only he, fills the order. But we have to be up there before day shift starts at eight. Too many eyes on the day-shift, half of them are in love with the company,"

"How do you do it?"

"Once we got the truck up to the loading dock, all kinds of things just fall into the box. Save a lot of money that way. Me and my old friend split the difference,"

"That's stealing, isn't it?"

"Stealing? No, no, not at all. Reallocation of Resources is what it is,"

"'Reallocation of Resources'? What the hell is that?"

"Yukon General Warehouse is part of a worldwide corporation. We could empty the whole damn warehouse and they wouldn't notice a thing was missing. So me and my old friend we watch out for each other. He cuts me some room on the order, and I deliver him a load of firewood. He saves money on heating his old cabin; I save money on feeding my crew. And nobody gets hurt,"

"How did you figure all this out,"

"Which part?"

"The part about how nobody gets hurt,"

"I seen enough of the big guy fucken' over the little guy. It's an old story, old as history itself. Warehouse pays shit wages, won't let a union in without threatening to shut down and put everybody out of work. My old friend works for peanuts, and he's got three kids and can barely feed them. This way me and my old friend take care of each other. When you steal, you take something that belongs to somebody else. Nobody owns what we get. If you want to get fussy about it, it all belongs to some board of directors, or some stockholders group, or maybe just a bunch of assholes in New York, or London or Paris or Rome or upper bumfuck Iowa. They never notice the difference, but we sure do,"

"How'd you figure this out?"

"Easy, I used to work there. And then we go over to Yukon Lumber Supply where I have another old friend, and we do the same damn thing. It's not as easy with Lumber Supply. I have to order so much wood, and then pay for it. That gets me a slip to get into the yard. Then I have to make sure my friend is the one who does the loading. It says on the slip I paid for ten two-by-fours and he loads twenty. And he gets load of firewood for doing it, too. He's got two kids, but his old lady is out of control,"

"And I guess Yukon Lumber Supply is part of some worldwide corporation, too,"

"No, just Canada and the States,"

"What happens if you get caught?"

"We don't get caught,"

"What do you mean 'we' don't get caught? Listen Rolly; you hired me to cut wood, not steal stuff,"

"When you steal you take something from an individual. We used to do this in the marines, it's how you get things done, you have to be creative, or you don't get anything done,"

Steve narrowed one eye in suspicion as Rolly continued.

"Listen to this Steve: to survive in this world you have to have a guerrilla mind-set, I learned that in the 'Nam; you have to be able to live by your wits, to think ahead and see what you can do with what you've got. I've got a truck and a slip for the warehouse and I'll get one for the lumberyard. Those are my resources. The question for a guerrilla is what can you do with what you've got, using your wits. Corporations steal from each other all the time, they do it with lawyers. If what they're doing is illegal, they change the law to make it legal. I can't do that so I work outside the law. Stealing is when you take something out of somebody's pocket. That's criminal. What I do is being an outlaw,"

"So what's the difference between a criminal and an outlaw?"

"Jesus Christ, Steve, criminals hurt people. I don't,"

"So you have a philosophy that allows you to steal,"

"You still haven't got it. I do it to survive, not to stop somebody else from surviving. You were in university, what is the study of history all about,"

"Wars,"

"You got it. Armies coming into somebody else's country, killing everybody in their way, then stealing everything that's worth picking up and carrying away. You think I'm doing that? Who gets hurt?"

"Let me get this straight; history is armies killing and stealing, but what we're doing is having a guerilla mind-set,"

"Ya, that's about it."

"Okay, fine, let's go."

Rolly's pick-up was a rough looking and rougher sounding old four-by-four three-quarter ton crew-cab Chevy. There was a wrap-around bush-bar bumper, built up to the hood, with a heavy-duty power winch bolted down in the middle. The rusted winch cable was tangled with broken branches and browned leaves, giving the impression that it was well used and not well maintained. The two-tone paint job was flat black and sky blue, chipped and rusted along the dented fenders and door bottoms. The windshield was cracked, the wheels over-sized, the rear bumper hung lop-sided, and the doors had to be slammed hard to keep them shut. A shiny silver and black sticker was fixed to the passenger window:

ASS GRASS OR CASH - NOBODY RIDES FOR FREE

The truck had a plywood box over the back, which was full of truck parts, assorted tools, empty beer cans and oily rags. The box had holes drilled through the bottom and into the truck where binding wire held it to the truck's frame.

Steve threw his bag in the back seat of the truck and jumped up front. Dog was curled up on the back seat, tail across his nose to keep out the cold, and fast asleep. On top of the transmission hump, wedged under the dashboard, were two large truck heaters, stacked one on top of the other. Both blew a fierce hot blast into the cab. There was no radio.

They made it to the Yukon General Warehouse by seven o'clock and pulled up out front. The warehouse was an old barn-like building, painted yellow, set on cement blocks and framed with plywood. Rolly hopped out of the truck and rang a bell by the truck door entrance.

The door creaked open and he walked in, while Steve jumped into the driver's seat and backed in the truck. Rolly scrambled up an old wooden ladder onto the dock where a tall, curly haired blonde man met him.

Rolly yelled out, "Yo, Teddy!"

Teddy yelled out, "Yo, Rolly!"

Teddy had an ear-to-ear grin, filled with perfect shining white teeth that didn't look at all real, a chin that was as square as a box, a nose that looked formed out of putty, and blue eyes that snapped and sparkled in the reflection of the bright lights of the warehouse dock. Rolly and Teddy hugged each other and took turns lifting each other off the ground and giving each other bear hugs, while they both took turns howling out in playful pain. They walked out of sight into the warehouse and Steve heard loud voices and more playful howling.

Steve sat in the truck and fidgeted. No matter how many friends Rolly had at the warehouse, he was still nervous. He looked all around and saw nothing. He looked into the back seat at Dog snoring. He fidgeted more, then jumped out of the truck and climbed onto the loading dock. Rolly was standing in the middle of five men, all of them laughing and passing a joint. Rolly turned and saw Steve walking towards him.

"Hey, guys, this here's my new crew. Say hello, Steve."

Steve said 'hello' and shook hands with all them. He got all their names quickly and forgot them all quickly.

"How long are we going to be here," he whispered to Rolly.

"No longer than need be,"

"Is the order ready?"

"We got time," then Rolly turned quickly and looked over his shoulder. "What the fuck's he doing here?" he asked Teddy, motioning towards a corner of the dock where a well-dressed man in a business suit stood. He was looking at all of them in a very agitated manner.

"Shit, Wilson's here an hour early. Shit." said Teddy.

"Who?" Steve whispered to Rolly.

"General Manager,"

"Shit." Steve said.

The general manager was short and chubby, balding with a jet-black strip of hair around the back of his shiny head and over his tiny ears. He was perfectly shaved and dressed in a formal three-piece suit and red tie. His shoes had elevator heels to make him look taller. They glistened. His glasses were too thick for his fat face.

They were the same jet black as his hair and covered the bottom half of his eyebrows and the top half of his cheekbones. He cuddled a clipboard to his chest and his fingernails were perfectly manicured. He walked like a duck. He eyed Rolly and walked right up to him.

Rolly led off, "Good morning Mr. Wilson, Sir. And how are you this fine morning,"

Teddy and his crew did a lousy job of not chuckling.

Wilson stood still for a moment. "And just what are you doing here? I thought you weren't allowed on the property."

The crews' job of not chuckling was getting worse.

"Don't you men have work to do?"

They all separated in different directions. Teddy stood behind Mr. Wilson, made some funny faces, then moved out in front of Mr. Wilson and said, in a clear and steady voice, "I'll supervise the loading."

Mr. Wilson nodded, and then turned to Rolly "Get your order and be on your way,"

"Just saying 'hello' to my old friends. You must have some friends somewhere, don't you?"

Wilson looked Rolly in the eye, put the back of his right hand on his hip, gripped his clipboard hard to his chest with his left hand, then shifted his weight to his left foot.

"Do you want me to call the R.C.M.P.?"

Rolly turned to Steve, "Don't you wish Rosie was with us? Guess what she'd do?"

Steve looked down between the shelves and watched the crew passing another joint. They made funny faces at Wilson like they were a bunch of school kids.

"Do you have your order loaded," Wilson said to Rolly.

"Well, actually, no,"

"Well, got on with it then." He turned and waddled away.

Teddy came back and supervised Rolly handing boxes and bags to Steve. When they finished loading Rolly gave Teddy another hug, jumped off the dock onto the truck roof and did a dance. Steve jumped out of the truck, thinking Rolly might crash through the roof.

Dog jumped out, sat beside Steve and started howling. Wilson came back and stood there, amazed and shaking his head.

The crew returned, broke up laughing again, got sent back to work by Wilson again, so Rolly jumped down to the ground and back in the truck, all in one bouncing move.

He leaned out the window, shot his fist into the air, and yelled out, "Fuck you very much," He slammed his foot on the gas pedal and screeched off in a cloud of black smoke and flying gravel.

"Damn, I miss those guys. What a bunch of fuk-ups,"

"Why'd you get fired?"

"Reading skin books in the shit-house, couldn't take it anymore. Was losing my edge, worst thing a man can do is lose his edge, but it was good while I was here,"

"Losing your edge?"

"Too long in the same place, got a bad case of itchy feet."

Rolly drove up to the front gate of Yukon Lumber Supply. Surrounding the entire two acre compound was a twelve-foot high chain-link fence, topped with three strands of razorback barbed wire.

He ran into the office, and in a moment he ran back out with an entry slip to the yard and jumped into the truck. He handed the slip to the guard at the gate.

"First things first, now we find my other old friend." He drove around the yard in circles until he waved to a man in blue coveralls with a Lumber Supply Yard patch on his pocket.

"Just the guy I'm looking for,"

"Morning, Rolly, ya'll ready to load up?" Ricky's hair was long and black, stringy and greasy.

His beard was a collection of peach-fuzz scattered on his acne-scarred, blackhead covered face.

His teeth all went in different directions. They looked like a rotten picket fence. Steve gagged from his cheap wine breath.

"Okay, Ricky. Let's do it," Rolly jumped out of the truck.

"Follow me, Steve." Steve drove the truck through the yard and backed it up to a pile of two-by-fours.

"Get out Dog, go shit in the corner." Dog walked ten feet, lay down and watched.

"What's the slip say, Rolly,"

"Ten,"

"Count twenty." And they did.

Steve jumped into the truck and backed further into the yard. "Rolled roofing," Rolly said.

"Right," said Ricky. He grabbed three rolls and threw them into the truck.

"Three more," said Rolly and Ricky threw in three more.

"Three-inch nails,"

Ricky ran over to a tray of nails, poured some into a heavy paper bag and tossed them into the back of the truck. Ricky spotted a chain saw lying on the ground.

"Rolly, you see anybody watching,"

"For what,"

"New chainsaw."

The chain saw flew into the back of the truck.

"Okay, we need plywood now,"

"Right," Ricky and Rolly started heaping plywood into the truck.

"We're getting full." Rolly dropped to his hands and knees in the ice and snow and looked under the truck at the springs."They're not too sagged yet, more plywood."

Ricky and Rolly kept throwing plywood into the back of the truck as Rolly kept dropping to the ground and watching the truck springs sag."Okay, we're full."

Rolly and Steve jumped into the back of the truck and started sorting through the mess and stacking it properly, and then roped it all down.

"Dog, in," yelled Rolly, and Dog jumped back in.

Rolly climbed in behind the wheel and put the truck in gear as Steve scrambled into his seat.

Rolly turned the truck onto the Alaska Hi-way and started heading west."You have to admit this, Steve, was that fun or what?"

Steve nodded, "Ya, that was fun."

Rolly opened a bottle of sipping whiskey, had a drink as he watched the bubbles rise up to the bottom of the bottle. "Enough of the Alcan," he said, turning off the Alaska Hi-way onto a smaller road. It was full of ruts, rippled washboards, and potholes full of frozen mud and ice. "No more west; now its north on the Klondike Road."

Rolly's old truck shook and rattled over the potholes, pitching and rocking with every corner and bend. Steve put his feet up on the dashboard, half for comfort, half for stability, and stared out the window.

The sun was rising up behind them in the southern sky, and over the eastern mountains, casting a dim pink glow throughout the river valley. Over the bare rock faces of the hills Steve saw the sunlight streaking down across the flatness of the frozen marshes. He watched as the jack pines and scrub spruce thinned out as the valley narrowed.

They rattled over a shaky old wooden bridge, browned with age and coated in ice that swayed with the wind and pushed the truck from side rail to side rail.

Rolly cursed the wind, the rails, the bridge, but talked sweetly to his truck. "Come on sweetheart, that's it, hold her tight, no wild bounces, that's it, nice and tight, hold on now, that's it, we're clear."

With every curse, and every sweet talk, Steve became more and more confused with the advice he got about Rolly. He seemed really happy behind the wheel, at the warehouse, the lumber yard, with Larry and Rosie and Sammy, just all around happy.

The slippery road that took them out of the lower valley wiggled back and forth, slowly making its' way up the hill, while Rolly continued with his non-stop talking to the truck. When the road would allow, he pulled on his whiskey bottle, yawned and scratched.

They topped the hill onto a wide high mountain plateau, the wind picked up, and the truck wandered all the more.

A ravine opened up and they quickly dipped back down. Rolly rode the brakes down the south side of the valley, slipping and sliding, grinding gears, spinning the wheel and singing out his curses. Steve looked down into the valley and saw wolves playing along the riverbank, chasing something around in the muskeg brush.

All along the side of the road he saw wolf and rabbit tracks, all criss-crossing and tying themselves in knots and mazes.

"Look down there!" Rolly screamed over the whine of the truck. "That's the 'Marge'."

"The what,"

"The 'Marge of Lake Lebarge', where Sam Magee got cooked. You know, Robert Service's poem,"

Steve sat up in his seat and pressed his face to the window. He looked down into the valley, to a small spit of land that reached out into the lake. That was it! He was at the 'Marge of Lake Lebarge'. He remembered class, yesterday, but it seemed like long ago in some forgotten lecture hall, sitting next to Sheila.

Steve put his feet back up on the dashboard and settled into his seat. He watched the few trees flying by the window, looked down to the ground and imagined wolves running alongside the truck, jumping up to say hello like friendly dogs welcoming their master home. The sun flashed through the scrub brush in splashes of red and pink, yellow and blue, green and white, leaving after-images in Steve's eyes like a TV set in a darkened room.

Rolly was leaning back comfortably in his seat, enjoying the ride and the warm blast coming out of the double heaters stacked on the transmission. He looked up to check his rear view mirror.

The rising sun hit the mirror straight on, blinding him with a bright yellow glare, and in the middle of that bright yellow glare, a burning black spot, just like an incoming mortar round.

Rolly's entire nervous system went into massive overload. An electric shock rammed through every cell in his body as he was taken over by the brute will to survive.

INCOMING he screamed out.

He spun the truck off the road into midair, it crashed down into the bush, then bounced back up as snow covered broken branches flew aside. Steve's eyes shot wide open. He looked through the windshield, through the bush, to the edge of a cliff, and the sheer drop below. Rolly's arms were a flying blur as he fought the steering wheel and furiously pumped the brakes.

Steve grabbed at the door handle. It jammed. The truck flipped up and onto the drivers' side, hit a tree, slammed back down again, then stopped.

Rolly flung his door open, grabbed Steve by the collar, dragged him across the seat and out the door. He ran through the knee high snow, hauling Steve by the collar, all the time screaming,

INCOMING, INCOMING, INCOMING

Rolly was in the middle of a mortar barrage, and he had to get away, quickly. There was one tight opening in the bush, between wounded out. Charlie was walking in the rounds, two at a time, each pair exploding fifty feet ahead of the other, three seconds apart. The only way out was down the middle. He had his wounded by the collar, ran for the middle of the rounds.

He felt his foot pull on a twig, no, it was a trip wire; he got down quick, face first in stinking rice paddy muck. He spat out a mouthful of snow. It didn't taste like shit; it was cold.

He lay quiet, no more incoming; Charlie's going to rush him.

He almost panicked, trying to get his gloves off, trying to find his weapon. Why is it so goddamn quiet, he thought?

He heard a voice, not the radio, not the corporal."You're in the Yukon; you're in the Yukon,"

"'The Yukon'? What zone is that?"

Soft and gentle, reassuring and warm, he heard. "You're in the Yukon. You're in the Yukon."

Rolly was wondering why was there snow in the rice paddy, why the sun was so low, why it was cold. Who's talking? What's that over there? It's not a jeep, it's my truck.

MY TRUCK

Rolly sat up and shook his head. Steve took some snow, gently rubbed it on Rolly's face and calmly said, "You're in the Yukon, you're in the Yukon."

Rolly started shivering, his sweat soaked body started to cool as his heart hammered in his chest. Steve sat next to him, wrapped his arms around him, just like his mother did for his father, and rocked him back and forth. "You're in the Yukon, you're in the Yukon."

They both looked over to Rolly's truck, still running. The engine coughed once, twice, shuddered, then quit. Steam hissed out of the radiator.

Rolly blinked quickly, squeezed his eyes closed, shook his head, opened his eyes. "You okay, Steve?"

Steve was seriously happy to hear the sound of his own name. "Ya, I'm okay, Rolly. You okay?"

Rolly was still shivering. "Ya, I'm okay." He turned to smile at Steve. "My truck." he said.

He stood up, helped Steve to his feet, as they brushed off the snow. "I'm gonna get the whiskey."

He calmly walked over to the hissing truck, climbed into the cab and started digging around in the mess, "Where the hell is that damn thing." he muttered.

Steve watched and wondered, 'what the hell is that guy doing?

He's just gone through all this shit with the truck and his flashback, and he's carrying on like nothing happened, like this is all normal stuff.

Rolly found the whiskey and climbed out. They stood there, watched the hissing radiator, passed the whiskey.

The sun had now fully risen in the southeast and the clouds had cleared.

"Nice view, eh, Steve?" Rolly said.

Twenty feet from where the truck stopped there was a sharp embankment, with a sharper drop into the valley below. He carefully walked along the cliff edge, found a spot, sat with his boots dangling over the side. Dog picked his way through the brush and came up for a nuzzle. He sat in the snow, breathing heavily, and looked up at Rolly.

"Jumped out first chance, eh, Dog?" Rolly said. "Should send the government a bill for the road we cleared." He took the bottle, held it high, "Thanks, God. Saved my beloved ass once again."

He had a long drink, followed by a loud burp. Steve took the bottle and very carefully joined Rolly on the cliff edge. He took a long drink and burped out, "Thanks, God."

They sat on the cliff edge, enjoyed the view and finished the bottle. Rolly stood up, leaned back, and for all he was worth, threw the bottle and watched it sail down into the trees. He walked back over to the truck and started checking the damage.

"We got a torn rad hose, one mirror flattened out. Windows are all okay, that's important. That's all I can see for now."

Steve watched the blue and green anti-freeze drain out of the radiator and into the snow, then turned back to study the view. He looked again at the fluid draining out of the radiator, the truck sitting up to its' axles in the snow, the open door creaking back and forth in the wind, Rolly wandering back and forth, figuring out what to do next, then he started laughing. He laughed so hard he lost his balance on the cliff edge, had to flipped over onto his stomach to keep from falling.

His legs flapped over the edge, toes desperately trying to find something to dig into, hands frantically grasping in the snow.

He felt himself slipping down, lifted his head to cry out, looked up and Rolly was in mid-air.

He landed on Steve's head, grabbed him, again, by the collar, and flipped him clear of the cliff face. "Once is enough," he said. "What are you laughing at? You're lucky we didn't roll, would have been a hell of a mess."

Steve crawled away from the cliff edge, got up and brushed off the snow, then sat down again. "If I had any brains, I'd be at home working on my term paper. But no, I had to say 'fuck it' and fly up to this frozen place, lose all my money playing pool, nearly fall off a cliff, now I'm stuck on the side of the road, probably going to freeze to death, and I still don't know why. Now what the hell do we do?"

"Change the rad hose, thaw some water, and put the truck back on the road. Ain't no point in wondering why you're here, you're just here, and that's what you got to deal with. Rest of that stuff don't mean shit to a tree. Be happy you're not dead,"

"Well, that makes me feel a whole lot better,"

Rolly sat down in the snow next to Steve, took a deep breath, let it out slowly. Dog came over and nuzzled into Steve's arm.

Rolly nodded. "You scared,"

Steve nodded, "A little,"

"Scared shit outta me, I thought we were history. Well, you saved my ass, I saved yours, we're even,"

"What?"

"Just back there, I was getting mortared and you was falling off the cliff, we're even,"

"What?"

Rolly was calm about everything. "The mortars, I thought they was coming from the west," he said, pointing into the trees,

"so I headed west, if it was the other way, I could've dragged you off the cliff. Seems you wanted to go there anyways. Where'd you lean to deal with that shit of mine?"

"From my Mom and Dad, he was in the war,"

"Ya, I remember you telling me that. Good."

Steve changed the topic. "You did a pretty good job of not rolling the truck,"

Rolly turned to stare out over the cliff again." You know, I didn't even know the cliff was there, isn't that something? I'll usually pay attention to those things. Of course, all that weight in the back helped; sometimes it works for you, sometimes it works against you. This time it was on our side. Stand up,"

"What for,"

"Just stand,"

Steve did.

"Bend over and touch your toes. Uh-huh. Arms over your head. Uh-huh. Twist from side to side. Uh-huh. You got a bump on your forehead, otherwise, you're okay."

Steve felt the bump on his forehead. He knew there were more, he just couldn't tell where.

"Roll us a joint." Rolly handed Steve a bag of weed and some rolling papers, then walked around to the truck box. He dug around in the mess, threw out a one gallon metal bucket, a five gallon plastic pail, the chain saw, a few two-by-fours, and a plastic tarp.

He took the tarp over to Steve. "Here, sit on this. If you sit in the snow it'll thaw and soak your ass. Then you get frost-bite of the butt."

Rolly started up the chain saw and cut the two-by-fours into short pieces, then dug a hole in the snow, down two feet to dirt, and piled the pieces of two-by-four in the hole.

He turned off the saw, opened the fuel port and poured fuel on the pile. He took out a match and lit the pile, grabbed the metal bucket, filled it with snow, set it in the fire.

"Keep putting snow into the bucket until it's thawed and full of water. Then pour it into this pail, and do it all over again till we got enough water to fill the rad. Keep the water in the pail hot or it'll freeze."

Rolly walked back and forth beside the truck's under-carriage poking and jabbing, turning and pulling. He patted the truck on the hood and hollered at Steve. "This is my truck and it's a beautiful truck." Then he turned to the truck, "You are a beautiful truck, aren't you, truck."

Then he went back to the mess in the box.

He pulled out a six foot truck jack, wedged it under the truck, jacked it up as high as he could, then pushed the truck off the jack, moving the truck three feet closer to the road.

He kept doing that, going from the front bumper to the back, jacking it up and pushing it off and forward, slowly working his way back to the road.

"Got that joint rolled, yet,"

"I wish I had a camera. Nobody back home would believe this,"

"I would,"

"You're not from back home,"

"You're not back home, you're here, what's done is done. Don't mean nothin'; don't mean a damn thing,"

"'What's done is done'? What the hell is that supposed to mean? We almost got killed here,"

"'Almost', don't mean shit either. You got a bump on your head, that's it. Now quit your pissing and moaning and roll that damn joint,"

"Shit." Steve sat down on the tarp and spit a little blood onto the snow."Bit my lip, too,"

"Should we call in a dust-off?"

"What's a 'dust-off'?"

"Helicopter medical evacuation,"

"A helicopter medical evacuation for my lip?"

"I don't think a bit lip would qualify. How about a medical evacuation for your brain,"

"What's wrong with my brain?"

"You been complaining about it, how it doesn't work. How's the fire doing?"

"It's burning down,"

"And you want to know what's wrong with your brain. What do you think you should do about that fire that's burning down? You said you could run a chain saw,"

"I didn't say I could run it, I said, well what the hell did I say,"

"You said you could outwork anybody. Let's see you do just that. There's the saw,"

Steve picked up the saw and looked at it. He turned it one way, then the other.

Rolly took it, showed him how to start it, "Be careful," he said.

"Fuck off," Steve said.

"Oh, such language."

Steve cut up some of the two-by-fours and piled them on the fire. Rolly came over to the fire and warmed his hands. He bent over to look closely at Steve's boots.

"What?" Steve said, looking at his boots, wondering what Rolly was looking at.

"You did a good job,"

"I know,"

"No, you don't. Any asshole can run a chain saw, but look what you did."

Rolly was still staring at Steve's boots. "You still have your feet where they belong. You didn't cut them off, good job. Got that joint rolled yet?"

"Fuck off again,"

"Such language, I'm gonna tell your mom on you. Keep that fire going, you got that joint rolled yet?" Rolly went back to jacking up the truck and kicking it off.

"Now the rad hose." Rolly dragged a piece of plywood from the pile and slid it under the radiator. He climbed back into the truck, reached around behind the seat and pulled out a toolbox. Then he crawled under the radiator and pulled out the broken hose.

"Got that joint rolled yet?" Rolly was looking at the broken rad hose and scratching his head. He dug into the pile at the back of the truck and fished around in the mess for a while.

He pulled out an old rad hose, another bottle of whiskey and a small jug of anti-freeze. "I always keep everything," he with a grin, then went back under the truck and put in the old hose.

Steve poured the anti-freeze into the pail of water, and then emptied that into the radiator. Then they both went over to the fire and warmed their hands.

"Think the truck will start," Steve asked.

Rolly put his finger to his lips, almost whispered, "Don't talk nasty about my truck, it'll hear you."

Rolly climbed into the truck, turned the key, the engine coughed once, twice, blue smoke poured out the exhaust, and the engine started its familiar whine.

"Got that joint rolled yet," he yelled out the window as he drove the last few feet back to the road. "Off your ass, buddy. Come on, Steve, get up."

Steve staggered over to the truck, couldn't work the door handle. His fingers were cold, rigid and white. Rolly opened the door for him and he climbed in.

"I'm going to roll this joint if it kills me." Steve was fumbling with the joint and spilling weed on the floor.

He managed to pull a rolling paper out of its packet, fold it in his fingers and started putting the weed in it. He dropped some on his lap, picked it up and put it back in the paper. He fumbled some more, dropped some more, picked it up again, and kept rolling. Finally, he got the joint rolled.

"Well done, my boy. You'll be a Yukoner yet, even if it kills you trying."

Steve put the joint in his mouth, and Rolly leaned over with cupped hands and lit his Zippo. Steve tried to light the joint, but his lips wouldn't form an airtight seal. His face felt like he'd been to the dentist.

"Froze your face," Rolly took the joint out of Steve's mouth and rubbed his cheeks. "That'll teach you to shave this time of year. Your cheeks is bit."

Steve's cheeks felt waxy, and were forming red blotches. "Wrinkle your face. Stretch the muscles. Come on Steve, put some work into it. You got to get the blood back in your face." Rolly rubbed more to keep the blood moving into Steve's face.

Steve started shaking, "Bit," he mumbled. He tucked his hands under his armpits, snuggled his head down into his chest, pulled up his knees and rolled over on his side.

"Okay, let's go." Rolly carefully laid him over the seat, pulled off his coat and put it over Steve, massaged Steve's hands, finger by finger, then sat Steve up so he could put his hands over the heater vent.

He took off Steve's boots and massaged his feet.

"Can you drink," Rolly held the bottle to Steve's lips. He drank, and then spit it out.

He lurched for the window, got it down just in time to puke.

Rolly leaned forward, held Steve's forehead with one hand and the other massaged Steve's stomach as he puked out the window.

Rolly sat back, took a drink, looked at the bottle, capped it and dumped it on the floor. Steve sat back and closed the window.

""Hmm,"

"You were standing still and getting cold, while I was jacking up the truck and staying warm. I should have given you more wood for the fire."

Rolly massaged Steves' stomach some more. "I should have seen your face changing color,"

"I shouldn't have drunk so much that I didn't feel the cold,"

"Sure as hell you're not the first to drink your way to frostbite,"

"I'm okay now," Steve wiped his sleeve across his mouth.

"Jesus Christ, that's my coat your wiping puke all over,"

"Your fault, your coat,"

"Shit. Put your hands back on the heater."

Rolly listened intently to the sounds of the engine, his head cocked so his right ear was aimed at the engine. He stared at the gauges, watching for any changes that could signal more trouble.

"How's your face?"

"Burning,"

"It's my fault, I'm sorry." Rolly almost scared Steve with that. He seemed shook up.

The truck rattled and shook as it had before, but Steve didn't daydream or gaze out into the mountains. Every bend was a quick slip into a snow-bank; every valley waited to swallow the truck.

Every hill to crawl up or slide down was a roll-over waiting to happen. When Rolly pulled on the wheel, Steve held tight to the door handle. He kept working the latch, and his fingers, open and closed, open and closed. Next time it wouldn't jam. He wanted to pay attention, to be ready if the truck left the road, but he couldn't stop the memories of his mother cradling his father, saying, "You're in Canada," after "Tanks," now it was "You're in the Yukon," after "Incoming."
Why was Rolly so calm about everything? Rosie said he was a mirror, Larry told him he had flashbacks. Steve wondered about his father and why he never talked about his flashbacks. Rolly said that was because he never asked?

Was it too painful for his father to talk about it, or was he too embarrassed over his crying. What would Rolly say?

"Rolly, I want to ask you a question."

Rolly knew what was coming. He knew when people asked him about the war, they didn't want his answers. They wanted stories of glory, good guys against bad guys, simple stuff; Saturday morning cartoons stuff.

He knew they didn't want to listen to him say the war was a waste of time and lives and suffering for nothing; that the war was a bunch of slogans thrown out by hot-headed and dim-witted politicians giving speeches about patriotism and sacrifice, while other people did the dying; that the war was only about power and the grab for it, and it's always been that way and always will. They only wanted Saturday morning cartoons. Despite everything Rolly had been through; the frustration of people asking him questions they didn't want his answers to; arguing with him over things they knew nothing about; blaming him for the war, like he himself started it, and he himself was losing it; not honoring his dead friends because they didn't agree with the war; he was still willing to answer their questions, if only they were willing to listen to his answers.

Rolly turned to look at Steve and the look in his eyes calmed Steve. "Okay, Steve, let's have it."

Steve saw the gentleness that Rolly showed when he joked with Rosie or Larry; when he checked that all was well with Sammy; when he didn't get upset that Hank took all his money.

Sure Rolly was noisy on the surface, and he did have a sense of humor, but there was no bullshit with Rolly, he was genuine, he cared.

"Tell me about incoming,"

Rolly nodded to himself; seemed to agree that this question was worth answering. "Incoming is what you yell out when mortars or rockets come in. Some fucking new guys couldn't tell incoming from outgoing. Outgoing is what you send to Charlie; incoming is what he sends back; and Charlie sends it back whenever the hell he wants to. Day, night, you never know how much, how long; you don't know 'till it's over and you never know when it's over. If you don't know the difference, if you don't get your head down and keep it down, you lose it. I got real tired of putting people in bags because they couldn't tell the difference. Does that answer your question?" Rolly knew it didn't.

Steve was still not sure about another thing. He knew that Rolly had a sense of honor, what was wrong and what was right.

Rolly was also clear on the difference. He didn't care about stealing from a company, but he did care about the well being of his friends, and would do anything for them.

Steve sometimes wasn't sure what honor was, but he was sure what it wasn't. Hank didn't have it, but that didn't bother Rolly; he understood that Hank had no choice, he couldn't work, he had to hustle pool, that's how he got fed and Rolly knew that. But Rolly still wouldn't play pool with him.

Steve knew that Rolly had a sense of pride, but he didn't let it get in his way. When he looked out for Sammy, he let Sammy know he wanted some smoked jerky in return for getting him moose meat. This helped Sammy keep his own pride; that he was paying Rolly for what he did for him. Steve knew that you had to have pride in order to recognize it.

His father taught him that coaching soccer; play with pride and respect it in the opposition.

Don't play dirty; you dishonor yourself and your team.

Rolly was a Marine and Marines had pride. That much Steve did know. Even though he and Rolly had just gone through a flashback together, and Steve was never in a war, he still knew things other people didn't know. Rolly was strangely calm about the whole thing, but Steve was still not sure how to ask the question that bothered him the most, but he had to ask.

"Rolly, why'd you desert?"

MAY 30, 1968

Sergeant Rolly McGarret stood up and wiggled his toes to get the blood flowing. He heaved his duffel bag up to his shoulder, climbed down the steps of the Air Force transport and turned his collar in from the rain. The protestors were at the gates, waving signs and hurling insults. He didn't care what they had to say, he'd been there, he knew what was and what wasn't. He'd been warned about them.

Standing on the airport tarmac, with a bunch of other troops he didn't know, all returning home after their tours, he felt very alone. He'd dreamt of this moment, even prayed for it, every day and night since his tour began, now it all seemed like nothing.

When he first got to Vietnam he was proud; of himself, his unit, his mission, his country. Now he was only proud of his unit. Only the men he served with meant anything to him, and a lot of them were dead.

Rolly was a ground pounding grunt. His job was to find the enemy and kill them; or take them prisoner, get information from them, turn them over to the appropriate authorities. If they surrendered, he took them, if not, he killed them. That was his job for the marines. His job for himself was to get home to his family, and if he had to kill the whole god damn Viet Cong and North Vietnamese Army to get home, then that was what he was going to do. He took no pleasure in his job; actually it made him quite sick. He tried not to think about it too much, but, sometimes, he couldn't help himself, he couldn't make the memories go away. He had no choice with what he did, or what he thought about what he did.

On the tarmac that day he wondered what had happened and why. It was the answer he would spend the rest of his life looking for. On that day he was only interested in getting home and seeing his family. He was homesick, that much was for sure, but it was his kid brother that he worried about.

He had to get to him quick, each day counted now, his kid brothers' clock was ticking. He was almost eighteen, almost old enough to join up.

When the plane refueled in Hawaii, Rolly phoned home. He looked at his fingernails. Bitten to the quick, and under what was left of them, the red clay of 'Nam.

When he showered back at the base, before he caught the 'Freedom Bird' home, he tried to scrub them clean, get the clay out, get the memory out. He scrubbed them 'till they bled, but still the red clay remained.

They hurt when he dialed the phone.

"Peter, I'm in Hawaii. I'll be at the airport at five. Pick me up,"

"All right, I'll be there. How many commies did you kill? I'm old enough next month, I'm joining up,"

"One from this family's enough. We'll talk when I get home. Can you get into the bar?"

"I can get into any bar,"

"Meet me there."

Rolly thought about nothing but his kid brother on the flight to San Francisco. How many commies did you kill? What kind of question was that? He's got absolutely no idea what he's getting into. I'll tell him: the only way to know is to go, and then it's too late.

'Gotta save his ass, one from this family's enough', that same thought repeated itself, over and over again, like a broken record that kept playing the same line.

Rolly went to the bar at the airport and took a seat in a distant corner where he could see everything. He looked out the door and saw Peter walking down the hallway.

Peter stretched to look taller and swaggered into the bar like he owned the place. He tossed his coat into a chair, dropped his cigarettes on the table, dumped himself into a chair and leaned back.

He pushed his voice down low, "Two whiskeys, two beers." he yelled at the waitress.

Rolly sat and watched Peter, how much he'd grown over the last year and the show he put on of being all grown up.

He didn't recognize the clothes he wore; the bell bottom blue jeans, the flowered shirt, the wide leather belt. When Rolly left for the 'Nam; Peter wasn't even shaving and now he had side-burns and hair over his ears. He did look taller. Was that really Peter?

He couldn't take it any longer, the wait was too much. He decided to sneak up on him. He quietly walked over, tapped him on his left shoulder, while standing at his right.

Peter spun to look to his left and nobody was there. He was rattled, then turned to his left. He jumped up and hugged Rolly.

"What's with all the hair," Rolly said.

"It grows. Look at all your medals,"

"Uh-huh,"

The waitress came over with their drinks.

"Thanks, honey pie," Peter said. "Give my brother a kiss; he just got home from Vietnam."

The word 'Vietnam' made Rolly wince. He hid the look of pain.

His face twitched. The waitress looked bored. "Why don't you kiss him? That'll be four bucks,"

"What do you mean, 'me kiss him', he just got home from Vietnam."

Rolly winced again.

"He's a hero, kiss him 'Hello'. Kiss him 'Welcome home,"

"Four bucks, please."

Rolly reached into his pocket and pulled out the four dollars and offered it to her.

"No way," Peter said, grabbing Rolly's outstretched hand. "No brother of mine fresh out of Vietnam is going to pay for his own drinks. He should get them on the house.

The waitress put her hand on her hip and looked to the ceiling, then turned down to glare at Peter. "Listen, kid, in this bar I get guys straight out of 'Nam every fucken' hour on the hour. If I start giving away drinks, this place would go bankrupt and I'd be out of a job. Four bucks, please,"

"You bitch," Peter said.

Rolly stood up and put his hand on Peter's shoulder. "Settle down, I'll take care of it." Rolly handed her the money and she took it. "Peter, I'm not ready this. Take it easy, will you,"

"What do you mean, 'take it easy'? There should be a parade for you, ticker tape and everything. Fuck those anti-war commie lovers,"

"No, don't fuck anybody. Listen Peter, I was in the field, and in the field it's different than what you think," Rolly looked up.

A woman was walking over to the table. She looked very angry. She stopped at the table and stared at Rolly. She stared at his uniform. "Did you just come from Vietnam," she demanded. "Did you,"

Rolly rubbed his forehead, hiding his eyes. He shook his head. "Fuck," he said.

"Did you kill women and babies?"

Rolly sat still and silent. He didn't move, didn't answer. He looked away and closed his eyes. Peter was stunned.

She screamed at Rolly. "Baby killer, fucken baby killer." She grabbed his beer, threw it in his face. She spat on him.

Rolly picked up a napkin and wiped the spit and beer off his face. He was silent.

Peter sprang to feet screaming, "You bitch, you fucken' bitch. Who the hell do you think you are? What kind of American are you, he's a hero, not a baby killer."

He turned to Rolly, "Tell her, Rolly. Tell her." He leaned across the table and grabbed at the woman.

She jumped back. "He tried to hit me, he tried to hit me. See, see, I told you so. They're both baby killers."

The bartender ran over and shoved Peter back into his seat. He pulled the woman back, locked his arms around her, pinning her arms to her side, then wrestled her screaming through the bar and pushed her out the door.

He returned. "Sorry about that," he said. "We try to get them out as soon as possible, but we can never tell who's going to do it next. The hippies are obvious, but she didn't look like one,"

"It's okay," Rolly said, "I was warned,"

Peter was almost crying. "What do you mean 'its okay', Rolly? How can you take shit like that? It's not 'okay',"

The bartender said."Listen, Welcome home Marine. Let me buy you guys a beer,"

"No, thanks, time to go." Rolly said. "Peter, let's get out of here,"

"Warned," Peter said.

"Lot of guys get shit like that. Come on, let's go,"

"I haven't finished my drink,"

Rolly grabbed Peter's drink and slugged it down. "Now you're finished."

They left the bar, went out to the front of the airport, flagged down a taxi.

"Where' ya going soldier," the driver said.

"Richmond,"

"Finish your tour,"

"Uh-huh,"

"Bring any horse with you? I'll give you a good price on some horse,"

"Didn't have time, just got my papers,"

"Shit. You guys are the best thing that ever happened to me. All day long I just pick up you guys fresh from the 'Nam and buy your horse. You should 'a brought some back with you, great money to be made from this war."

"What's horse," Peter said.

"Heroin,"

"That's illegal,"

"So's killing without a permit, that's how a lotta guys survived the war,"

"What are you talking about?"

"Nothing, let me think."

Rolly stared out the taxi window watching the sights of his hometown roll by. They were different now, something he couldn't put his finger on, something he didn't understand. These were the streets he grew up on, the streets he went to war to protect; the corner store where he stole cigarettes as a kid. The pool-hall where he hustled a few extra dollars and the bar he snuck into when he was under-age. The empty lot where he played football and baseball; the abandoned building where he and Mary Lou Wilson played naked games, old man Haggartys' general store where he worked afternoons and weekends during high school; all the same, yet somehow different.

What played with his mind, on top of his fear about Peters' joining up, was what he was going to say to his father.

How could he convince his father, a career marine that Peter should stay out of the marines, stay out of Vietnam, and go to college where he belonged.

He was the smarter of the two brothers; they always laughed about that.

The taxi pulled up in front of his parents' home. They stood on the porch, waiting for their son, the one they didn't know if they'd ever see again. His father stood proudly wearing his uniform; his son was home from the war. He remembered when he came home to his parents, after his own war.

Rolly's mother ran down the steps and across the lawn to hold him, sobbing out tears of relief.

He'd come home, and thank God, in one piece. He wasn't in a wheel chair like the Anderson boy down the road. He'd come home alive, not like the Tucker boy who came home in a box. And he hadn't turned his back when his country was in need, like the Brenner boy, sneaking off to some foreign place, leaving his family behind to bare the shame.

Together they walked arm in arm into the house with Peter carrying Rolly's duffel bag. The neighbors looked out their windows, happy for the McGarrets', sad for the Tuckers, and angry with the Brenner's.

"I'd like to propose a toast," Rolly's father said as they settled down in the living room. He reached into his liquor cabinet, underneath the bronze American eagle that was next to a thirteen star flag of the United States; all surrounded by his military medals and pictures him and other family members in uniform, including Rolly. He pulled out a part bottle of Scotch.

"This bottle was given to me by my mother, God rest her soul, when I got home from Japan in '45. We had a toast then, her and my father, your mother and me. The war was over and I had a home assignment. I had done my job and was lucky enough to come home in one piece, as you, Rolly, have done. We each had one drink out of this bottle. When you were born, Rolly, we had another drink, and then again when you, Peter, were born. I think it's time now for another drink,"

Mr. McGarret pulled out four shot glasses and put one ounce into each and passed them around. "A prayer," he said. They stood in a circle, holding each other's hands and bowed their heads.

"Thank you, Lord, for watching over Rolly and bringing him home safe and sound and we pray that you watch over all our boys defending democracy and fighting communism in Vietnam; that you guide our President in this time of need; that you watch over Peter when his time comes and bring him back home safe and sound. Thank-you, Lord, Amen."

They raised their glasses and drank.

"What now, Rolly, another tour?"

"Not a chance, still owe the Marines six months,"

"You've done your duty, Rolly," said his mother. "I'm proud of you. Did Peter tell you he's joining up next month?"

Now was the moment that Rolly feared the most. He knew he had a good chance with Peter, if he could get him alone; he could hopefully talk some sense into him. But his father was definitely 'old school'; he didn't stand a chance with him.

"I think Peter should go to college," Rolly said.

"After his service," his father said.

"Instead of his service. One from this family is enough,"

"'Instead of his service'? Everybody does their service,

Rolly stood up and walked around his living room. He looked out the window, up and down the street. He knew it was coming, it had to be done, and there was no other way.

"Vietnam is a waste of time. I don't want Peter there,"

"Waste of time? What's that mean, 'waste of time',"

"We're not doing any good there, nobody wants us there, and we don't want to be there,"

Rolly's mother was silent until then. She was usually quiet, left most of the talking to the men, but now she wanted answers.

"What are you saying, Rolly? That we shouldn't be there? Are you one of those...?"

"Mom, you waited for Dad and it damn near killed you, you waited for me and what did it get you? Now you want to wait for Peter?" He took another drink and looked around him.

Nobody was saying anything. Nobody knew what to say.

"Dad, know how many dead friends I got? Know how many of them died in my arms? You want that for Peter,"

"You don't have to put it that way. You're scaring your mother,"

"Good. She should be scared. There's a hell of a lot in 'Nam to be scared of," then he turned to Peter again,

"I can never explain to you what happened on my tour, but if you can believe one thing, this is it, there is nothing for you in Vietnam. Nothing, go to college,"

"He's not going to Vietnam for himself," Rolly's father said. "He's going for his country. He can go to college when he gets back,"

"What if he doesn't get back? He's not going,"

Rolly's father put down his glass. "What do you mean, 'he's not going'? Of course he's going. He's due to enlist next month."

He sat in his chair and looked to his wife as she looked to him, then she spoke, "What are you talking about, Rolly? It's his duty, as it was your duty and your father's. Everybody in our family, mine and your fathers', has been in the service."

"Mom, that's all different times in different places. Maybe it was worth it then, but it sure as hell isn't worth it now. I've been to Vietnam. It's a waste of time, of people; one from this family's enough. I'll take him to Canada myself,"

"You can't go to Canada. Your discharge isn't due 'til next year,"

"They might send me back. My training, experience,"

"They can't, you've done your tour,"

"I know lots of guys who weren't supposed to go back, and they were sent back."

Now Peter stood directly in front of Rolly and said, "I'm enlisting next month. I'm going to request combat duty in Vietnam, just like you did,"

"As God is my witness, you're not going to Vietnam. None of you really know what is happening over there. I don't even know what's happening over there,"

His father stood. "I don't believe it! Is my son turning his back on his country, on his family, generations of family?"

"Don't make it sound like that, Dad. The government lied to us. We're not saving anybody from anything; we're just killing and being killed. I don't want Peter there,"

"My son is talking treason. Were you captured? Did they brainwash you?"

Hs mother now stood. "Leave him alone, honey, he's been to war, he's not well,"

"What happened to you, son? What did they do to you?"

"They didn't do anything. I did it all and saw it all. Vietnam is one big sewer pipe,"

"Rolly, do you know what you're saying? Have you thought all this through?"

"Thought all this through? You know how many nights I sat in the pissing rain, waiting out an ambush, or a mortar barrage, or a sniper to take another shot? I've had nothing but time to think it all through."

Rolly's father put down his drink, leaned over to Rolly, went nose to nose.

"You think you've cornered the market on the old war-is-hell routine? You think you're the first marine to taste combat? You think you're the first marine to hold dying buddies,"

"Dad... Dad...!"

"God damn it, Guadalcanal was hell, Bataan was hell, the whole damn war with the Japs was hell, but we didn't turn our backs, we didn't run off to another country. Vietnam is just a little shooting match, it's not a real war, you don't know what hell is, I know what hell is, and I was there,"

"You weren't in Vietnam and I wasn't in Japan. In the airport I was spit on, in the taxi home the guy wants to buy heroin off me. A lot of guys won't be coming home, Vietnam killed them, and now you want it to kill my kid brother,"

"This is your country, Rolly. And it's mine and your mothers and your brothers, and we all love it,"

"I love my country, too, but our government fed us a pack of lies and lies aren't worth dying for. I won't let Peter get caught up in that. One from this family's enough. Peter's going to college."

Rolly was as drained as if he'd just come off another long dark night patrol, but he wasn't finished. "Dad, I know this is hard for you and Mom, but I didn't want Peter to die for nothing,"

Rolly's cheeks twitched, he shook his head, struggled with his emotions. "Remember 1776, Dad? Why that happened? It has to happen again because our government has gone bad. I've been to Vietnam, you haven't."

"If I have to leave my country because it's gone insane I'll do that.

But I won't let Peter waste his life there,"

"Get out. Get out of my house." his father said.

Rolly's mother shook and rattled. "I cooked dinner, his favorite, where's he going? Why didn't he say good bye...?"

Mr. McGarret held Mrs. McGarret as she slumped to the floor.

Peter stood numb, had no idea what to think.

Rolly picked up his duffel bag, heaved out a sigh of exhaustion and walked out the door of the house that was once his home.

He hurried as he walked along the streets of his hometown, trying to remember some good memories, trying to remove the confusion and pain of the last few minutes. It certainly wasn't what he'd expected, but he didn't know what to expect. Others had gone before him, he'd been warned.

Walking further into town, he bought a bottle of whiskey and rented a room. He changed into civilian clothes, dug into his bag and brought out his .38 special. He placed it on the table and looked at it. He took out the gun oil, clean white cloth, small brush, set them next to the gun on the table. He unscrewed the cap to the whiskey bottle, drank straight out of it, then started dismantling the 38. Each piece was taken in its turn, held up to the dim light bulb for a good look, wiped free of dirt with the cloth that he folded and refolded to make sure the dirt was coming off and not going back, and then oiled carefully.

Each part was laid in sequence on the table so that when he was finished the parts of the gun were perfectly laid out like a diagram. When all the parts were clean and oiled, he carefully reassembled the gun, double-checking for cleanliness, loaded it and rolled the cylinder to make sure it spun smoothly.

He held the gun up to the light bulb, turned it side to side, watching the light reflect off the barrel, then turned it and put it in his mouth. He didn't like the taste of gun oil. He took one more drink, tucked the bottle into his belt, put on a light coat; just enough to cover the gun and bottle, then left the hotel and started walking.

He strolled easily down the street, stopping to look over the old neighborhood. He felt better. A good decision settles the mind, he thought. His kid brother would never go to Vietnam.

He walked quietly up the driveway to his parent's home. Nobody saw him return. He knocked on the front door. Peter answered.

"I don't think Dad wants you here. Mom's very upset,"

"Are you still intent on going to Vietnam,"

"Yes, Rolly, I'm going. I'm sorry for you if you can't understand that."

Rolly grimaced and his eyes watered. He reached into his belt, pulled out his 38, pointed it down, pulled the trigger and the gunshot echoed throughout the quiet neighborhood.

Rolly McGarrets' mother and father ran to the front door. Rolly was gone. Peter sat on the ground, holding a bleeding foot.

No charges were laid. Very soon after that, Peter was ruled unfit for military service.

THE CZECK

Rolly leaned on the wheel and smiled. "Does that answer your question?" He knew it didn't.

`"Who's that," he yelled to Steve.

Steve shot up once more, fought his way out of the tangled blanket, grabbed the door latch, sprung it open. Then he calmly closed it. Rolly pumped the brakes, downshifted, pulled over. Somebody was hitchhiking.

"Get in," Rolly yelled out the window. Steve moved to the middle of the seat. Whoever it was threw his duffle bag into the back, and hopped in.

The hitchhiker had a young, fair, and weathered, wind burnt face, shoulder-length white-blonde hair and bright blue blood-shot eyes. He had a thick red bandana covering his forehead, black imitation-fur ear-muffs, a crisp new green canvas parka with wolf trim collar, baggy black pants tucked into bear-fur knee-high mukluks, and hanging on a strip of raw leather around the neck of his parka, a peace sign. His gloves didn't match.

"How far you going?" he spoke clear English with a European accent.

"Pelly Crossing," answered Rolly.

"I'm going to Elsa,"

Rolly reached across Steve and extended his hand. "Name's Rolly McGarret, this here's Steve Kovacs,"

The hitchhiker reached across Steve to shake Rolly's hand, "My name is Jan Havlat."

Then he turned to Steve. "Kovacs, you Hungarian?"

Steve sat up." Yes,"

"Your Daddy in Elsa?"

"What?" Steve said, taken aback by the hitchhikers' calm comment.

"Your Daddy. He's in Elsa?"

"What," Steve stared at Rolly, who shrugged.

"Guy in Elsa looks just like you, only a whole lot older,"

"I don't know anybody in Elsa, and my fathers' in Vancouver,"

"Name Joe Smith mean anything to you?"

"Nothing," Steve said.

Jan shrugged. "Well, maybe he's your aunt, but she got no tits and a beard,"

Steve handed him the bag of weed. "What country you from?" he said.

"Me? I'm from Czechoslovakia, Bohemia,"

"Long ways from home," Rolly said.

"Yukon is my home, Canada is my home. Czechoslovakia don't want me anymore,"

"'Don't want you anymore'? What's that mean?" Rolly knew what it meant to have your home not want you.

"Means just that," he turned to Steve, "you are from Hungary," and then to Rolly, "You are from the United States, which state?"

"California,"

"You are surf bum?"

"Not much. Why'd you leave home?"

"I told you, Yukon is my home,"

"Okay, fine. Why'd you leave Czechoslovakia?"

"Revolution, we lost, time to go,"

Rolly turned to Steve, "Sound familiar?"

Steve was still stunned about the idea of his father being in Elsa. "Where's Elsa?"

"Past Pelly Crossing, another hundred miles," Jan said. "Why you leave California?"

"Same as you, time to go,"

"You run away from Vietnam?"

"Nope, did my tour,"

"You're American, you went to Vietnam. Why are you in the Yukon?"

"Like I said, time to go,"

"You're here for the beautiful weather?"

Rolly started laughing, "Ya, that's it. I left my life as a surf bum to roll around in the snow in the Yukon,"

"Well, Rolly McGarret, you are the first American I meet in the Yukon not running away from Vietnam. Every American here is running away from Vietnam,"

"Well, I'll tell you this much, if I knew what I was getting into before I went, I just might have run away too, matter of fact, I probably should have,"

"No, you shouldn't. You were right to go to Vietnam, all you Americans run away from Vietnam, communists take over Vietnam, then they go on to the next country. I fought the communists in Czechoslovakia, wanted to kick them out, go home to Russia, you pigs, but they had bigger guns than us, so we had to leave, or go to Siberia. Everybody needs salt for dinner,"

"You fought the communists?" Steve said. "My father fought them in Budapest,"

"Yes, I know, you're Hungarian. That's why we put down our guns in Prague; we didn't want another Budapest in Prague. We didn't want tanks in the streets,"

"What happened?" Steve said.

"Tanks in the streets."

KILIAN BARRACKS,
BUDAPEST, NOVEMBER, 1956

Janos Kovacs sat stunned in the cellar of the Kilian Barracks. He peered through the thick dust. He struggled to stand up, steadied himself as he climbed up the long barrel of his empty anti-tank gun, stretched to grab the window ledge, and carefully peek out. He watched the Russian tank grinding up the broken pavement as it clanked its treads towards him. He worried if the tank knew he was out of shells. It swung its barrel around, aimed at a point ten feet above his head and fired. When the shell hit, he was halfway to the floor.

His ears roared, the shock wave pushed him into the corner and he couldn't hear himself scream out, "Save me, God. Save me."

He curled up, covered his head with his hands and waited for the cement floor to collapse and crush him.

The five floor brick and cement building shocked back under the hit, swayed slightly, then steadied. He couldn't stop shaking.

The plaster fell down in sheets, sent up thick waves of sand and powdered cement. A thick cloud of dust hung in the air, plugged his nose and coated his face with grit. He tore off a piece of his shirtsleeve and used it to cover his mouth and nose. Taking short shallow breaths, his dry mouth tasted of sand and cement. He tried to breathe through his wide open mouth, but the smell of burned sulfur and backed up sewage fouled it worse that the dust.

Seeing only in quick blinks, he made out where the window was, but the dust stung his eyes. There was pain in his left leg, he reached down, his fingers came up bloody.

He listened closely as he heard the familiar sound of bottles breaking, the 'whoosh' as the Molotov cocktails blew up in flames, the tank hatches opening and the Russian soldiers screaming as they burned and the instant rifle fire that quieted them. Janos kept his eyes shut as he cradled his rifle to his side, flipped the selector switch from safety to automatic.

Slowly and quietly, he crawled up the wall to the window and peeked out again. Across the boulevard, the burning tank blocked the main entrance to the Kilian Barracks.

Sprawled across the turret hatch was the tanks' captain; the forward hatch held the burning body of the soldier who pulled the trigger on him.

High above the bullet scarred barracks, the Hungarian tri-color flag, with a hole cut in the middle where the hammer and sickle used to be, still proudly flew. Strewn about the avenue were blown-up tanks, burned-out personnel carriers, collapsed barricades, dead bodies, piles of broken glass and shattered boards.

Clanking and grinding noises signaled more tanks and Janos held his rifle tight. He watched two boys, maybe fifteen or sixteen, run to the side of the first tank. The boys ducked under the machine guns, and stuffed lead pipes into the tracks. The tank lifted up on one side and crashed back down, belching black smoke. The tracks let out a high- pitched screeching wail, then the tank stalled. As the boys ran for cover, more Molotov cocktails poured down from the roof of the barracks and the tank exploded. Janos leaned on his bleeding leg. It hurt, but not enough to stop him from climbing through the boarded-up window and peering out further across the boulevard.

He watched the tank burn, listened to the anguished cries from the crew inside, and was quiet until the flames died out.

'You have your orders, I have mine', he thought. 'You are conscripts, I am a volunteer. We are all soldiers, and I pray for your souls'.

One of the boys waved at him to stay down. It was good they knew he was there, they would tell his older brother Stephan that he was okay. It was important that Stephan knew; then he wouldn't worry.

Stephan trained the boys how to stop tanks with lead pipes salvaged from plumbing; how to fill glass bottles with petrol and stuff rags in their necks for Molotov cocktails.

All guerrilla tricks Stephan had taught Janos and their little brother Josef, when they were fighting in the Mokan Army to rid Hungary of Nazis.

Stephan's boys in the Kilian Barracks still had important work to do; the last days of hard fighting had left few of them alive.

The dust was settling, the air was beginning to clear, so Janos relaxed a little now that Stephan knew he was alive. A new and more troubling thought occurred to him. His stomach tightened again. What if Stephan hadn't made it through the last tank assault?

Janos suffered the loss of his parents the last time the Russians invaded, and if this time, if it was Stephan? He didn't want to think about that.

Janos stared long and hard at the hammer and sickle on the side of the burned out tank and thought back to when he was a child soldier and first saw that kind of tank.

It rolled into Budapest just hours after the Nazis fled. Russian soldiers set up camp in front of the Kilian barracks, just feet from where he was now.

He and Josef had jumped on the side of the tank for a victory ride. They were their new friends, these Russian liberators; they gave Janos and Josef chocolate and cigarettes, then took away their rifles. The war was over, they said, and children didn't need rifles anymore.

CARMACKS, YUKON

"Not your Daddy in Elsa?" Jan went on, still not believing
Steve.
"No,"
"You never heard of Joe Smith?"
"No,"
"I knew he was a liar. No Hungarian is named Joe Smith,
he's somebody else. Turn your head sideways,"
Steve turned his head sideways while Jan studied his
profile.
"Might be your sister,"
"Maybe he's not Kovacs," Jan said. "What kind of work
you do, Rolly?"
"Cut wood,"
"Good job for soldier,"
"I'm not a soldier, I'm a marine,"
"You're still a marine, after you left California?"
"Once a marine, always a marine,"
"I was in the Czech army, no longer a soldier. But you're
still a marine. You get called back, you have to go?"
"I don't go back, the government doesn't want me. No,
that's wrong, they do want me, but not for the service,"
"You a deserter?"
"Yes Sir,"
"Me too, and they want me back, but not for the army,"
"What happens if you go back to Czechoslovakia?"
"Work camps for sure, maybe shoot me. And you, what if
you go back,"
"Just like you, jail for sure, but they don't shoot me,"
"Good country, United States. Bad government,"
"You got that right. You working in Elsa, Jan?"
"Yes, Elsa, with the other Czechs, and some of your
American countrymen, they all run away from Vietnam. And
Germans, they fight all the time, nobody likes the Germans,
some of them were Nazis, I hate the Nazis more than the
communists. Some Germans are okay, but I hate all the
Nazis,"

"Your Daddy fight the Nazis, Jan,"

"My Daddy was Nazi. I hate them all,"

Rolly whistled at the window. "Okay, Jan,"

"Who your Daddy fight?"

"Japs,"

"And we got Jews in Elsa, some from the camps, they keep trying to kill the Nazis, sometimes they do. No Germans go underground, too easy to die underground,"

"I thought that war was over?"

"Not in Elsa. And we got lots of Hungarians, Steve. They all got out in fifty-six, that when your Daddy got out?"

"With my Mom and me,"

"Any other family gets out?"

Steve thought of the stories his father told him about his Uncle Stephan, how the family escaped Budapest and the communists. It always seemed like an adventure story, with his heroic uncle leading them to freedom. He thought about the pictures his father showed him, the look in his mothers' eyes when his father talked about his Uncle Stephan, and the look in his fathers' eyes whenever Steve said the word 'uncle'.

"Don't have any other family, just the three of us."

"Uh, huh," Jan said and Steve knew he didn't believe him, but he listened closely; he knew there was something missing.

"Good place to work, Elsa," Rolly said, "I got friends up there. We're going to pull into Carmacks for a while. Steve here got frostbit on his face. Gonna drop him at the nursing station. Wanna have a beer and wait with us,"

"Yes I do."

Rolly pulled off the Klondike Hi-way, turned down a small hill to the settlement of Carmacks. To the west was a large old brown barn that was cafe', bar and hotel. Behind the bar was a forestry station that was closed for the winter, next to that the only R.C.M.P. detachment for the next two hundred miles, and scattered about a few cabins and small tarpaper shacks. Behind that was the Yukon River, and on a low hillside across the river, an Indian village.

The frozen river had a footpath from the settlement to the village. The nursing station was next to the R.C.M.P. detachment and that's where Rolly dropped Steve.

"We'll wait for you in the bar. Don't get hung up on the nurse, I think she's got a boyfriend."

Steve stood on the road and watched as Jan and Rolly drove over to the bar, steaming exhaust pouring out of the tail pipe reminded him of how cold it was. He felt his face burning. His ears began to prickle and his fingers were going numb.

He walked up to the door and banged once and his knuckles flashed pain. He kicked the door and waited for some sign of life. No one answered, so he kicked again. Still no answer.

The lights were on at the R.C.M.P. station so he went over and kicked the door. A constable answered right away.

"I'm all frozen and nobody's at the nursing station,"

"Get in,"

Steve stumbled in the door and leaned his elbows against the counter. He was weaving and had to steady himself. His head was spinning and he broke into a sweat. "We put our truck in the bush and it took a long time to get it out and we had to unload everything so we could jack it up and push it over to get it back on the road and then we had to load it again and by then I was freezing and I puked, but I have to see a nurse or doctor or something 'cause my face is freezing and it hurts bad and I,"

"How much have you had to drink?"

"Some whiskey for the cold,"

"Come with me."   The constable took Steve through a door and down a hallway. He opened another door into a cellblock, took a ring of keys off the wall and opened a cell.

"Get in,"

"What? I need a doctor or nurse or something. My face is freezing,"

"You're under arrest. Get in."

Steve stumbled into the cell, trying to figure out why he was under arrest. The constable locked the cell door, hung the keys on his belt and walked away. Steve sat on the bunk and shivered.

There was a blanket there and he wrapped himself in it, then lay down and drifted into a sleepless haze.

He didn't know how long he'd been there when the door opened again. It was the constable with a young woman.

She had a large tote bag over her shoulder, her face mostly hidden under a toque that came down to her eyebrows, and a scarf that wrapped up to her chin. She had the same color eyes as Sheila, and her nose curled the same way.

She came up to the cell bars. "Let me see your face,"

Steve moved to the edge of the bunk, closer to the bars. She examined his face and reached into her tote bag.

"Put some of this on your face." She reached through the bars and handed him a jar. He tried to open the jar, but with his frozen fingers he couldn't grip it hard enough to turn off the lid.

"You'd better let me in the cell." she said. The constable pulled out his keys, unlocked the cell door. She walked into the cell, picked up the jar, opened it; spread some cream on Steve's face and hands. The burning started to go away. His face felt cool and he began to relax.

"What am I doing in a cell," he asked the constable. "Why am I under arrest?"

"Let's see some I.D.," said the constable.

Steve reached into his pocket, but couldn't grip his wallet. The constable came into the cell and pulled Steve's wallet out of his back pocket.

"You stink of whiskey. You're under arrest for public drunkenness. Got any idea of how many people freeze to death from being drunk outside? I'm going to check you out. If you don't have any warrants, you can go."

"I don't have any warrants,"

"Uh-huh. I'll be right back." The constable locked the cell door and he and the nurse left the cellblock. In a few minutes he was back.

"You don't have any warrants, but you're listed as missing in Vancouver. What are you doing in the Yukon?"

"Going to work in the bush. Got a job cutting wood,"

"If I was you, I wouldn't be working outside till my face healed. I can't hold you just 'cause you're missing. That's your business. I told Vancouver you're here, though. They don't like stupid people causing them useless paperwork,"

"I'll have to phone home,"

"That's your business. Anyways, you're not missing anymore. Where you going from here,"

"I have to meet some friends in the bar. We have to get up to Pelly Crossing,"

"If your friend is driving and he's drunk, I'll lock him up. If you drive, I'll lock you up again,"

"That's okay, there's three of us. The other guy hasn't been drinking,"

"He's in the bar isn't he?"

"Well, yes,"

"If any of you have any brains you'll get a room in the hotel. It's cold today and it's going to be colder tonight. Might hit fifty below. There's too many cliffs beside the road, you go off the road, you go off a cliff, you disappear in the snow drift, I pull out your stiff in the spring,"

Steve thought quite a bit about cliffs beside the road. He decided not to mention anything more about that.

"You've been warned. You understand?"

"Yes, and thank-you,"

"Don't thank me. The nurse took care of your face. I'll take care of you if you fuck-up in town; but you fuck-up on the road, you're on your own. It's a long way to anywhere on these roads and its near a hundred miles to Pelly Crossing. I get a real tired of having to identify frozen stiffs."

It was now early afternoon, and the sun was already on its way down when Steve got to the Carmacks Hotel bar. Rolly and Jan were deep into conversation, and drinking heavily. Steve sat down and stayed quiet. He didn't want to drink or talk.

He sat next to the heater and wondered what he would say to his family. He had been gone only two days and already he was on the missing persons list. Or at least he used to be.

Steve leaned over to hear what Jan and Rolly were so intensely discussing.

"When I left Czechoslovakia, my father, my mother; they were communists, they thought all the rebels should be shot," Jan trailed off.

Rolly straightened up, "All rebels? That include you?"

"They never said so, not in those words. When they say all rebels should be shot, and I'm in a rebel battalion,"

"I had to shoot my little brother in the foot." Rolly let the words fall out of his mouth. He put no emphasis on what he said, he just said it.

"Did he let you?"

"Sure as hell wasn't his idea. Only thing that kept him out of 'Nam,"

"Why not send him here?"

"He wanted to go to Vietnam. I already done my tour, I knew better."

Jan stopped talking and picked up his drink. He brought it to his lips, and then he put it back down. He tried to say something but he couldn't form the words. His hands shook. He tried again to say something, tried to get the words out, but nothing came. Rolly sat quietly and let it sink into Jan.

"You fought in Vietnam,"

"Volunteered, family thing,"

"In the jungle,"

"Lots, was there for Tet, January, February, 68,"

"We read about that in Pravda; but we also had many papers from America, Washington Post, New York Times, all smuggled in, easy to get,"

"From Pravda to American papers, what did they say,"

"We know American papers all propaganda, because we read Pravda, and that was all propaganda,"

"Gotta get confusing,"

"Oh, no, it's quite simple, very easy. What they say is true, is really not true,"

Rolly looked up from his beer, "The opposite is true, everything else is, propaganda,"

"That's correct,"

"Didn't know it was that easy,"

"Very easy, I had a close friend back in Bohemia, we grew up together, won a soccer championship together, he went to Russia for training, then Hanoi. Was killed fighting in Hue,"

"Fighting my friends, my marine brothers, in Hue,"

"Yes, in Hue. February 16, 1968,"

"Why didn't you go to Russia?"

"Pretend to be stupid. I played soccer all the time; I played stupid all the time, stayed out of Russia that way,"

"Well Jan Havlat, you don't seem very stupid to me,"

"We learned very young to play stupid. Wrote the wrong answers on tests, the Russians are stupid, they're easy to trick. We all read smuggled books; Russian history is a pack of lies. If they caught us with the books, it's off to jail,"

Rolly nodded and stared at the hundreds of baseball caps nailed to the ceiling. "Go to jail for reading books." He paused again, reflected on Jans' words. "Lot of guys, good guys, on both sides, died in Viet-fucking-Nam. Your friend in Hue, he was a white guy?"

"Yes, a Czech,"

"You know we heard a lot about Russians with the N.V.A., advisers, but we could never get any bodies,"

"No, my friend was buried in the military graveyard in Bratislava, full military funeral, fighting the evil Americans, hero of the international socialist pack of lies, they're all pigs, all those communists. I saw his body,"

"But your folks were communists, what happened to you?"

"I got in the army, not like in America, where only some go, in Czechoslovakia everybody goes, on your eighteenth birthday you join. You're a boy in school, then you're in the army and you come out a man. We had more smuggled books in the army than in the school,"

"No draft, everybody goes,"

"Oh, yes. In America you call it 'draft', only the poor boys go, the rich don't get drafted,"

"Oh, no, the rich get drafted, too,"

"Then they sneak out of the army with money,"

"Well, I guess you're right there. If your family has money, you get college deferments, all kinds of outs if you have money. You can buy the right doctor for a medical release,"

"That's what I said, only the poor boys go, the rich boys don't fight and die for American Imperialism."

Rolly bristled at the words 'American Imperialism'. These were some of the key words of communist propaganda. Why they were told they had to fight the communists, why he was told he was in Vietnam.

He knew long ago that the newspapers were full of shit, they never told the true story, they claimed defeats that were victories; he knew that because he fought in those victories.

But he didn't like some guy from another country rubbing it in his face. He glared at Jan, who saw it right away.

"Us rebels in the Czech army, we felt close to you marines in Vietnam. We knew you didn't want to fight, but you'd get shot if you didn't. Same with the Czech army,"

"Some of us wanted to fight, we wanted to win,"

"But American government won't let you win,"

"What?"

"American government wants to fight all the time, good for money. What is it your protesters say 'War is good business, invest your son'."

"You know, we'd fight for a piece of land, then walk away and give it back. We'd go into a village, be good to the villagers, give them medical supplies, help them with their rice crops, train the locals to fight the Cong, then they'd turn on us,"

"Turn on you?"

"They'd take the weapons and training we gave them, then attack us. We'd 'Zippo' the village, burn it to the ground. Next day the village gets bombed. We did it all the time, we busted our asses, trying to do good, trying to help these fucks, then bang, they're shooting at us."

"That's what we did in Czechoslovakia. The Russians trained us, gave us rifles, and then we 'turned' on them, tried to take our country back,"

"Jesus Christ, it's the same all over,"

"We didn't make it up, we didn't invent it. That's the history of guerrilla armies, take what you get from the invader, turn it against them. That's why we in the Czech army felt close to you marines in Vietnam. You're fighting and dying for good things, but get shit in return,"

"What about the Russians in Czechoslovakia,"

"It was very difficult to fight the Russian soldiers; many lived in our towns and villages. We played soccer many times, after we go drink, but don't let them chase our women. But they're in one uniform, we're in another."

"They're under orders; we're fighting for our country. It was very difficult,"

"I never met a live Cong or N.V.A., sometimes a prisoner, but we wouldn't drink or talk. Well, we talked, but not that way, we had to get information, we had to know what they're doing,"

"You don't want to kill one prisoner to make the others talk, but the prisoner has friends, they kill your friends, yes, it's a very bad spot, I know that spot, I was there."

Jan paused now, he too stared at the hats nailed to the ceiling, thought over what they were saying, "I'm sorry for you, marine, you're a good man, doing a bad job. Same as me."

Rolly didn't believe him, wasn't interested in his pity. Sure, he made some interesting points, seemed to have a handle on history, went through a revolution, got caught up in things over his head and out of his control, knew a fair bit about things that other people knew shit about, but still, he wasn't in the 'Nam, he wasn't a marine. But there was one thing Rolly did like about him; he was a veteran and he called him 'marine'. Rolly didn't like it when he was called 'marine' by somebody who didn't know what they were talking about.

Jan knew what he was talking about when it came to being a soldier, but Rolly wasn't a soldier, he was a marine.

"Good man in a bad job, heard that before, heard that many times before. So, Jan Havlat, how'd your revolution go?"

"Same as you, lost."

There he goes again thought Rolly. Saying things he don't understand, saying things that hurt. They weren't losing in Vietnam, they weren't allowed to win, the odds were stacked against them, they kept getting the rug pulled out from beneath them.

Every time they took a step forward, they were forced to take two steps back, the same old story. They weren't allowed to win, doesn't anybody get that?

"We ain't lost that war, not yet, there's still a chance,"

"No, you lost when your army went in; you lost when your politicians didn't want you to win. Your soldiers want to win, you marines want to win, but your politicians won't let you win. They have too much money invested in guns and bombs.

They want to use them all, get more money from the government to build more bombs, then sell them to the army, that's how they get rich. If you want to win this war, and you still can win this war, your generals have to get away from your politicians, you have to have an independent army in America, one that won't take orders from men who have been elected by lying to the people of America. That's what you get with democracy."

Rolly held tight to his beer glass, held tight to his ideals. He couldn't get a grip on everything Jan was saying, some of it made sense, sort of.

He understood politicians being liars, that much was true, and the part about military contractors getting rich sure was true, he'd seen a lot of that in the 'Nam, but to blame all that on democracy?

"I thought you said you weren't a commie,"

"I'm not, I fought a revolution against them and I lost,"

"You think we should have an independent army in the States,"

"I don't think we should have an army anywhere, but as long as the Russians are in the Kremlin, and the Americans are in the Pentagon, they both want the whole world.

What choice do we have? We're just a bunch of peasants, doing what we're ordered to do,"

"Well, that much is true. You were a part of your revolution, did you want it,"

"I was eighteen years old, what choice did I have? I was a member of that battalion; they had my loyalty, my ass. We were given rifles, ordered to get ready to shoot Russians,"

"Did you,"

"Not, but we got ready, if we got the order, we would have,"

"What happened?"

"Same as Budapest, they came in with their tanks and said put down your rifles or we blow Prague to hell and back. In Budapest they didn't put down their rifles and the Russians blew Budapest to hell and back. We said, no thanks, and put down our rifles."

BUDAPEST, NOVEMBER, 1956

Janos slid back down into the cellar, rested his head on a flat brick and tried to make sense of the latest Russian invasion. 'Should've kept my damn mouth shut', he thought.

Just days ago, it was Janos' turn to speak at his at his weekly Workers' Committee Meeting. "Why are we hungry and cold, when we produce more than enough food and clothing for ourselves? Why is everything shipped to Russia?"

Janos' shop supervisor, Sandor, narrowed his eyes and glared at Janos. He pushed out his enlarged gut and stuck his thumbs in his belt. "Watch what you say, you could get yourself in trouble,"

"Fuck you," Janos snapped. "Why do we work an extra day every week to pay for the damage the Russians caused when they bombed our factories?"

Sandor pushed Janos aside and yelled, "Don't listen to this man! He talks subversion. The Russians are our friends. They helped us rebuild our factories."

"Get down, Sandor, or you will get yours," yelled one man.

"Who said that?" shouted Sandor. "Who would say that to my face,"

All the men moved towards Sandor, who quickly backed down.

Sandor stabbed his finger into Janos' chest, "Watch what you say, Janos Kovacs, or you'll pay for it!"

"Pay for it? You son-of-a-bitch I have paid for it, and my father and his father before him! We have all paid for our factories and our country many times over. Who else in this hall fought the Nazis?"

Men shot their hands into the air, stretching out their arms to reach as high as they could. They all called out together, "We fought and we won."

"Janos Kovacs," Sandor snarled. "You are a family man. I would watch very carefully, what you say."

Janos felt the anger he had kept in check for so long fly out of him. "You threaten my wife and baby? You are a pig of a man!"

Janos jumped toward Sandor, who quickly ran out the side door.

All the men in the meeting hall laughed at Sandor as Janos stood on a chair and yelled back, "Our courageous shop supervisor, our leader and party Commissar has left us." "Who among you will be with him, and sneak out the door?"

The men laughed again and one yelled out, "Sandor is a coward."

"Communist pig." yelled another.

With Sandor gone, Janos saw in the men a renewed sense of self; they had stood up to Sandor, and his reports to the hated Secret Police, the AVO.

Janos extended both hands, "Why do the products of our factories go to Russia when we have them rationed here? Why do our farms produce so well and yet our children go hungry?"

Janos felt the flood inside him, and watched his co-workers feel it too. They stood tall, stamped their feet, and clapped their hands. With every declaration of Janos, they cheered him on.

"Why are Russian troops still here? We all know the Warsaw Pact; we know what it means and what it asks of us! Who do we need protection from? America? They're not at our border!"

The men stopped their cheering and went deathly quiet as Janos felt his stomach lock. Their smiles drained away, replaced by the fear they all knew too well. Janos now knew he had gone too far.

By speaking of the Warsaw Pact, he had openly admitted to listening to the banned radio station, Radio Free Europe. The broadcasts always promised support for anti-communist rebellion, but no man could admit to listening to it. That would mean immediate arrest.

An angry silence spread through the meeting hall. Long suppressed emotions were ready to boil over. Each man had a decision to make. Cheer on Janos and be reported by informers for applauding subversive speeches, or remain quiet and cheer only when ordered to.

A foul smell crept through the same doorway Sandor fled out, and every man stared at the doorway. Fear swept through the meeting hall, followed by a wave of hushed whispers, and sweat drenched foreheads.

Four uniformed men blocked the doorway; AVO. All the men's eyes focused in tight stares. Jaws tightened and fingers twitched.

The AVO stood motionless. Dark blue uniforms, wide black leather straps running up their backs and down their fronts, shining metal hooks fitting into tight black belts, knee-high black boots, hats cocked at just the right angle.
Pistols in holsters, truncheons in hands, shoulders thin and stooped, faces narrow. "Kovacs, now!" Janos froze. His knees wavered. The cold sweat ran prickly down his neck. One AVO in front of him, one at his back, one on each arm and Janos was hustled away. The meeting was finished, but the AVO were not.

CARMACKS, YUKON

Rolly turned to Steve, "Hey, you getting all this,"
Steve hadn't missed a word. "Go on Jan, then what,"
"You listen to me, Hungarian. This could have happened to you and your family,"
Steve held his breath and leaned forward as Jan went on.

"They took my whole battalion, from the generals on down, and put us in cattle cars. I had a general standing right next to me, they were going to send us to all to Siberia. Would have died there, but the Czech police were running the trains, the Russians didn't trust the train men, they were on our side, they threatened to strike, so they were taken from their jobs and our police took over. The Russians locked us all in the cattle cars and off we go on the train to Siberia. Don't say goodbye to anyone, no one knows anything, so we travel a few miles, nobody can sit, were jammed in as tight as the Russians can get us, some older guys had heart attacks, thinking over what's coming. I'm too young; I know next to nothing about the camps, I've heard a lot, but we're not allowed to talk about them. The guys that had heart attacks just stood there, there was no room for them to fall down,"

Jan took a drink of his beer, caught his breath and continued. He wasn't upset, he wasn't crying, he just told his story. "Then the train stops and the doors open. The only thing I knew was that we got some fresh air, the air was real bad, guys were fainting now, but us young guys were hanging on, it was the old guys giving out. I was deep in the group, couldn't see the door, then I hear cheering, and I think 'what's this cheering all about', we're on our way to Siberia and it doesn't look good, and then the cheering. I finally get out of the cattle car, fall out because my legs are cramped up and I can't stand without help, and we're surrounded by Austrian police and they don't have rifles, and I think, 'Austrian Police, what's this all about'? Everybody is cheering and then the sergeant tells me the train has been re-routed to Austria, by our Czech police. We're not going to Siberia, we're now in Austria and we're free men."

"I think, 'What's a free man, and what the hell do I do now?' I'm eighteen years old and free and I don't speak Austrian or any other language, and what does a free man do? The Austrian police say 'Welcome to Andau', then they gave us beer and sausage and told us stay away from their women. "

Jan caught his breath and drank his beer. He was almost angry, almost yelling, when he turned to Steve and said, "You getting all this, Hungarian? You know how close your family was to this?"

Steve couldn't say anything.

Through Jan's entire story, Rolly was watching Steve closely. He leaned over, felt Steve's forehead, and looked at the cream on his face. "Nurse was good to you,"

"Yes," Steve said.

Rolly turned to Jan. "Well shit, you're a lucky man, Jan Havlat. That close to Siberia,"

Jan put his forefinger and thumb a fraction of an inch apart, "That close, and now I'm a free man in Canada. Rolly McGarret, are you a free man in Canada,"

"Am I a what? 'A free man in Canada'?"

"You're not in Vietnam, you're not in the marines, you got three meals a day and nobody's shooting at you,"

"You got that right,"

"You work when you want to, sleep when you want to, eat when you want to,"

"Never quite thought about it that way, this is one hell of a country,"

Jan held up his beer glass, "One hell of a country," then he hollered out, "more beer, please," he continued, "and in Canada, they let you at their women,"

Rolly started laughing and fell out of his chair. "Yes sir, they certainly let you at their women,"

"Tell me, Rolly McGarret, did you march in the streets of America, to stop the war,"

"Never got the chance, when I left the service, I came straight to Canada. Don't know if I would have; might have."

"Lot of guys I knew in the 'Nam said they were going to march in the streets, some went to Washington and gave their medals back,"

"I read about that in the Washington Post, and I read the Pentagon Papers, about all the corruption. That amazes me, that's what's great about your country, you Americans can do that and they don't lock you up. They even give medals to the journalists. If we tried that, off to Siberia,"

"Ya, I never left my country, I left my government,"

"You know how we know our government is corrupt?"

"Tell me,"

"When they tell us there is no corruption in Czechoslovakia, we think, everybody is corrupt. Very simple, I told you that,"

"Yes, you certainly did tell me that. How to read the news,"

"What about all the protestors that opposed the war, what do you think about them?"

"Bloody peaceniks, they don't know shit. Listen, Jan, who do you think is more opposed to the war? Some kid marching down a street carrying a sign that says 'hell no, I won't go'? If things get really tough a cop might take a Billy club to his head; then he won't make it to the bar on time and he won't get laid that night. That's tough for him. Or how about some other poor shit of a kid sitting out a mortar barrage nose deep in a shit filled rice paddy hoping to hell he lives through the next few seconds, and if he does live through the next few seconds he knows he'll have to fight off a squad or a company of Cong while wondering if his sixteen is going to jam 'cause it's been under water with him in the shit? That's tough for us. Who do you think is more opposed to that war?"

"You make a good point, Rolly McGarret. How was the war for you?"

Rolly paused, thought about it, "This is what the war was for me; one time we spent a month training the locals to fight the Cong. When it was over we had a big party and everybody got shit-faced drunk. First light they attacked us. The whole fucken company we trained went over to the Cong. They had some M-16's, but mostly they had pitch forks and machetes."

"They fucking attacked us with pitch forks and machetes, we're all hung-over, and we had 30 and 50 calibers. Turned them all to hamburger, we took some casualties. But it's all over now and I don't want to talk about it anymore."

"Fine, no more questions. Why isn't the Hungarian talking?"

Rolly turned to Steve. "Hey Steve, you run out of words,"

"I got words; just don't know which ones to use,"

"Just like a Hungarian," Jan said. "First you can't get them to talk, then you can't get them to shut up."

Steve was trying to imagine his father in Budapest, what he must have gone through to get him and his mother to Canada. What Jan told him made him shiver in a way the cold never could. And now here he was 'missing', what kind of hell had he put his parents in? How was he going to explain what he'd done to them; all he could think about is what they'd done for him.

"Hey, talk to me buddy," Rolly said. "What took you so long?"

"Had to spend some time in a jail cell,"

"We dropped you at the nursing station, not the damn jail. How'd you end up there?"

"Nobody at the nursing station, had to go the R.C.M.P. He put me in a cell 'cause I stunk of whiskey. Said we shouldn't drive, going to get cold, maybe fifty below. Said we should get a room here,"

"Government agents," Jan snorted.

"I think it's time to go anyways," Rolly said. "My Canadian woman is waiting for me,"

Jan perked up, "She got a Canadian woman friend for me,"

"I can ask. I'm supposed to meet her in Pelly Crossing tonight. A man doesn't want to deal with that woman when she's pissed off."

PELLY CROSSING

"Where's Rosie?" Rolly said as they pulled into Pelly Crossing.

The bar was empty, save for an old Indian woman bartender. She looked up from her book, glanced at them, "Hi, Rolly," she said, and then went back to her book.

The bar had a wooden floor, four round wooden tables, no covering, table-tops carved with initials and hearts. All the tables were bolted to the floor. There was on old jukebox in the corner with a cracked glass front and most of the buttons missing. The broken windows were covered on the inside with plastic sheets to keep the cold out. In the middle of the bar was rusty forty-five gallon barrel, lying on its side propped up with bricks. It had a door on the front and a metal chimney on the back, going up through the roof. Inside the barrel a fire was blazing away throwing heat and flickering orange and red light on the far wall.

The three of them sat at the nearest table to the barrel stove and ordered beers. The Indian woman didn't look up from her book. She picked it up and walked over to the beer cooler, book in one hand, and pulled three beers out, never lifting her eyes from the book. She put the beers down without saying a word and went back to her seat.

Steve asked her, "Do you have a phone,"

She looked up from her book and eyed Steve; blinked once, twice, looked him over from head to toe, scratched her nose, yawned, scratched her nose again, said, "Yes," and looked back into her book.

"Can I use it?"

She sighed, looked up from her book, and scratched her nose again. "Where you gonna call?"

"Vancouver,"

"Why?"

"Its home,"

"Long ways from here, I was there, didn't like it. You like Vancouver?"

"What,"

"You like Vancouver?"

"Its home, it's where my family is,"

"Didn't ask that, asked if you liked Vancouver,"

"Never thought about it,"

"You never think about your home?"

"Well, not that way,"

"What way do you think about it?"

"Jesus Christ, can I just use your phone?"

"My name's not Jesus Christ, it's Eleanor,"

"Can I use your phone, Eleanor?"

"You don't have to be rude,"

"I wasn't rude,"

"Yes, you were, and you are now,"

"I'm sorry if you thought I was rude, but I certainly didn't mean to be,"

"Yes, you can use my phone," she sighed. "Only collect calls, don't charge nothing here." She reached under the counter and lifted up an old phone. Stuck in the dial was a note. She read it, thought it over, then said, "Message here for you, Rolly."

"What's it say?"

"Rosie says that her truck is getting fixed and she'll be here tomorrow afternoon, by five o'clock."

"That truck of hers is more a piece of junk than mine is,"

"Whatever it is, she won't be here today," Jan said. "If I pay for the gas, can we go on to Elsa? Three hours, I'll drive, you sleep. I'll get you a meal and a room in the bunkhouse,"

"What say to that, Steve? Want to go on to Elsa for the night,"

"Elsa? That where the guy that looks like me is,"

"That is where Joe Smith lives," Jan said.

"I wanna see this guy. Only I gotta make a phone call first."

Steve sat down at the bar and started dialing, then stopped and hung up. He stared at the phone, then picked it up again and started dialing again. The operator came on and he gave his parents' number and his name for the collect call.

Fifteen hundred miles away the phone was ringing. Steve broke into a sweat. What to say, what to say?

"Hello?" crackled the phone.

"Collect call from the Yukon Territory, from Steve Kovacs. Do you accept?"

The operators' voice had a disembodied sound to it, mechanical and dead, threatening and alive.

"The goddamn Yukon Territory! What the hell is he doing there! Yes, I accept,"

"Dad,"

"What the hell are you doing up there?"

"I've got a job,"

"A job! How the hell are you going to university in the Yukon?"

"Dad, I couldn't take it anymore,"

"Couldn't take what anymore? What the hell does that mean?"

"I want to work; I want to pay my own way,"

"Great, 'pay my own way', he says. What about all that over-time I put in? This is going to do wonders for your mother's heart. She's not as strong as she used to be,"

"Dad, I want to take a break, I want to work," Steve listened to quiet, then a sigh in the background.

"I got a choice in this? Talk to your mother; she's worried sick about you,"

Steve shuddered as he listened to his father call his mother.

"TARA, your son's on the phone. He's in the Yukon Territory,"

"Steve? We've been worried sick. Thank God you called,"

"Mom, how are you?"

"Fine question! What are doing in the Yukon?"

"I've got a job, Mom. Working in the bush,"

"You quit university,"

"Just for now, I can go back,"

"You're just like your father. Why didn't you tell us you were leaving? Sheila came in yesterday all in a flap. She said you walked out of class and ran away from home,"

"Mom, I'm a little old to be running away from home, and me and Sheila broke up,"

"Well, that's between you two. She's been very good to you, you could have said something, you could have said 'goodbye'. Why didn't you phone me?"

"I was in a hurry, the plane was leaving,"

"You're always in a hurry, but where are you going? I didn't sleep all last night and l couldn't eat a thing,"

"Mom, I'm sorry. I am, but I just had to go,"

"Very well, Little Stephan, if this is why we left Hungary in such a hurry, so you could quit university in such a hurry, and run off to the Yukon Territory in such a hurry, well I guess I'll just have to understand because I don't have any choice, do I?"

"Listen, Mom,"

"Don't you 'listen mom' to me. If you have to work instead of university I understand. You have to grow up some more; you're still too impulsive. You have to think things through before you act. You have to understand that whatever you do, it will affect somebody else. I knew you were okay when Sheila came in. I told her, my Little Stephan's impulsive; he does things without thinking, I knew that you would call, but why so long?"

"It's only two days, Mom. Sometimes I didn't call for two or three days when I was in school,"

"A lot can happen in such a short time. But Sheila never used to come in a flap like she did. When you didn't show up anywhere she went to the Police and told them you were missing."

"What did she do that for?"

"You scared her and you hurt her, she's been very good to you, you should have called her. Have you called her yet?"

"No,"

"Are you going to?"

"I don't know. She'd just get upset,"

"Just like your father and I,"

"Mom, I just don't want to talk to her anymore. Can you call her for me?"

"No, you can do that. If you want to grow up and stand on your own two feet, that's fine. But you should make your own phone calls,"

"I'll call her when I get settled in,"

"Settled in where? What is this job you've got?"

"Cutting firewood, I met this guy in the bar in Whitehorse and he hired me to cut wood in the bush. Fifty dollars a day and room and board,"

"Cutting wood in the bush? What do you know about that? It could be dangerous,"

"Its' okay, Mom, I can learn,"

"And that supposed to help me sleep at night,"

"Mom, I'm eighteen. I can handle it,"

"Not as though I have a choice, is there? Well, we can send you money and you can come home right now,"

"No, Mom, I'm staying,"

"I'll call Sheila and tell her where you are. Your father wants to speak to you,"

"Stephan, what are you going to do?"

"I told Mom all about it,"

"Are you going back to school?"

"Sure, I can go back. You can't feed me forever,"

"I know. I miss you, son. You take care of yourself on this job. And you can fly home whenever you want. We can wire you the money in one day. You know that, don't you?"

"Yes, Dad, and thank-you, but I've got to do this,"

"I know, son, I know. Your mother wants to speak to you now. Listen, write often and phone collect whenever you want,"

"One more thing, Dad,"

"What's that, Stephan?"

"I love you, Dad. I do,"

"Great. And that's supposed to help me sleep at night, is it? And I love you, Stephan. You take good care of yourself, now. Here's your mother,"

"Stephan, I want you to write real often. And phone collect and we'll send you money whenever you need it,"

"I know, Mom, I know. Listen I have to go now, my ride is waiting. Please don't worry,"

"How can a mother not worry? Take good care of yourself, write and call often and remember we can send you the money for a ticket home. Right now would be a good time,"

"No thanks, Mom. I'm staying put; you take good care of yourself,"

"Myself? I care for you and your father, that's what I do. Good-bye, my Little Stephan,"

"Bye, Mom." Steve put the receiver back down in its cradle and fought back a tear.

"What's that call about," Rolly said.

"Called the folks,"

"Shit," said Rolly to Jan, "you called your folks since you've been in Canada,"

"No,"

"Same here," Rolly said.

"I have to wonder about my family," Jan said. "What can I do? They said, shoot all the rebels, and here I am in Canada. I didn't ask for the revolution, but I was ready to fight the communists."

He shook his head, looked to the floor.

"Why don't you call them," asked Steve. Rolly and Jan exchanged nervous glances. Their eyes opened wide, and they both glanced down.

"Not that easy, Steve," Jan said. "Too much politics in the way. Every school day you have to say, I love the Russians, and everybody hates them, except my parents,"

"Why do your parents love the Russians," Steve said.

"They chased the Nazis out of Czechoslovakia, but they stayed and took over,"

"Same as Budapest," Steve said. "Dad said the secret police were going to shoot them if they didn't leave Hungary,"

"Secret police shoot everybody," Jan said.

"F.B.I. don't shoot anybody," Rolly said.

"I told you America was a great country." Jan said.

MARINE CORPS TRAINING FACILITY
CAMP PENDLETON, CALIFORNIA
FEBRUARY, 1969

A corporal ran up to Colonel McGarret.
"Sir,"
"What the fuck do you want?"
"Sir, General Stratford wishes to see you, Sir."

McGarret waited in the hallway outside of General Stratford's office. The floor were waxed and shining maple hardwood, the doorknobs and hinges all highly polished brass, ashtrays clean and empty, the antiseptic smell of ammonia fumes wafted through the air.

A corporal showed McGarret into the General's office. He strode up to the General's desk, and briskly saluted, "Sir,"

The General sat behind his oak desk, pulling at his shortly cropped mustache. His blue eyes twitched and the skin over his cheekbones tightly vibrated. His hands were folded in front of him and his thumbs rolled over each other.

"At ease, McGarret. This is not easy for me. I have a son of my own,"

McGarret felt the blood rising in his throat.

"According to the F.B.I., your son has applied for Political Asylum in Canada. According to the Marine Corps he's a deserter,"

The blood in McGarrets' throat locked. His knees went solid, his back rigid and his chest out. "Sir,"

"It is my duty to inform you that your son is wanted for desertion. I'm very sorry to hear that Colonel, very sorry. If he returns to these United States, he will be sent to the military stockade at Leavenworth. If he doesn't do that, he is no longer American."

McGarret stood at attention. He said nothing, did nothing. He stepped out into the rain, stood at attention and sharply saluted the flags. Once more for each generation before him that had served their country and their Corps with pride.

As he entered his barracks, a corporal approached him, stood at attention, saluted.

"Colonel, Sir. May I have a word with you, Sir?"

"Is it important, Corporal?"

"Well, Sir,"

"It can wait then. I don't want to be disturbed,"

"Sir?"

"Fuck off, Corporal."

McGarret stepped into his room, shut the door tight, stared at a picture of his wife and two sons. "What did I do wrong?" His tears dropped to the tight-as-a-drum blanket.

In the morning he showered, shaved, ironed his uniform, polished his medals, didn't eat breakfast, went to see General Stratford.

"What can I do for you, Colonel?"

"A week's leave, Sir. The wife is sick,"

"Granted, take two if you need it."

His wife, Lucy met him at the airport. She had lost a lot of weight over the months since Rolly had come and gone.

Her face had new lines and newer wrinkles. Her hair was tied up at the back, hidden under a scarf; she wore sunglasses, no make-up.

Rolly had used up his thirty days leave, then thirty days Absent

Without Leave, then sixty days before he was legally declared a deserter. No one in the family had ever deserted before. No one in the family would tolerate a deserter.

Lucy's voice shook as she met George. "Your father called," she said.

"What did you say?"

"What could I say? He's his grandson. He's worried about your mothers' heart. He doesn't know how she's going to take it,"

McGarret stared into nothingness. "Does she know?"

"He said he told her,"

She drove through the city, with him staring out the window and saying nothing. It was the first time that she ever had met him on leave that they didn't talk continually, the first time she did the driving. When they got home he poured a drink and stared out the kitchen window.

"You know," she started. "Vietnam Veterans Against the War marched again; it seems they're all against the war,"

"They didn't desert, they earned the right to demonstrate, that's their business,"

The phone rang, she picked it up. "George, it's your father,"

"Dad, how's Mom... Oh, Jesus, Oh God."

They buried his mother next to her mother in the family graveyard. All who attended agreed it was a nice funeral and nobody spoke of the grandson that was missing.

ELSA

Steve peered into the distance and saw a small scattering of lights sparkling across a westward sloping hillside. They drove closer, turned a corner, then he saw the fully lit mining camp of Elsa. Everywhere there were the same billowing clouds of smoke and steam pouring out of chimneys and car and truck tail pipes. The center of the small town was lit up by strings of light bulbs running back and forth across the roadway, lighting up doorways to wooden buildings.

The buildings were all painted a drab green or gray, and many buildings were covered with layers of tarpaper or wood slab planks. Steve heard a loud bang and spun his head to the right just in time to see a small ore-train smash its way through a set of double doors that flew open on loud squeaking hinges. The doors fronted a small shed that backed into the hillside, looking as though the shed grew out of the hill.

"Watch out," Steve yelled. "It's going to hit us,"

"No, it ain't," Rolly yawned back. He kept the truck lumbering on slowly, and the ore-train passed the rear of the truck without hitting. The train had a battery-powered car at the front that pulled five large rusting ore cars, each one over flowing with rocks and mud. There was a small seat in the front car of the train with a miner in a muddy yellow rain coat and pants.

He had an electric light mounted on the front of his muddy yellow hard hat.

As he sat lazily in the seat, he aimed his hat-light down onto the tracks in front of him. It looked like he was asleep. He looked up to Rolly's truck, sneered, then saw Steve staring at him.

He stared back through a muddy face and his eyes focused tight on Steve. Steve shuddered and looked away. He felt his stomach jerk tight and his throat lock.

The train rumbled across the road and smashed its' way through another set of double doors that led into a large wood building.

The man never dropped his stare until he disappeared into the building.

All around the camp were small groups of miners, in their muddy yellow pants, coats and hard hats, hurrying in and out of the double doors.

"Shift change," Jan said. "Bar's going to fill up soon."

There were many more people, not in miners' gear, but in the usual parkas, toques, and heavy boots. They too, were in a hurry to get from one building to another. All trailed streams of fog breath.

Jan pointed up the hillside, to a large square building. "That's where the boss man lives,"

"Who," Steve said.

"The boss man, King of Keno Hill Mines, General Manager, ugly old Nazi."

Steve looked up to the top of the hill, a long winding stairway criss-crossed its way up the side of the hill, stopped in front of the largest of all the buildings. In bold block lettering a sign said:

UNITED KENO HILL MINES
ELSA, YUKON TERRITORY
OFFICE OF THE GENERAL MANAGER

At the bottom of the stairway, a small sign in rough lettering,

Now Hiring.

The sign was old and weathered, like all the buildings.

Rolly drove on through town letting the truck bounce slightly and shudder as it went into and out of the potholes in the road. Steve looked at the long, narrow bunkhouses, perched on the side of the hill.

Each bunkhouse showed its' age with peeling paint, broken windows covered in faded plywood and tar paper patches flapping in the evening wind. Steve counted eight bunkhouses, and between them was a ramshackle network of stairways running up and down the hillside connecting the bunkhouses with each other and the lower town.

The walkways had patches of plywood covering broken sections, and many of the patches were broken. Each step looked slippery as the snow and ice was piled high all around. The lower town had a cook shack and snack bar, as well as the Engineering and Exploration buildings and they all sat on a small plateau at the bottom of the hill. Behind the snack bar, a wobbly walkway was tacked along a long log cabin. It started at ground level, and as the hillside dropped away, it finished twenty feet above the ground.

At the end of the walkway was a sign, 'Elsa Bar'. Rolly parked under the sign and said, "First round's on Jan."

The Elsa Bar had a bare plank floor, worn smooth, unpainted and unswept. The walls were covered in pictures of the first miners to prospect the surrounding mountains. Many more pictures were of the camp in older cleaner days. There were pictures of hunters with the hunted; moose hung upside down to bleed dry, bears with lips drawn back to show their teeth, and fishermen with racks of drying fish.

The ceiling was covered with hats tacked to the planking. Some were baseball caps with the names of sports teams, or trucking and mining companies. Some just had bad jokes. More were cowboy hats, all old and worn out, and fur caps, many of them molded to thin shreds. The entire ceiling was covered and in some places the hats had spread down to the upper walls.

A heavy oak bar was varnished clean and polished. The brass foot rail was dented and shining. Behind the bar sat an old man, with long shoulder length gray hair, and a thick gray beard. He puffed at his pipe, filling the air around him with a thin blue haze. The wall behind him was covered with paper money from all over the world. The bills were autographed and dated by whoever had put them there. Some of the dates went back to the 1920's, the same age of the Elsa Bar.

The bar was full of miners, dirty, tired, noisy and stinking of sweat and diesel fumes. A few office workers were clean. There were card games, chess games and a pool table. Loud voices echoed with European accents.

Rolly and Steve sat as Jan chatted with the bartender. At the next table, one of the miners with a Hungarian accent was loudly boasting to his friends, "You have to be seeing mine working place. You are putting your light on ore-vein; you must be wearing sunglasses,"

Another Hungarian accent added, "At mine working place you are needing two pair."

They all laughed loudly and then turned to look at Rolly and Steve, then were quiet and stared. Jan arrived with beer, looked coldly at the Hungarians who returned his look. Nobody said anything. One of them stood up and looked closely at the long hair and beards on Jan, Rolly and Steve. He walked over, pointed at them. "First I think there is one Jesus, now I see three."

Jan looked directly at Rolly and very slightly shook his head. Rolly, just as slightly, nodded back. Steve didn't see it.

The man said "My name is John Wayne. This is Peter and Henry," he said, motioning to his friends. "Looking for jobs, company needs miners,"

Rolly and Jan said nothing, but Steve couldn't keep his mouth shut, "We're not looking for work,"

John Wayne glared at Jan, "We fight communists in old country, America fight communists in Vietnam. Some people don't fight communists, they run away,"

Jan whispered to Rolly, "Not my fault we ended up in Austria. These guys hold grudges forever,"

"Beats Siberia," Rolly whispered back.

John turned to Steve, "You are Hungarian,"

Steve thought for a second, "Canadian,"

"You look Hungarian, what's your name,"

"Why,"

"I gave you my name, you give me yours,"

Steve shrugged, "Kovacs,"

"Kovacs is Hungarian name. When did your family come to Canada?"

Steve didn't like his attitude. "That any of your business,"

"Miner here looks like you. Joe Smith, you know him,"

Steve looked at Jan, who firmly and quietly shook his head.

"Never heard of him," Steve said.

"You say you're Canadian, but you name is Hungarian. You say you're Kovacs. You look like Joe Smith. You know Joe Smith,"

"Listen, I said, 'No',"

"You family! When they come to Canada?"

Steve felt the flush flow through his cheeks.

Jan whispered, "Be cool, Steve. It's only questions. He's from the old country and these guys take it seriously,"

Steve nodded." '56, or 7, somewhere around then,"

"You don't know,"

"Shit, I was just a kid; I don't remember the bloody date,"

"Date's very important. Month's very important. Your family communists,"

"No,"

John sighed, and said with a shrug, "Is old country, you too young, you Canadian now."

Rolly stood up, "I'm going over to that table, see some old friends. You safe here, Steve? These old guys gonna eat you alive,"

"Don't think so,"

"I join you," Jan said.

Steve put his feet up a chair, but couldn't keep his mouth shut. He turned to John. "So who's Joe Smith,"

"Maybe he's your Daddy. He never comes out. We call him 'Yappy'. You speak Hungarian,"

"No," Steve lied. He never lied or liked liars. These guys were fellow Hungarians and he lied to them. He'd done something terribly wrong, but somehow it seemed right. He spoke Hungarian all the time at home.

He thought over why he lied, he thought about this Joe Smith, this guy that looked like him.

John Wayne went into a conversation in Hungarian with Peter and Henry. They were quiet and determined and spoke in hushed tones. Steve stared away, but listened intently.

"I say he's Yappys' family," John said.

"Leave him alone, it's too many years now," Peter said.

"So what if he is Yappys' family? Leave the kid alone," Henry said.

"The AVO took my family to die in the camps, your families, too. Yappy was AVO," John said.

"We can't kill Yappy in Canada. The RCMP, they'll lock us up for a long time," Peter said.

"Many ways to die underground." John said.

John got up again, asked Steve quietly, in English, "You run away from Vietnam,"

"What,"

"Jan ran away from Czechoslovakia. He's a long hair like you and him," he said, pointing over at Rolly and Jan. "You run away from Viet Nam,"

"No, I'm Canadian. I'm not a draft dodger,"

John stood still and thought about Steve's answer. "You Daddy fight the communists in Hungary,"

"Yes,"

"Where he fight,"

"Budapest,"

"He People's Army of Hungary?"

"No,"

"All of us here fought the communists in Hungary. I fought them in Vietnam with French in 1954. AVO find out, take my family to work camp. Then I came home to Budapest, try to find my family, but they gone in the camps. I fight the communists again in Budapest, then I came to Canada. My home now, your home now,"

"Nice country," Steve said.

John sat down again and was quiet. He said nothing in either language. He put his hand in the air and ordered more beer, and one for Steve. When the beer came he had more to say. "You like communists?"

"Listen, I wouldn't know a communist if one jumped up and bit me on the ass. But my Dad fought them, so I guess I don't like them,"

"Then why don't you fight the communists in Vietnam?"

"Not my fight,"

"Your Daddy fight communists, you should fight the communists. Jan ran away from Czechoslovakia, he's no good. The other long hair, he run away from Vietnam?"

"No, he fought there,"

"You tell him I want to talk to him."

Steve thought this over and didn't think it was a good idea. Nothing he could immediately understand, but from the same place where he lied about not speaking Hungarian, he just didn't like it. Rolly made the decision for him by returning to the table.

"Didn't mean to leave you, buddy. Just bullshitting with the guys,"

"This guy here wants to talk to you," Steve said, pointing at John.

"That right," said Rolly, turning to look at John. "What's up?"

"You fight communists in Vietnam?"

Rolly stared at him, as though he was sizing him up for a fight. "What's it to you?"

"I fought in Vietnam, 1954. With the French,"

"Why?"

John was stunned. "You fought the communists?"

"Yes," Rolly said.

"Why?"

"Was the thing to do,"

"Hungarian communists took my family to work camps when I went to Vietnam with the French. They died there, in the camps,"

Rolly's tone changed, he became very serious. "I'm sorry to hear that, I am. They killed some of my friends' families in Vietnam. Guess they don't fight fair all over the world,"

"That's why I fought the communists,"

"Good reason,"

"Why do you have long hair if you fought in Viet Nam?"

Rolly picked a lock of hair off his shoulder and looked at it. He scratched his beard with his left hand, while still looking at his hair in his right hand.

"Never really gave it that much thought; stopped shaving and haircuts when I left the Marines,"

"You friend Jan ran away from Czechoslovakia. He's a long hair. Long hairs don't fight,"

"That's Jans' business, what he does ain't my call,"

"Kovacs here is Hungarian, his Daddy fought in Budapest, same as me. Long hairs don't fight,"

"Ain't his fight, he's Canadian," Rolly stood up. "Going back to the other table, nice talking to you, what'd you say your name was?"

"John Wayne,"

"Hell of a name you got there, John Wayne. See you later.'

Rolly gave Steve one of his looks that said he was serious. "Steve, you going to join us?"

Steve felt that Rolly wasn't asking, he was ordering him.

"Okay," Steve quietly said.

When they got to the other table, Rolly turned to Steve, "I shouldn't have left you. I won't do that again; looks like you were cornered,"

"They're like that, they have long memories," Jan said.

"They don't like communists; that's for sure," Steve said.

"They lost their families to communists, who can blame them?" Rolly said.

"They're still fighting the war," Jan said. "Only thing they agree on is they all hate the Germans. They think every German is a Nazi. Rest of the time they fight amongst themselves. Steve, you gotta watch you don't get caught in the crossfire,"

"Crossfire?" Steve said.

"Inquest last year, German geologist fell down a ore chute, got crushed to death.

No way to prove murder underground, accidents happen,"

"You're shitting me,"

"I'm not," Jan said. "Like I said, they're still fighting the war,"

"I left my war back in 'Nam," Rolly said. "and I'm about done for this day,"

"It's been a long one," Steve said.

"'Bout as long as yesterday," Rolly said. "Listen, Jan, you get us a room in the bunkhouse,"

"No problem; got an empty right next to mine. Fully loaded with bunks, blankets and pillows, sorry, no women,"

"No women? What kind 'a bunkhouse you running here,"

"Grab your gear. You can leave the truck plugged in where it is."

They unloaded their gear and carefully carried it up the slippery steps to Jans' bunkhouse. Dog wandered up with no problem. When they got to the top of the steps and through the double wind-tight doors, Steve got a good look at the inside of the bunkhouse. It had ten rooms on each side of the narrow, dimly lit hallway. Steve was sure the floors were warped. In the middle of the bunkhouse were the washroom; five toilets, five urinals and five sinks. The shower room had five nozzles.

The toilets, urinals, sinks and shower room floor were stained so brown the white was hardly visible. None of the faucets worked properly. Steve tried some and the handles unscrewed right off. Others simply spun around doing nothing. A few others burst out water that was steaming hot or freezing cold. The floors creaked, the linoleum was worn away from the corners, the paint was peeling off the walls, only half the light bulbs worked, and the doors all hung crooked. The place stunk of urine.
The old steam heating howled through the building and the windows were patched so many times with pieces of plywood and planking that the original glass was long gone.

The gaps were stuffed with fiberglass. Every time the wind blew, the whole building groaned and leaned with the wind.

Jan showed them the room next to his. "No work tomorrow, I'll bring up breakfast. Cooks don't shine on tourists. What's Dog eat,"

"Whatever we don't,"

Dog lay on the floor by Rolly, who grunted his way onto the bunk. Steve sat on his bunk with a sigh.

He looked around the room. It was small, with two bunks and a footlocker at the end of each bunk.

The room was lit by one old light bulb hanging on a string.

They stretched out on their bunks, Rolly yawned and said, "Don't forget to grease your face,"

"What,"

"Cream, use the cream on your face. Frostbite will burn in the morning,"

Steve put more cream on his face. "Pretty much of a dump, eh, Rolly,"

"Holds heat, sheds snow. Shut up and go to sleep,"

Rolly pulled the string and the light went out. "Only thing that works in this 'dump', as you call it,"

"Think the bunkhouse will hold up through the night?"

"If the wind don't pick up. Shut up and go to sleep,"

"Think it'll slide down the hill?"

"If you don't shut up, you'll slide down the hill,"

Steve took a deep breath and then blurted out, "Rolly, the Hungarians are going to kill Joe Smith,"

"Joe Smith ain't the only guy who's going to get killed if you don't shut up and go to sleep,"

"I mean it. I heard them say it in Hungarian,"

Rolly leaned up on one elbow, pulled the string to turn the light back on. "What's that?"

"I heard them say in Hungarian that they wanted to kill Joe Smith,"

"You speak Hungarian?"

"Yes,"

"So, they want to kill Joe Smith,"

"Yes,"

"What's this got to do with you?"

"Don't know,"

"Well then, Stevie my boy, what are you going to do about it?"

"What?"

"I said, 'What are you going to do about it?' "

"Do about it? What do you mean 'what am I going to do about it?'"

"Shit, if you're not going to do anything about it, why are you worried about it?"

Rolly dug into his ruck sack and brought out his whiskey.

"I've had enough to drink," Steve said.

"It's not for you." Rolly had a drink, put it back in his ruck sack, then said, "Shit, kid, you better lay off the smoke,"

"No, I mean it! They don't know I speak Hungarian. I heard them say it,"

"Call the cops,"

"What's that supposed to mean,"

"Let me get this straight. You have a couple beers with some Hungarians you never met before. They get on your case about family history and tell you this guy here looks like you,"

"Yes,"

"Then they say in Hungarian, and they don't know you speak Hungarian, that they want to kill this guy that looks like you, that you never met,"

"Yes,"

"What for?"

"Don't know,"

"You don't know why they want to kill him, but you're worried 'cause this guy looks like you. That's a pretty piss poor reason, if you don't think these Hungarians are full of shit,"

"I don't think these guys are full of shit. If you grew up Hungarian you'd understand,"

"Well, I didn't grow up Hungarian, I grew up American, and that's confusing enough for me. You wanna worry about somebody you don't even know, just 'cause he looks like you, then I think you're nuts,"

"Think so?"

"Fuck, what do I have to say to get through to you? Yes, I think you're nuts. Remember what Jan said, about these people still fighting the war?"

"Yes,"

"And remember what Jan said about not getting caught in the crossfire?"

"Yes,"

"And you want to join in on this old war, do you?"

"No,"

"Then just what do you want to do?"

"I don't know,"

"Steve, there's one hell of a lot you don't know,"

"I know,"

"Okay fine, this is what you do,"

"What?"

"Shut the fuck up and get some sleep. You can't join in on wars that have been over for years without getting a good night's sleep. Now Good Night, Steve,"

"Good night, Rolly."

Rolly pulled the string and the light bulb, socket, plaster, plywood and some old wires all came down and crashed on the floor.

Dog jumped up and howled, then curled up in another corner and started snoring again.

"Well, I guess that'll put the light out," Steve said.

"Ya, I imagine so." Rolly said.

Steve kept thinking over the conversation the Hungarians had. Why did that guy say, 'Leave the kid alone'? Why does he want them to leave me alone? They think I'm related to him! That's why all the questions about my folks.

Just as Rolly began snoring, Steve said, "I think I know why they want to kill Joe Smith,"

"Fuck you,"

"No, I think I've got it,"

"Okay, what is it?"

"They said they knew he was AVO,"

"What's AVO?"

"I heard my Dad talk about them. They're the Hungarian Secret Police,"

"Well shit, you don't want nothing to do with no secret police. Not from any country,"

"Think so?"

"Absolutely fucking yes!"

JANOS KOVACS AT AVO HEADQUARTERS

A fat AVO yelled in Janos' ear, "Got a big mouth, Kovacs". His pock marked face fell straight down to his neck and flopped over his collar, while his belly hung over a tight belt.

Tufts of coarse hair on his knuckles dripped sweat as they smashed Janos to the floor. Three other AVO, boots flashing in the intense interrogation lights, repeatedly kicked him.

Janos curled up, but they pried him open in a spread-eagle position, laid him across a table, and strapped him down.

The fat one wore gloves with weighted knuckles. The other three picked up truncheons and the beating continued. They stood him up, hands tied behind his back.

"Stand on one foot!" Janos tried but neither leg could hold him. They tripped him and the boots continued.

"Who are your associates?"

"I have no associates,"

"What are your plans?"

"I have no plans,"

"Don't lie to us, we know everything!"

Blood poured out of his nose, his eyes swelled shut and the pain in his balls clawed into his stomach.

"You want water? You'll have water."

The fat one threw a bucket of ice water on him. They turned off the lights and left him in the dark and the cold. He got little food, water, or sleep; no contact with anyone, no charges, no trial. After five days, he was released. Janos said nothing because there was nothing for him to say.

"We're watching you." is all they said.

Janos limped home under a gray overcast sky, the same color of his tenement. He thought about the border and how to carry Little Stephan while Tara could carry the food. It would be a long hike, but they could make it out. Maybe he could do it alone and send back for them, but how would they get out? Even if he did make it, Stephan, Tara and Little Stephan would all be arrested. He was needed him here at home, he had to stay. It was still too far, too cold, and the border guards shot to kill.

The hallways in his tenement were cold and dark and always smelled of mould. He stopped at his door, not knowing if his family were safe, or if they too had been arrested. He was afraid when he opened the door, but Tara jumped out of her chair.

"Thank God, you're home. I thought Little Stephan and I were going to be alone," She fell onto their broken old couch pulling Janos next to her and held him as she cried.

"I would be here for you, Tara," Stephan said. "You and Little Stephan, I would be here for you,"

"You'd probably get arrested too, Stephan,"

Stephan slowly nodded his head. "Janos, we could do nothing for you, nobody can take the risk,"

"I know; it's too dangerous," Janos said.

Tara shook slightly, "We wanted to try to do something… but with Little Stephan, what could we do," Tara held Janos at arm's length, "You must eat,"

Tara went through the blanket that hung over the doorway to their tiny kitchen and got some cabbage stew and potatoes.

"Tara, get me the Palinka, please," Janos said.

"That's rotten plums, it's bad for your stomach, you get drunk quick, I don't like it when you drink that,"

"It's not that bad, Tara," Stephan said. "I'll get it and have a drink, too."

Janos slowly limped about the room. He stopped at the wall covered in family pictures. He pointed at one of his father and mother. "Have we lost our home, our country, Stephan?" Janos said.

"You call this tenement a home," Stephan said. "This little dirt hole? With what all of us make, this is all we get. Hardly enough food to feed one child and the four of us have to survive on it. We are slaves at home. Yes, my little brother, we lost our country when the communists took over."

"What about my job? Do you think I've lost it,"

"I don't know, they'll want to make an example of you, that's for sure. Today you eat and sleep, tomorrow you go back to work. No matter what, every god damn day you go back to work."

In the morning, at the machine shop, Supervisor Sandor called up Janos in front of all his co-workers.

"Janos Kovacs! Put down your tool and step forward,"

Janos turned off his metal lathe and stepped up to Sandor.

"You left your place of work for five days without consent or excuse. You let down all your co-workers and selfishly forced them to do your share,"

Janos bit his lower lip until he could taste blood.

"Take this," Sandor said, shoving a broom at Janos. "You are no longer a machinist. You are now a clean-up man and you will be paid as such,"

Janos' co-workers stared at the floor and gritted their teeth. They glanced at each other, the floor, then turned away and went back to their machines.

After Sandor went into his office, some of Janos' co-workers quietly gathered together. All veterans of the Mokan Army and friends of the Kovacs family for generations, they pretended to discuss the job.

"Every day, ten hours of work and nothing to show for it,"

"Every night political meetings, I never see my children,"

"Janos is right. My children grow hungry as food trains go east,"

"They take everything we make, everything we grow, and give us back nothing.

"To think we fought alongside those Russian bastards,"

"They rid us of Nazi pigs, now they are communist pigs,"

"We have little choice; they run our country now,"

"Look what happened to Janos, to all the others the AVO took,"

"The AVO are all Hungarian, they have turned our own against us,"

"They will pay for their treason,"

"We have to do something, but they took all our guns,"

"Yes," they all nodded, "we have to get our guns back,"

"Then we get the traitorous AVO, every single damn one of them."

Janos thought of his younger brother, Josef, and his stomach choked. He swept his broom away from the men, and quietly finished the floor.

That night Josef came to visit. Stephan heard the knock on the door and was immediately suspicious. "Who is it," he said through the closed door.

"It's me, it's Josef."

Stephan carefully opened the door, and peaked up and down the hallway. He looked coldly at Josef. He was out of his usual army uniform. He carried a large duffel bag over his shoulders.

"What do you want?" Stephan said.

"I have some things for you," he said.

"Come in, come in," Tara said, as she hugged him.

Janos hugged him, then held him at arm's length, "Why haven't we seen you for so long,"

"Yes, why," snapped Stephan.

"I have been away, ordered away,"

"Back to Moscow," snapped Stephan again.

"I was under orders, I had to go; I had no choice,"

"How many times is it now? No choice you say?" Stephan said.

Josef stammered. "I have some bread, some sausage and cheese, and some warm clothes for Little Stephan,"

"How can you bring us these things when we can't afford them ourselves," Stephan demanded

Josef motioned to a chair. "Can I sit?"

"Yes, of course," said Tara. She glared at Stephan who wouldn't move for Josef.

Janos took a chair and gave it to Josef. "Please sit and tell us…"

Josef sat and pulled out a rolled cigarette. He offered one to Janos.

Stephan reached out and put his hand on the pack of rolled cigarettes. "We can't afford rolled cigarettes, Josef. We have to roll out own,"

"I'll take one, Josef," Janos said. "Tell us more about… Moscow,"

Stephan jumped in. "Yes, Josef, tell us about Moscow and how only the favored few go there,"

"I only guard the border, that's all I do. I don't do anything else,"

Josef took a long drag on his cigarette. "I had to go, I was ordered. You don't understand…"

"What don't we understand, Josef? That you go to Moscow, that you receive special extras, that you bring these extras to us," Stephan's anger was growing.

"Stephan," Tara said quietly, trying to calm Stephan.

Stephan wouldn't stop. "If you guard the border, you shoot escapers, Josef. Is that what you've become?"

"No, I don't shoot anybody. I never have,"

"If you don't shoot them, you will be shot. We know how these things work,"

"That's not true," Josef said.

"Then," Janos asked, "What is true,"

"Many of us, we don't do those things, we have been conscripted, they own us,"

"How did you get these extras for us," Janos said.

"From storage, in the armory. They won't know they're gone, I saw to that,"

"How did you 'see to that'," Tara said.

"They have records on everything, I got into the records, they're not missing,"

Stephan jumped up, "You can change the records, you can steal from the armory, you can smuggle extras to us, for Little Stephan. How nice. What about the rest of Hungary, what about your fellow countrymen, what can you smuggle for them?"

Josef held up his hands in defense. "There's only so much I can do. They're watching me, and you and everybody else."

"They watch everything and everybody. They watch each other. I haven't done anything wrong,"

Stephan was now yelling at Josef. "Except work for the Russians, I'm glad that our parents are not alive to see this day,"

Janos again told Stephan, "Sit, and let him speak. Go on Josef; tell us what we need to know,"

"Be careful what you say, there are informers everywhere. They will take what you say and turn it and twist it and use it against you. They make wives spy on their husbands, they can get to anyone."

Josef was sweating; he dragged heavily on his cigarette. "You have to be careful, watch what you say at all times. Watch who you talk to and what you say."

"We know all that, Josef. Look at the bruises on your brothers' face. Know where they came from, how he got them,"

"Yes, I know how he got them. That's why I have come here, to tell you these things, these things you need to know,"

"And to give us things you stole? To try to buy our forgiveness? I can never forgive a traitor and that's what you've become, Josef. I am ashamed that you are my brother and I cannot look you in the eye."

Stephan stood up, grabbed his coat, stomped out the door, loudly slamming it shut behind him.

Tara jumped in her seat at the sound of the slamming door. Janos turned to his younger brother; he tried to speak, but Josef wouldn't let him. "I wish I could stay longer, I want to stay longer, to tell you more, you need to know more, but I have to go now, the neighbors have heard the door, they will want to know what is happening, they might inform on you if they see me here. I will go out through the cellar door, out the back way; I have to leave before they see me."

Tara reached out to hug Josef.

"No time, I must go now," Josef said. "Watch what you say, what you do, there are informers everywhere. I don't know who they are, but I know they are everywhere."

He opened the door slowly, peaked out, then turned back to Janos and Tara, "I don't know if I can come back, it's too dangerous; for all of us, it's too dangerous." Then he was gone.

ELSA BUNKHOUSE

"You guys awake?" Jans' voice boomed through the door.

"I'm not, but Steve is," Rolly said.

Jan came into the room and sat cross-legged on the floor, holding a brown paper bag. Dog put his head in Jan's lap and started chewing on the bag.

"Here you go, Dog," He put a few sausages on the floor and Dog slurped them up, gave Jan the eye for more. He emptied the bag on the floor and Dog quickly ate them.

"Where's mine," Rolly said.

"Dog ate them. The sausages here are only good for dog food,"

"Not the first time he's beat me to food,"

"Not to worry," Jan said. "I will get you real food. Did you sleep well?"

"Ask Steve here,"

Steve sat up quickly, "Listen, Jan, you know this Joe Smith guy,"

"I know who he is; I've never talked with him. He doesn't talk to anybody,"

"Where is he?"

"Working,"

"When does he finish?"

"Four thirty,"

"Can you introduce me to him?"

"You don't need me for introductions. He can tell you to fuck off all by himself,"

Rolly reached down to where Dog was chewing on the sausages and quickly grabbed one. "Ha, ha. Beat ya." Dog ignored him.

Rolly looked at the sausage, bit off a piece and chewed it, looked at it some more, then finished it. He let out a small burp and said, "Your right, only good for dog food. " He paused for a minute then said, "Jan, we got a problem here,"

"Who's got a problem?"

Rolly pointed a sausage Steve. "Steve here got a stick up his ass on Mr. Joe Smith,"

"I told you he was a Kovacs," Jan said.

"What do you know about this Smith guy," Steve said.

"Very little, Hungarians are still at war with each other. I know they all hate the Germans. You guys want to eat now?"

Rolly started counting off on his fingers, "I'll have a stack of pancakes, maybe five, six high, handful of sausages, say ten, big steak well done, few handfuls of hash browns, half a gallon of milk, pail of coffee, and a few fried eggs, thank you very much. And a stack of toast, with jam and honey,"

Jan yawned with his mouth wide open. He turned to Steve. "And you, Sir, what would you like on this fine and wonderful morning? Eggs Florentine? Belgian waffles,"

"Hey, whatever you can get is fine with me," Steve said.

Jan took off for the cook shack and Rolly started digging in his sack. "Going for a shower." he said.

Steve looked out a small opening in the boarded up window, the only place where there was any glass left. The sun had not come up yet. He looked at his watch. Nine thirty and no sun. He tapped his watch to see if it was still working. It was.

Joe Smith would be back in camp about four thirty. He knew Rolly would want to be on the road right after eating. Could he talk Rolly into staying long enough for him to meet Joe Smith?

Rolly returned from his shower." You go take one, lots' of hot water, use the nozzle on the far left."

Steve stood in the hot water and tried to think up ideas he could use to talk Rolly into staying one more day. Go fishing? No, too damn cold, all the creeks are frozen over. Truck broke down? Nope, Rolly keeps lots of spare parts and is a good mechanic. Then, the brilliance hit Steve! Just ask him. Tell him it's important. It's family stuff. He would understand. He's busted up with his family. He has to understand.

"Really? How surprising," Rolly said.

"I have to meet this guy. Maybe he is some long lost family or something,"

"Rosie'll have my ass on a platter, but that's nothing new. I'm already a day late for work and I got contracts to fill. Also, I was wondering how long it would take you to figure this out. If I was a betting man, I would have bet that you'd have sprung this on me yesterday, but you're kind of slow, so it took you all night to think it over."

The door flew open and Jan yelled out, "Breakfast is served." He struggled through the door with an over-loaded tray.

Rolly happily complained "Steve wants to stay all fucken day,"

"Like it here, do you," Jan said.

"I gotta meet this Joe Smith guy,"

"That should be fun, time to eat."

Jan laid out the food on Rolly's bunk. It wasn't quite what Rolly ordered, but there was lots of it. Plus a pail of coffee.

"Plenty damn good there, Jan. Plenty damn good," Rolly said as he started to stuff his face. "Better dive in Steve, before I eat it all,"

"I will, I will. I've seen this show before,"

"This is what I figure," Rolly said between mouthfuls. "To start with, how long can Steve stay in the bunkhouse without getting in shit?"

"Till Klutzfuck finds him,"

"Who's Klutzfuck?"

"General Manager. The King of Keno Hill, ugly old German. Even the few Canadians here hate him. He will toss you out and fire anybody who puts you in their room,"

"How long's he got?" Rolly said.

"Noon, Klutzfuck misses nothing,"

"Why don't I wait in the bar? When he gets off work I'll find him and introduce myself. See what happens. Then I can hitchhike back to Pelly Crossing. You can meet me there,"

Rolly raised his fork in a salute, "The kid's brilliant! But, you wanna hitchhike at forty below? With frostbite already? Ain't nobody driving anyways, 'cept me,"

"Can I pay for a night in the bunkhouse? Like a hotel,"

"Nope, get a room in Keno City and how you gonna do that?" Rolly said. "Thought you lost all your money shooting pool,"

"Shit, you're right," Steve said.

Between mouthfuls Rolly reached into his pocket and pulled out a wad of money. "Advance on your wages." He handed Steve a small roll of dollar bills.

"I haven't even started work, yet,"

"You will, family's important. You find him, you find out what his story is, you stay out of his war, you get a room in Keno City. Now eat, you got a long day ahead of you,"

"What's in Keno City?" Steve said.

"Not much, few miners, few trappers, few hippies. Hotel there hops on the weekend; got a real good old jukebox. Italian guy runs the café', great food, taxi service for the drunks, too." Jan said.

"So this is what I do," Steve said. "It's cool for me to wait in the bar, right,"

"Right," Jan said.

"So I wait in the bar till Joe Smith gets back from work. I meet him and see what happens. Then I taxi to Keno City,"

"Then what," Rolly said. "I'm ten miles into the bush from Pelly. How we gonna get back together,"

"Jan, what's the food like at this cafe in Keno City?" Rolly said.

"Not bad. Damn good if you phone ahead and order something special," Jan said.

"Okay, Rolly," Steve said. "You tell Rosie you're going to take her out for a special night on the town. Just don't tell her which town. Phone ahead and order what she likes. I'll reserve you a room in the hotel, and I'll pay for it,"

"And you'll pay for dinner,"

"And dinner,"

"And gas,"

"Okay, and gas,"

"And the bar bill,"

"How much money you give me?"

"Didn't give you any money, lent it to you,"

"Your girlfriend will agree" Jan said, "She will like a three hour ride for dinner,"

"Jesus," Rolly said. "She's part Cree. She can put up with anything, long as there's a good reason,"

"Tell her it's a sightseeing tour," Steve said. "Tell her it's... what's to look at here, Jan,"

"Hell of a juke box at the hotel,"

"She like music," Steve said.

"I can talk her into it,"

"Special date? Special dinner? Meet your old friends?" Steve said.

"She don't like any of my friends. But the dinner date thing might work,"

"So, is she your girlfriend or wife or what?" Steve said.

"Oh well, hell, you know, well she's, you know," Rolly started to blush.

"God damn it, Rolly," chuckled Steve. "You can't tell me a Marine is afraid of a little girl,"

"Hey," Rolly barked. "Go easy on the Marine thing,"

"Okay," Steve backed off quickly. He was worried he's upset Rolly. "We cool?"

"Ya, we're cool. You're Canadian, you don't know the Marines. Let's do it then. Food's done, I'm done. So I meet Rosie at Pelly Crossing today and come back here tomorrow,"

"And I wait in Keno City 'till you get there," Steve said.

"Go to the Administration office and ask the number of his room." Jan said.

Steve packed up his bag and snuck out the back door of the bunkhouse. He slipped most of the way down the hillside to the Elsa Bar, walked in and dropped his gear in a corner by the door.

The same bartender, the old man with the long gray hair and beard, sat at the bar drinking coffee and smoking his pipe, making the air around him a thin blue haze. He was reading a newspaper. Steve sat at the same table he sat at the night before. The seat the Hungarians had cornered him in.

The bartender didn't look up from his newspaper. "Coffee's in the pot," he said. "Help yourself,"

"How much," Steve said.

The bartender looked up from his paper, then at Steve's bag in the corner. "You ain't going anywhere, pay up later." He put his paper down and refilled his coffee. He eyed Steve slowly and fully, then picked up his paper, left the bar and sat down at Steves' table. He said nothing. Steve looked at the front page of the paper.

PEACE NEGOTIATIONS BREAK DOWN IN PARIS
HANOI AND VIETCONG WALK OUT
PROTESTING CONTINUED U.S. BOMBING

Steve thought about the conversation he had with Larry when he first arrived in Whitehorse. "Some day this war will end," Larry had said, "and then we can all go home."

Better tell Rolly about that, he thought, then yawned, stretched out, and promptly went to sleep. He was startled awake by a loud noise. It was the door slamming shut. He reached for his coffee and spilt it.

"Get another," the bartender said.

Four miners walked in and sat down. They were in their underground work clothes; muddy yellow raincoats and pants, muddy yellow hard hats with head lights. They left muddy boot prints on the dirty floor.

"Four beers and we ain't here," one of them said.

"Four beers and you ain't here," the bartender said.

Steve closed his eyes and went back to sleep. He was startled awake again. Four more miners walked in. He looked at his watch. It was four o'clock, time to go to the Administration building and find out Joe Smith's room number.

"Can I leave my bag by the door," he asked the bartender.

"'Less you wanna carry 'em," he said.

"No,"

"They're fine where they are."

Steve headed for the administration building, on the top of
Keno Hill, at the end of a long winding wooden walkway. It
was dark now and the lights on the ropes across the road flew
back and forth in the wind, casting jumping shadows across
the snow banks. He stood at the bottom of the stairway and
watched as the wind blew the dry snow around in circles and
swirls, moving it over a few feet, then bringing it back.

The wind had a calming feeling. There was nothing
complicated about it. It just blew. He smiled into the biting
cold wind that stung his frost bit face and enjoyed the peace
that it gave him.

Then the calming feeling blew away in the wind and a
scary thought took over. "What the hell am I doing here? Do I
have to see this guy?

Why not just leave him alone, catch up with Rolly and get
on with work? How much do I owe Rolly and how long do I
have to work to pay him off; before I get to make any money
of my own?

I don't need to do any of this; nothing here needs to be
done. Stay out of his war? How do I do that?"

Steve stood in the howling wind, felt the frostbite on his
face begin to burn and watched as his legs began the long
climb up the stairs. He couldn't see the administration
building; it was wedged between two hillocks. All he could
see was the snow and ice covered walkway winding its way up
the hill and disappearing into the blowing snow.

Along the walkways, more light bulbs strung up on ropes
jumped around in the wind and threw flashes of light across
the steps and snow banks. White and black, visible and
invisible; a step in the light, a step in the dark; after images in
his eyes blinded him before the lights came back.

He turned into the first switchback walkway and gripped
the railings as the wind caught him and pushed him back.
When the walkway switched back again, the wind pushed him
forward. He steadied himself, but then the wind gusted and
changed directions. The higher he went, the stronger the wind
got. He stopped halfway up and looked back down.

The walkway was gone in the blowing snow, lost and found again, in the whiteness and the blackness of the jumping lights.

He turned and continued up, fighting the wind and the snow, shielding his eyes from the cold and the flashing lights. When he got to the top he was gasping for air, but couldn't take a deep breath. The air was too cold, it froze his lungs. He stepped out of the wind at the door.

He took a close look at the only building in camp that didn't look like it was going to fall down, or collapse in on itself.

It didn't need a paint job, none of the windows were broken, and the doors weren't frozen shut. He opened the front door without a struggle, walked in and closed it. He couldn't hear anything, or see anybody.

He shook the snow from his boots and coat, and then walked straight up to the front desk and stood there, looking down. A pair of feet rested on the top of a typewriter. They had no shoes on, just heavy woolen socks. A head popped up from further behind them. It was a young woman and she had a book in her hands.

"Bitchin' weather, eh? Why didn't you wait 'till tomorrow?"

"Wait for what?" Steve said.

"We're hiring," she said. "You can start tomorrow. Fill this out." She put down her book and handed him a piece of paper.

"No," Steve said, shaking his head. "I'm not looking for work,"

She looked startled. "Then why are you here,"

"I'm looking for Joe Smith,"

"You gotta be shitting me,"

"I need his room number,"

"His room number?"

"Yes, his room number. You know who he is?"

"Oh ya, I know who he is. Question is, who are you?"

"I just want to meet him," Steve said.

"Meet him? You want to meet Joe Smith? Why the hell do you want to meet Joe Smith?"

Steve let out a sigh. "I just want to say hello,"

"Oh, I got it," she said. "You must be some long lost son or something,"

Steve shook his head. "I don't think so,"

She shrugged and went over to a filing cabinet and pulled out a piece of paper. "He's in Bunkhouse five, room seven,"

Steve headed back to the door, but the secretary called out, "Hold it, not so fast,"

Steve stopped and turned to face her.

"Have a seat," she said.

"Why,"

"Mr. Von Klutz will definitely want to talk to you,"

"Why?"

"Oh, he's the boss of...well the boss of everything. You sit, I'll get him." She took off down the hallway and was back quickly. "He'll be right out." she said with a smile.

Mr. Von Klutz came into the hallway. He carried his short, stocky frame with a military briskness. He was fully bald and his jowls hung over his shirt neck in deep furrows. His small blue eyes were sunk behind heavy hairless eyebrows. "What do you want with Joe Smith?"

"I want to talk to him,"

"About what,"

Steve was stumped. Just what did he want to talk about? The weather? "I just wanted to say 'hello',"

"'Hello?' You came all this way just to say hello? That's it? Are you family,"

"I don't know,"

"You are either family or you are not family,"

"I may be family. I don't know,"

"And that is what you are here to find out,"

"Yes,"

Mr. Von Klutz turned to his secretary, "Have Smith sent here."

He looked back sternly at Steve. "You will wait here."

Then he turned and marched down the hallway.

The secretary looked at Steve, smiled, and shook her head. She picked up a phone, dialed and said, "Send Smith to Von Klutz... yes, that's what I said,"

There is a Season   J. Harding Montgomery

"... guy here says he might be family... no shit, that's what he says... Well, he sure looks like him."

She hung up and looked at Steve. "You don't know if you're his long lost son?"

"No,"

"Maybe little brother?"

"No,"

"Nephew?"

"I'm told he looks like me and we're both Hungarian,"

"Ya, you look like him, that's for sure. He's on his way."

She shrugged her shoulders and went back to her book.

Steve stretched out in his chair and began to wait. He couldn't get comfortable in his chair. The legs were too short, he looked at them, they weren't; maybe they were too long, he looked again, they weren't. The back was too stiff, how stiff should the back of a chair be? Maybe he just needed a foot stool; that might help.

The air was getting stuffy, he couldn't get a lungful. It tasted bad, something was wrong with the air.

Maybe she could turn the lights down low, they were too bright, but she had to read her book. Did she have something for him to read?

Shit, he thought, maybe I should have brought some text books, that way when I go back, I won't be so far behind. I'll have to start all over, be a good idea to do more studying, could use a bit more work and a bit less drinking beer.

I should be nicer to Sheila, she helped a lot with my algebra, I'm going to need help with my trigonometry, damn that stuff is complex, I could get another place, closer to campus, so I don't spend so much time on the bus, give me more time for studying. I really should get back to school, maybe I could get some more money from Dad, pay off Rolly and fly back, that way I won't miss too much time. I could be on the plane tomorrow if I got out of here now, I have to leave soon, no, right away, then I won't be so late and I can get back to... the door was kicked open and slammed shut.

A man stomped in, walked right past him, and went directly to the secretary. He left a trail of snow on the floor. "What's Klutzfuck want," he demanded.

Steve heard something familiar in the voice and his heart started thumping.

"Its okay, Smith. There's nothing wrong," said the secretary.

"Then why the hell did I climb a thousand fucken' steps in a hundred fucken below to say hello to Klutzfuck,"

"His name is Mr. Von Klutz,"

"I don't give a shit what his name is,"

He turned around and glared at the door. He looked right through Steve. He turned back to the secretary, "What's he want from me?"

Mr. Von Klutz came out of his office, marched down the hallway, pointed his finger at Steve, and in a cautious tone said, "Smith, this man... wants to talk to you."

Smith turned to look at Steve, who slowly stood up. Steve didn't see Smiths' nose or mouth or chin. He didn't see his forehead, ears, hair or anything else. He didn't see Von Klutz and the secretary standing nervously behind Smith. All he saw were the eyes.

Tight eyes, narrow and focused; fearful, like those of a frightened child; and deep, like those of a wise old man; and in those eyes Steve sensed something he should be very afraid of, like looking into eyes that have been in hell and refused to die. He felt his throat tighten, he was about to cry, but couldn't. He didn't move. Smiths' eyes changed and he looked confused.

He stared deep into Steve's eyes, then... leaned forward for a closer look. One slow step at a time he walked over to Steve and reached out his hand to gently touch his beard and softly rub his frostbit face. He took his hand back, let out a heavy sigh, sat down and calmly said, "You... sit."

Steve sat down. Smith sat next to him and wiped a single tear from his cheek as he quietly nodded to himself and stared at the floor. He sat very quiet for a few long seconds, eyes closed, as though he were praying.

Then he looked up to nothing and let his eyes wander. He squeezed his eyes open and shut and blinked a few times. Then he turned and pointed directly at Steve. "You," he said with a smile that warmed Steve and tightened his throat again, "are Little Stephan."

Steve wasn't ready for this. He wasn't ready for anything like this. He never imagined that this Joe Smith guy would call him by the name that only his mother ever used. He quickly shook his head, tried to regain some of the control he felt he was losing. "Who are you?"

"I am your Uncle Josef, Janos' brother."

Steve stopped breathing.

"You don't know me," Smith said.

"No,"

"Never heard of Uncle Josef,"

"Never,"

Smith got up and walked towards the door. "Good-bye," he said.

Steve was stuck in his chair.

Smith stopped at the door and turned, "Why did you come here,"

Steve jumped up, "I came here to see you,"

"Okay, you've seen me. Good-bye,"

"Why don't I know you?"

"You've come a long way for nothing. Good-bye," Smith slammed the door.

"Bullshit." Steve yelled.

Smith stomped down the steps with Steve running close behind him. Steve skipped two steps in front of Smith, reached up and grabbed him by the collar, screamed in his face. "You have to talk to me."

Smith grabbed Steve's' arms and tried to loosen his grip, but Steve wouldn't let go. Smith stopped struggling. He felt Steve's arms, almost massaged them. He nodded. "You want to talk,"

Steve held a firm grip. "Yes,"

Smith let out a long sigh and nodded again. "Okay... we talk,"

Steve let go and stood aside as Smith walked past him and down a few steps, then Smith turned back to look at Steve, who had hadn't moved. "You coming?" he said.

"Yes, yes I am," Steve stammered.

"Then let's get on with it. It bloody cold out."

Smith led the way as the two of them leaned into the wind and quietly began their long walk back down the slippery stairs.

At the bottom Smith stopped and turned to Steve. He had a puzzled look on his face. "You like this weather," he said.

"No, it's too damn cold,"

"You got that right."

Smith walked quietly to the bunkhouse, with Steve wondering what to say next. He felt like he was sliding down a dark hole and there was nothing for him to hold onto, then he felt like he was falling off the cliff again, but this time Rolly wasn't there to grab him.

They said nothing more until they walked through the door into Smiths' room. Next to the door was a bookshelf from floor to ceiling, next to that another floor to ceiling bookshelf, both stuffed with books.

In the middle of the room was a bunk bed, and on the top bunk were stacks and stacks of books. Along the wall where the window was supposed to be were planks laid across wooden boxes.

The boxes were full of magazines and the plank shelves held more books. Every wall was full of books, and the floor covered in boxes of books. From the door to the bed was a narrow walkway between boxes. Next to the bed was a big old chest that doubled as a bedside table. It was littered in scraps of paper and ragged notebooks. An old tin can served as an ashtray and was overflowing with hand rolled cigarette butts. Under the bed were piles of clothing.

Steve had to speak first, if only to slow his racing heart. "Why did you leave?"

"The office or Hungary,"

Steve was stumped. Smith noticed this and smiled. "You saw me. I thought that was enough,"

"I wanted to meet you,"

Smith sat on his bunk and folded his hands on his knees. He looked up, but not at Steve, who was still standing. He took another deep sigh, and as he let it out he started speaking with his hands moving in front of him, as though he was forming his words out of the air itself. "I never thought I'd see you again, ever, I tried to forget you, but I never could. Janos, Tara, then, there you are, standing in front of me, so many years," Smith turned to look at Steve. His eyes widened, narrowed, then widened again. "I didn't know what to do,"

"Why don't I know you?"

"So many years, no family, all alone, when I left Budapest I thought, no more home, no more family, all gone. Now you, why did you search for me,"

"I have to know you,"

"Now you know me."

Steve started looking over the books. Some were in Hungarian, others in Russian, German, French, and languages he didn't recognize, and many more in English. He looked at the magazines. Most he knew, Canadian and American weeklies, many others, European.

Smith sat quietly as he watched Steve look around his room.

"This is your home," Steve said.

Smith refolded his hands on his knees, then they came to life again as he swept them about the room. "For many years now, this is where I live. This is my home,"

"How long have you been here?"

"Since I came to Canada,"

Smith knelt down next to his bunk and pulled out a cardboard box, opened it, and brought a bottle of something Steve didn't recognize.

He pulled out two shot glasses, rubbed the dust out with his shirt sleeve, and said, "I want a drink. You want a drink,"

"Okay,"

Smith sat down at one end of his bunk and motioned for Steve to sit at the other. "You can sit here, I won't bite you,"

They were inches apart. Smith too, seemed not to know where to start. He looked at Steve in such a strange way that Steve didn't know how to respond.

Steve could tell that Smith was curious, but what scared him most was the look in Smiths' eyes. He'd never seen that look before.

It wasn't like his parents looked at him. Not even Sheila looked at him like that.

"You're a young man now. You look like your father. Where is Janos?"

"Vancouver,"

"Tara is with him,"

"Yes,"

Smith nodded. He seemed genuinely pleased, and then his manner changed. "Your Uncle Stephan?"

"I don't know much about him,"

"What do you know?"

"He died in Austria. 1956,"

"How?"

"Dad said he froze to death. Mom says it was his wounds that killed him. Neither of them talks about it. I had to drag it out of them,"

"They never talk about me; they only show you pictures of your Uncle Stephan, but never talk about how he died,"

"That's about it,"

"I know this causes them great pain,"

Steve thought about the pain he caused his parents. "What do you know about Stephan?"

"I know he's dead," Smith sighed.

"How do you know that?"

"You just told me,"

"You never knew,"

Smith shrugged. "They say why they left Budapest,"

"I know my Dad and Uncle Stephan were fighting in the revolution. They had to leave in a hurry. Couldn't take anything with them,"

"They bring any pictures?"

"A few,"

"What do you know from the pictures?"

"Nothing about you. So you are my uncle,"

"Yes,"

"Why don't I know about you?"

"Long story,"

"Listen, what do I call you?"

"Smith,"

"Why'd you change your name? Why aren't you Kovacs?"

"Revolution was very dangerous, changed my name. You'll see."Smith reached into his pocket and brought out a small set of keys. He pulled a locked trunk out from under the bed and opened it. He slowly and carefully moved things about in the trunk.

They were all wrapped in old rags and the time he took, moving them about and sorting them, made Steve very nervous.

"What are you doing in there?" Steve said

"You wait... I'll show you," he said.

Steve watched very carefully as Smith went on sorting and digging, looking for something Steve felt very afraid of. He took his drink, poured it down, and then quickly let out a gasp of air. "What the hell was that?"

"You like it," Smith smiled.

"Holy shit," Steve was still gasping.

"What is it?"

Smith started laughing, "It's a Hungarian drink,"

"What's it called?"

"Palinka,"

"Paaa...what?"

"Paa..linka. Brandy. Plum Brandy,"

"Plum Brandy, not bad,"

Smith held out the bottle. "You want another?"

"Well, hell. That was, well, hell, why not,"

Smith drank his, poured two more and went back to digging in his trunk. "I have to show you something, your family, when I find it,"

"What is it?"

"You'll see, when I find it,"

"Well, find it will you,"

"Calm down. You're just like your father,"

"What's that mean?"

"Don't wait for a damn thing; everything has to be right now. Here it is."

Smith handed Steve a weathered and yellowed black and white picture. Steve took one look and wanted to cry, but instead, he choked. He tasted the bile rise in his throat and swallowed it back down, then felt a burning anger rising up.

It was a picture of his mother and father. Both were holding a small baby. Next to his father were two smiling men. One man he recognized as Uncle Stephan. He had seen pictures of him before. Next to him was a man he didn't recognize. He turned and looked at Smith, who sat still, waiting to be recognized.

Steve felt the anger again. He wanted to tear the picture into a thousand pieces and burn it. He wanted to run out of the room and scream bloody murder at something he didn't understand. Knowing he didn't understand only made it worse. He carefully laid the picture on the bunk next to Smith.

"That is before I went in the army," Smith said.

Steve held his breath, and then let it out. His head started spinning and his stomach rose to his throat. He puked on the one piece of the floor that wasn't covered in boxes.

"You don't like Palinka," Smith said.

Smith got up and walked out of the room. Steve sat and wiped his mouth with his sleeve. Smith came back with some paper towels and started mopping up. "This is not the first time I cleaned up your puke,"

"I'll be right back," Steve said. He went to the washroom, washed his face, and gargled some. He kept taking mouthfuls of water, trying to wash out the taste of bile, but it didn't work.

He stared into the mirror and watched his face turn into his fathers', then his Uncle Stephan's. And now he saw Uncle Josef's. Only the eyes remained the same.

He puked in the sink again, washed out his mouth again; looked into the mirror, then returned to Smiths' room.

Smith sat on his bunk and said, "You have your fathers' patience and your mothers' stomach,"

"My mothers' stomach,"

"Puke a lot,"

"Why,"

"Ask your father. Here,"

Smith handed Steve a piece of chewing gum. "What do I call you?"

"Steve,"

"No Stephan, just Steve?"

Steve turned back, "No Kovacs, just Smith?"

Smith started laughing, great belly swelling laughter that came from far and deep inside. Steve thought Smith might rupture a muscle as he held his stomach and rolled over on his back.

"I didn't think that was so funny," Steve said.

"Yes, yes. Just like Janos. Damn funny and don't even know it."

There was a knock at the door. Smith looked at the door in shock. "Nobody knocks. Nobody ever knocks, nobody ever comes."

He went to the door, and yelled through it, "Who's there,"

"Mr. Von Klutz,"

Smith turned to Steve and whispered, "Nazi pig."

He opened the door and snapped out," What do you want,"

"I want to see how you are,"

"How I am? I'm having a drink with my nephew. That's how I am,"

"Just thought I'd look in on you,"

"So you looked. I'm taking my nephew to dinner,"

"You know we don't serve non-employees in the kitchen,"

"Fuck you. I'm taking my nephew to dinner,"

Von Klutz staggered back in amazement. His eyes almost popped out. "You know we have rules here, Smith. If I let you break them, everybody will break them,"

"Fuck you and fuck your rules. I'm taking my nephew to dinner,"

Steve was poorly trying to hide his grin. "Mr. Von Klutz, I would be happy to pay,"

Smith spun about to Steve, "You paying nothing. You are my guest."

He turned back to Von Klutz, "I've worked here long time, no problem. I'm taking my nephew to dinner,"

Von Klutz seemed totally lost for what to say or do. "Okay," he stammered. "Just this time,"

"Fine," Smith said. "Goodbye."

He slammed the door shut, turned to Steve with a smile as wide as his face could possibly stretch and started laughing again."Come. We go to dinner now."

Smith handed Steve his coat and put on his own. Steve wasn't sure what to do. "You think this is a good idea,"

He didn't want to cause problems for Smith, but he could tell that something was coming up, and he sure wasn't going to miss it. He felt that he'd missed far too much already.

When they got to the cook shack they hung up their coats and walked into the noisy overcrowded hall.

There were over forty tables, each seating eight men. Along the far wall were steam tables and each man grabbed a tray and walked along filling his plates.

In front of the steam tables were more tables, laid out with bread and sandwich meats, fruits, cookies and cakes. Everywhere there was noise and laughter, but when Smith and Steve walked in, it all went quiet.

Men with their backs to them turned and stared. It was completely quiet, followed by hushed whispers.

Jan was not far away, leaning against the wall with an ear-to-ear grin. He walked right up to them, shook Steve's hand, and said, "Welcome to the Elsa kitchen. Hope you enjoy the slop,"

Slowly the general level of noise returned.

"Jan, this is my Uncle Joe,"

Jan shook his head back and forth, never letting go of his huge grin. "Pleasure to meet you, Uncle Joe."

Jan put out his hand and Smith flinched.

"It's cool, Uncle Joe. He's my friend," Steve said.

"Your friend," Smith said.

"Yes," Smith slowly put his hand out. He was nervous and untrusting.

Jan saw this. "You've been here long, Uncle Joe,"

"Longer than you,"

"Join me at my table," Jan said

"No, I have my own table," Smith said.

"You have your own table?" Steve said.

"I always have my own table, never share with nobody,"

Smith straightened up, "I have dinner alone with Stephan,"

Jan nodded and bowed, "Have it your way," he winked at Steve.

"Nice to meet you, Uncle Joe,"

"Yes, nice," said Uncle Joe. "Stephan, you come with me. You pick what you want. I will talk to the cook,"

Smith led the way down to the steam table line. A skinny cook with his hair in a pony tail said with an American accent, "No tourists, against the rules,"

"I talked to Von Klutz. He said 'Okay',"

"Ain't my call, I'll get Tiny."

Out of the back of the kitchen stormed a huge man in a white smock. He was at least three hundred and fifty pounds with extremely fat arms fully covered in tattoos, a barrel chest and a gut that hung well over his invisible belt. He had a thick black beard, thick black long hair tied back in a pony tail, dark deep-set eyes and around his forehead, a bright red bandana. He carried a spatula in one hand and a soup ladle in the other like they were weapons. As he charged towards Steve and Smith the other cooks scrambled to get out of his way. He hollered out to no one in particular, "You tell that Nazi cocksucker Von Klutzfuck he can take a flying fuck at a rolling donut. He don't say who eats in my kitchen."

He charged over to Steve and Smith and came to a sudden stop. He looked Steve up and down.

"Smith," he growled. "Who's the fucken tourist," never once taking his eyes off Steve.

Smith straightened up, put his shoulders back, his chest out and said calmly, clearly and loudly, "This man is my nephew,"

"Your fucken nephew," Tiny bellowed out. "Well I'll be dipped in sheep shit. What's your name, boy?"

"Steve Kovacs,"

The cook stretched out his hand. Steve took it and got his hand squashed tightly and his whole arm shaken up and down.

"My name is Tiny. Okay, Kovacs, these here is the rules in my kitchen. You take what you want, you eat what you take. You don't like the cooking, you tell me. You don't like my crew, you tell me. You got any problems, you tell me, and I'll tell you what you can do with your problems. Got it,"

"Got it,"

Tiny leaned over and whispered to Steve, "Which state you from,"

"I'm Canadian,"

"You're not from the states?"

"No," Steve knew he didn't believe him.

"Ya, sure, whatever. Listen, you don't take no shit from these fucken D.P.'s. Understand?"

"What's a D.P.?"

"Displaced Persons; fucken Europeans what lost their homes after the war."

The skinny cook turned to Tiny, "I don't know what you're worried about, they'd never draft your fat ass, they ain't got a uniform to fit you,"

Tine spun around to face the skinny cook. "Get the fuck back to work, you skinny little shit."

Smith and Steve started moving down the steam table line, picking at the meats and potatoes and vegetables. All were well cooked and sitting under the heat lamps, where they'd been since early that morning. Steve squinted at some of them, poked his fork at others, and some he didn't even poke at. Even the colors had gone flat.

It reminded him of campus food, except worse. They were soggy and lifeless. The vegetables were mushy, the potatoes watery, the meats tough and heavy. Everything was soaked in grease and smelled the same. Steve shrugged and filled his plate.

Smith waited for Steve as he took his time poking at the food. Smith took no time at all loading his plate. He went for full piles without caring about color or texture.

He led them to the last table in the corner. It was empty.

"This is my table," Smith sat with his back to everyone.

"You sit alone,"

"Always."

Steve sat across from Smith and had a full view of the line of miners slowly working its way down the steam tables. He watched as the men loaded their trays, made strange faces at the food, built sandwiches and grabbed cookies and cup cakes.

He looked very closely, beards on some of the older men and a few longhaired younger men. He looked at their clothing, their moves, how they carried themselves. Then he saw that they all had a full view of him. They nudged each other to check him out, and as he watched them, they watched him. Most of them nodded and smiled, not so much at him and not so much at each other.

"Jan is your friend," Smith said between quick mouthfuls.

"Yes. How long have you been in Elsa?"

"1957. When I first come to Canada, I told government I was a miner in Hungary, they say 'Go to the Yukon'. So I came to Elsa,"

"Were you a miner in Hungary?"

"No,"

"What did you do?"

"I worked for the Hungarian government,"

"Doing what,"

"Jan is your friend,"

"Yes. What did you do for the Hungarian government?"

"Where did you meet Jan?"

"On the road, he was hitchhiking back here,"

"He ran away from Czechoslovakia,"

"He had to,"

"Why do you have long hair? Did you run away from Vietnam?"

"No," Steve shrugged again and started working on a pork chop with his knife. He kept sawing at it until he cut off a bit sized chunk.

"Why aren't you in Vietnam?"

Not this again, thought Steve. He chewed on his dinner and thought it over. Smith waited for an answer. "Vietnam is a whole lot different in Vancouver than it is here,"

"How is this?"

"Well, back there everybody I know is against it. Some older people think it's a good idea,"

"Don't you think you should fight the communists?"

Steve put a lot of work into chewing his pork chop. He was thinking over what Smith was asking, and wondering how his teeth would hold up against the tough pork chop.

"I never met a communist. I don't really know anything about fighting communism. Did you fight the communists in Hungary? Like Dad and Uncle Stephan,"

"Hard to say, I didn't fight anybody,"

"What did you do during the revolution?"

"I said before, I worked for the Hungarian government,"

"They were communist. Were you a communist?"

"Stephan, this is difficult question,"

"No, it isn't a difficult question. Were you a communist?"

"To work for communist government does not make one a communist,"

"Why don't you answer the damn question? What did you do for the Hungarian Government during the revolution?"

"I was a border guard."

Steve looked at Smith very closely. Why hadn't he been told about him? Why would his mother and father never tell him about his Uncle Joe? What was their reason? What stung him most was - what if they had a good reason? Was this uncle unbalanced?

"What kind of job is a border guard?"

"Military,"

"Army,"

"Yes, like the army,"

"Dad said the army went over to the rebels,"

"Mostly, not all,"

"So, during the revolution you guarded the border. From what,"

"You ask good questions, but you don't understand the answers,"

"That's right."

Smith smiled and returned to his meal.

Steve was feeling tired, he felt empty inside, there were no questions to his answers and the food wasn't helping at all. He finished working on his mouthful of pork chop. It didn't taste good, it didn't taste bad - it didn't taste at all.

It was just damn tough. He grabbed a bottle of ketchup and started unscrewing the cap.

Smith jumped up, "Don't use ketchup,"

"What,"

"Don't use ketchup on meat,"

"Why not,"

"Piss off the cook,"

Steve put the bottle down. "Ketchup pisses off the cook?"

"Yes, yes. You make him think you don't like his cooking. You piss off the cook, he cooks lousy food,"

"He already cooks lousy food,"

Smith almost panicked. "Don't say that,"

"Okay, so, why did you leave Hungary?"

"The revolution was very dangerous. Many of us had to leave,"

"If you didn't fight, why did you have to leave?"

"I pissed off the Russians," Uncle Joe said easily. "If I stayed they would have shot me,"

"For what,"

"Did some paperwork,"

"Paperwork? Like bookkeeping,"

"You could say that,"

Steve took some steak sauce and held it up for Uncle Joes' approval. Uncle Joe nodded.

"Piss off the cook," Steve said, "he cooks lousy food; piss off the Russians, they shoot you,"

"Now," said Uncle Joe, "you're beginning to understand the questions you ask,"

Steve needed a change. "Why don't you phone my father?"

"What,"

"I can give you the number. Talk to your brother,"

"What do I say?"

"Ask him why he didn't tell me about you,"

"You ask him,"

"What if Dad wants to talk to you? Give him the chance,"

"No,"

"Does he know you're in Canada?"

Smith shrugged.

"Does he know you're alive?"

He shrugged again.

Steve was getting impatient. "Well, at least tell him you're alive,"

"No,"

Steve put down his fork. "I'll tell him,"

"No,"

The 'unbalanced' idea was running through Steve's thoughts again. "Tell me why, or I'll phone him,"

"Why make me do what I don't want to do,"

"Why won't you talk to your brother?"

Smith put his head in his hands and choked back a sob, then seemed to give up. Tears rolled down his cheeks, but not a sound left his mouth, until "So many years, so much time."

Steve wasn't sure of what he was doing. He knew he had a question that was screaming out for an answer, but at what price?

Maybe I should just leave this old man alone with his memories. Maybe I should just walk out the door and go back to the bush to cut wood with Rolly.

He watched Smith with sympathy as he wept in his dinner. Nobody but Steve knew he was crying.

It was so quiet Steve felt totally humbled. "I won't, if you really don't want me to,"

"No, it's time."

Smith wiped his face, then said, "You didn't tell me, you have any brothers or sisters,"

"No, just me,"

"You married? Any kids,"

"No,"

"If you get married, have kids, will you tell them you have an Uncle Joe,"

"Well, of course,"

"Maybe I could meet them,"

"Well sure," Steve chuckled. "If I ever have them,"

"I don't have a family,"

"You have a brother and sister-in-law. And nephew,"

"No, they don't want me,"

"I do."

Uncle Joe wiped another tear from his cheek. "Janos and Tara, and Stephan, mostly Stephan, didn't know what I went through,"

"What did you go through?"

"No choice, I had to, or,"

"Or what,"

"You finished eating?"

"No, I'm hungry,"

"You eat more. I'll get you more."

Smith got up and walked over to one of the tables and started stuffing paper bags with fruits and cup cakes and cookies.

When they got up the noise of the cook shack quieted again. Steve felt hundreds of eyes watching him. He thought it odd he didn't care. At the door Smith grabbed his coat and handed Steve his.

Steve turned his back to put on his coat and when he turned around the three Hungarians had Smith backed into a corner.

Wayne spoke to him in Hungarian, in a hushed, snarling voice. "So, Smith, you do have family,"

Smith leaned into his face. "You leave him alone,"

"We don't forget our families, do we, Smith?"

"You touch him; I cut your throat! I swear to God you will die at my hand,"

Steve watched as Wayne slipped his hand into his back pocket, reaching for something. He jumped Wayne, twisted his arm behind his back and slammed him face first into the wall.

The other two Hungarians jumped back.

"You got a problem," Steve said, in Hungarian.

"You lie to me," Wayne said in Hungarian. "You do speak Hungarian,"

Smith and the other two Hungarians stood inches apart and glared at each other. Nobody moved for a frozen second..

"Let him go," Smith said firmly. Steve didn't.

"Now," Smith ordered, then Steve did.

Wayne's snarl turned into a smile at Steve, then he turned to Smith. "Nice to know you've got family, Smith. We used to have families."

Wayne kept smiling at Steve as they walked away.

"We go now," Smith said. Steve didn't move, but returned Wayne's glare.

"Now," Smith said.

"Okay." Steve quietly said.

When they got back to Smiths' room, Smith let out a tired sigh. Steve took Smiths' coat and hung it up with his.

"You want another drink," Smith said.

"I think I've had enough for now, thanks," Steve took a seat on the bunk. "So what's the story about families and throat cutting,"

Smith poured himself a drink and sat next to Steve. "Nothing, don't worry about it,"

He looked at Steve again in that way he did earlier, the look that so unnerved Steve. "I have a lot to say to you. I've waited a long time. I never knew if I'd get to say it,"

"I'm listening,"

"How did you find me?"

"Jan said you looked like me,"

"I was born first, that means you look like me, not the other way around. So you picked up Jan, and came looking,"

"That's about it,"

"And never knew I existed,"

"Nope,"

Smith shrugged, then pointed up.

Steve looked up, the ceiling needed painting.

"Somebody up there is looking out for you. And me," Smith said.

Steve looked up again. "Up where?"

"Not the bloody ceiling, up there, all the way up there. You got your fathers' brains as well,"

"Mom's said that a few times,"

"With good reason. What do you do?"

"I was a university student,"

"You're too young to graduate. Why are you not in class now?"

"The boredom was killing me."

Smiths' eyes changed. They narrowed and became sharper. "I have seen bullets kill men. I have never seen boredom kill anybody. Go back, now, before you lose too much time,"

Steve shook his head. "Don't want to,"

Smith leaned forward and tapped him roughly on the knee. "This is your life. You don't do what you want to do; you do what you have to do. I have not had a word with my brother since…, but this I know, you have hurt him, and your mother. You have hurt them both badly. They are both sick with this hurt you have given them,"

Steve didn't move, he hardly took a breath. He didn't dare.

"Do you need money? How much does University cost,"

"No, I don't need money. Dad took care of that,"

"You bet your stupid ass he took care of it! He is still a machinist,"

"Yes,"

"He works hard as a machinist so you can go to University, so you can get bored and quit. What does Tara do?"

"She works in a restaurant,"

"She is a waitress. She makes money as a servant. They've worked hard for you, for you. And you don't want to go because you're bored."

Smith took a drink and slowly worked it around his mouth. He never took his eyes off Steve. "'Boring', he says. Janos never told you about Budapest. He never told you about me. Ever wonder why,"

"Yes!"

Smith cupped his hands behind his head, leaned against the wall. "Ahhh, Little Stephan. You just don't know, do you?"

"I'm listening,"

"Well, at least that's a start. What do you know, so far?"

"Dads' brother died in Austria, after they left Budapest,"

"My brother, too. That you told me, then what,"

"They came to Vancouver. A lot of Hungarians were here at the University of British Columbia,"

"I also know about that, Sopron Forestry School, I have friends there. What else do you know?"

"My grandparents died in the Second War,"

"My parents. Do you know how?"

Steve shook his head, "They don't talk about it,"

"Your grandmother was killed by Russian bombs. Your grandfather was killed fighting the Nazis. I held him as he died. Your father and Stephan were about a hundred feet away,"

"What was happening? How were you beside him?"

Smith took another drink, a deep breath, and then carried on. "It was 1944, the Nazis knew the Russians were coming, and they were going to blow up our steel factories before the Russians could use them. They were trying to set the charges and we were trying to stop them,"

"Did you?"

"Yes,"

"How?"

"We killed them. Every damn one of them,"

"What happened to my grandfather?"

Smith took another drink. "There was about twenty of us. The Nazis had a squad dug in to protect their demolition teams. We had to kill them to get at the demolition teams before they set the charges off. There was a lot of heavy firing. We were dug in; they were dug in. We had to move forward, we didn't have time to wait them out. We had grenades; they had automatics. It was very difficult, we couldn't get close enough to use the grenades, and so we split into two groups. I lost a lot of friends, good friends, moving around the machine guns so we could get close enough to use the grenades. Janos and Stephan were on one side, your grandfather and me on the other.

They turned the machine gun on Janos; he dived down, and wasn't hit. Father went up on one knee to get a better shot, to try to protect Janos and Stephan. One of their riflemen hit him in the throat. He fell in my arms. Janos and Stephan couldn't see this; they were on the ground. I pulled Father out of the shooting, behind a pile of bricks. He couldn't talk; he had no throat. He looked at me, I looked at him, he smiled at me, then died,"

Steve stared at the floor. He looked up to the window, then out. Smith sat still. There was no expression on his face. He was watching Steve, who looked up to the ceiling and beyond. Steve wiped a tear from his eye.

"And Dad and Uncle Stephan, what happened to them,"

"While I was holding father, the Nazi machine gun jammed. Janos and Stephan, and the others with them, killed them all,"

"All dead,"

"We knew those Nazis personally. We knew their names. Some of them went out with our women. They had been in Budapest for a few years. Many times we wanted to kill them. We finally did,"

Steve was wiping tears as Smith went on. "This was a few days after your grandmother was killed. It was a very difficult time for us all,"

"Was the war over then,"

"No, it went on for many months after that. There were still a lot of Nazis in Hungary. We couldn't kick the Nazis out by ourselves. The Russians came in and took over. Nazis, then the Russians, occupied us. We had to fight beside them to get rid of the Nazis. We thought they would leave after that. But they didn't. They stayed and took over our country,"

"What did you do then?"

"I wanted to go back to school. When the war started Stephan had finished high school, Janos almost. For me it was different. I was the youngest. School was upset by the war. It was very difficult to have classes, to learn,"

"How far did you go?"

"Not very far. After the war, Stephan went right into Technical School. He became a machinist. Two years after that, Janos finished high school. Then he went to Technical School. He became a machinist, like Stephan. I was going to go to Technical School, too.
We were going to open up our own business. That was our dream.
It was our fathers' dream, too. We were all going to work together in our own business. Even after our father died, we still wanted to open our own business. That was what we had fought for. That's what Father died for. Our own country and our own business,"

"What happened then,"

"The Russians wouldn't let us,"

"Why not,"

"After they helped us kick out the Nazis, they stayed. We thought they would go back to Russia. They made false elections and turned Hungary into a communist country. That meant no businesses. Our family dream was over,"

"I don't get it,"

"The communist way is everything is owned by the government. The Russians said it was our government, but it was theirs. They ran everything, made five-year plans for us to fill. They took all the coal from our coal mines, crops from our farms; they took everything and shipped it to Russia. They ran everything, or it was run by those they made do it for them,"

"So this meant no family business,"

"You don't even own your own tools. They belong to the government. You can't sell your skills or your products. Everybody works for the government. Having your own business is the capitalist way and any kind of capitalism was outlawed. You couldn't even try, and once you can't even try, then you have lost everything. No business, no country, no freedom,"

"Can't even try?"

"If you did try, they would send you to work camps in Russia. And you don't come back,"

"What did you do?"

"I didn't become a machinist,"

"Why not,"

"I never went back to school. I had to work,"

"What kind of work did you do?"

"I told you. I was a border guard,"

"Why couldn't you go back to school?"

"Once the communists took over, school was only for children. I had fought the Nazis; I was a war veteran. They saw no need in my returning to school. I wanted to go back to school, to learn."

Smith took another drink and another deep breath. "I couldn't go back to school because I was conscripted into the Hungarian Army, with the Russians in charge. I had to do what they said. I had no choice against the government,"

"Conscripted?"

"You call it the 'draft'. You don't have the draft in Canada, you wouldn't understand,"

Steve quickly sat up and shot back. "I know about the draft. There's lots of Americans coming to Canada because of the draft! So don't tell me I don't understand the draft,"

Smith was calm and direct. He pointed his lit cigarette at Steve."You can't understand the draft, you're not at war. The United States is at war. You're Canadian, you can stay home." Smith did not let him think about it. "For you, the war is for someone else. You don't have to decide to leave home and live, or stay home and maybe die."

"For you, it is something you should study at the University you're going to go back to, because that's what you have to do,"

Steve sat back on the bunk."When did you get drafted?"

"Well, we all got conscripted, draft for you, into the army in 1943, then we were out of the Army after the war ended. Then I got drafted again in 1947,"

"And then you became a border guard,"

"Yes,"

"I still don't get it,"

"What part don't you get',"

"The part you played in the revolution. Why you left Hungary,"

"We were allied with the Russians, who ran the Hungarian Army. Because I didn't go to school, I had no trade skills. I couldn't say I was needed in industry. So this time I was in for as long as the Russians wanted me. This time I stayed until the revolution,"

"But if you didn't fight in the revolution, why did you have to leave,"

"I didn't want to leave, I had to. After Stephan took you to Austria, to freedom, I could finally leave, too,"

"How did you know Uncle Stephan took us to Austria? This afternoon you didn't even know if he was alive,"

"There are many things I don't know. And many things I do know. What I did know was that Stephan was capable of leading Janos and Tara through the swamps. It was very dangerous. Many people were killed. Many more got through to Austria. I knew Stephan could do it. What I didn't know until today was whether or not he was alive. This you told me. It is today I know that one of my brothers is dead." He let out another long sigh and took another drink. "I am tired now,"

"One more question,"

"You have many more questions. I will try to answer them, or some of them,"

"Why don't I know about you?"

"That is a very large question. Ask your father. It is not for me to answer that question. It was not my decision,"

"It was your decision to change your name. If it was so dangerous during the revolution, why didn't Dad change our name?"

"Canada was very good to Hungarians who fled the communists. Your father had nothing to worry about. Those of us who worked for the communists were not so well looked upon,"

"You said you weren't a communist,"

"I wasn't, and I'm not. I was conscripted. No choice. It was necessary for some of us to change our names. So we could enter Canada and become citizens,"

"You changed your name to enter Canada,"

"Yes,"

"You entered the country illegally,"

"No, I was a communist refugee, just as were two hundred thousand other Hungarians. But it was difficult to explain to Canadian authorities that I was conscripted into the service of the Russians. That I had no choice! Working for the Russians was not supporting the Russians. You had to do as you were ordered, or you and your family could suffer a great deal,"

"What would they do?"

"If you were in the military, as I was, and refused Russian orders, you and your family would be deported to work camps. Men would go to one camp, women to another, and the younger children sent to Russian orphanages. They would probably never see each other again. The family would be finished,"

"But if you don't have a family, how could they threaten you?"

Smith was quiet. He was tired, but still ready to answer questions he believed Steve had a right to ask. But his questions brought back difficult memories. "These were very dangerous times, as I have told you. I was in a very bad position,"

"How could you be in a difficult position' if all you did was guard the border,"

"That's not all I was ordered to do,"

"What else?"

Smith stood up and stretched his legs. He started to pace up and down the small room.

He took steps that would give him just enough room to turn around at the door, then to the wall behind his bunk, then back again.

Steve looked at the small rug on the floor. It was worn through right in the steps Smith took.

"Remember I told you that the Russians could cause great harm to your family. That you alone would not be the only one to suffer,"

"Yes,"

"That makes you a slave. They own you, and your family. You have to do what they say, no matter what it is; you have to do it,"

"What did they make you do?"

"I told you, I guarded the border,"

"You also said that's not all they ordered you to do. What else did they order you to do?"

Smith stopped his pacing. He stared at the floor, then at Steve, then poured himself another drink and sat down. "One day the Commissar, a communist party boss, came to our border camp. He talked of counter-revolutionaries, of fascists and capitalists, and all kinds of other people. We were supposed to be guarding the border against all these different people. There were many men like me working at the borders. We had no schooling, but we were not stupid. The Commissar thought we were stupid and talked to us this way. We knew there were no fascists or capitalists or anybody like that trying to sneak into Hungary. Nobody ever tried to sneak into Hungary, but many tried to sneak out. He talked of what a great job we were doing for the cause of international socialism, how we were protecting it and all kinds of propaganda like that. Some of us wanted to laugh at him. But we knew better, and pretended that what he was saying was worth listening to. Then he told us that some of us had been chosen, and this was supposed to be a great honor, to go to Moscow for special training. I knew what that meant and didn't like it, but as I've said, I had no choice."

Smith started pacing the room again, back and forth, forth and back.

Steve looked at the worn rug again and shook his head. "What was this 'special training'?"

"We went to Moscow, which was supposed to be a great privilege, and we were trained in interrogation,"

"How to make people talk when they don't want to,"

"Sometimes they want to talk,"

"What if they don't want to?"

"Then it would be different,"

"Torture?"

"Sometimes,"

"And the Russians forced you to do this?"

"They forced me to take the training,"

"Did you torture people?"

"That is not a good question. It is not a fair question. I have told you what I can. I have told you what the Russians could do to you, or your family, if you refuse any order,"

"But you didn't have a family they could threaten you with! It was just you,"

"Stephan, Steve, these things you don't understand,"

"I understand you became a torturer,"

"I was trained how to torture people. I did not do this,"

"You never tortured anyone?"

"Never, on my mothers' grave I swear this to you, my nephew,"

"What does my Father know about this?"

"He knows I went to Moscow. He knows I was transferred to the Secret Police,"

"The A.V.O.,"

"Yes,"

"Dad mentioned them. But he never mentioned you,"

"This is probably why you were never told of me. The Russians forced me to join the A.V.O., and Stephan thought I was a traitor. He refused to talk to me; he wouldn't let me visit you. They didn't know, and I couldn't tell them, but I tried,"

"Why couldn't you tell them?"

"Stephan wouldn't allow me to. Even if I did, he wouldn't believe me. He banned me from the family. He was ashamed of me, but he didn't know what I knew,"

"What didn't he know?"

"That if I refused the transfer to the A.V.O., I would be declared a traitor by the Russians, and all of us would have gone to work camps and you would have gone to a Russian orphanage,"

"Russian orphanage, me?"

"Yes. And your mother and father and uncle to work camps,"

"And you don't return from the work camps,"

"Probably die there,"

"Your brother didn't know this,"

"He thought only citizens found guilty of crimes against the state went to the camps. All the people had to think this. This is how the Russians kept control. But I knew that anybody who worked for the state could also go to the camps. If the people knew this, nobody would work for the state. Nobody would think they were safe. The Russians would lose control and they were very afraid of this. We were all very afraid. Stephan thought I was safe working for the state. I wasn't at all safe. Stephan didn't know this,"

"Stephan still banned you from the family,"

"Yes." Smith leaned over to his bedside trunk and picked up the picture of Steve as a baby. The one with his mother, father and two uncles. He put it on the bed, in front of Steve. Steve picked up the picture and looked at it closely. He stared deeply into it, trying to make some kind of sense of everything Smith had told him. He slowly shook his head and let it tilt from side to side on his shoulders. He felt his chin leading the tilt, his head leaning further from side to side, his eyes closed tight, opening them to look at the picture, closing them trying to see something, opening them to look again at the picture.

He put the picture down on the bunk, picked it up again, put it down again. "I want to phone my Dad," he said. "I have to know, I should call,"

"Yes," Smith said. "It's time."

Steve nodded, stood up and put his coat on. He turned to Smith,
who looked up from his bunk. Steve opened his mouth, trying to say something, but he didn't know what to say. He closed his mouth, he tried again but nothing came out.

Smith nodded, "It's okay, Little Stephan. Phone Janos,"

Steve stood at the door. He reached for the door handle but felt unable to turn it.

"Wait," Smith reached into his old trunk and pulled out a small bundle wrapped in brown wax paper.

"It's cold," he said. "Take this,"

Steve took it, unwrapped it. He stared at an old gray wool toque. On the side was a small, hand stitched tri-color Hungarian flag. He put it on."Fits," he said.

"It was your grandfathers'," Smith said.

Steve felt his scalp tingle, and then grow warm. "Warm," he said."Wait till you get outside. Then it will keep you warm,"

"What do you want me to say to, your brother,"

"Tell him I am happy to once again meet his son,"

Steve nodded and looked around the room. He felt like it was home, and he was leaving again. Smith got up and put the two bags of fruit and cakes into Steve's coat.

"Young men are always hungry,"

"Do you want to talk to him?"

"No, not tonight. I am tired. I must, like you, think about things,"

"I'm going to Keno City tonight. Get a room in the hotel,"

"I will see you again? Please?"

Steve felt the tightness in his throat. He looked at his uncle and wanted to cry; he walked forward and stretched out his arms.

Smith stood there and didn't know what to do. They stood inches apart, and then Steve put his arms around Smith and pulled him in tight. Smith put his arms around Steve and held just as tight.

Smith caught his breath and said, "You go now. Talk to your father,"

Steve nodded, "Good night, Uncle Joe,"

"Good night, my Little Stephan."

Steve walked out of Smiths' room and down the hallway. He stood at the door and looked through the ice-covered window and into the camp. Maybe Rolly hadn't left. Maybe he would be back in the bar. He would know what to do, how to handle things. The ropes of lights still ran up and down the walkways, still blew in different directions. They looked like wiggling snakes. Steve put his collar up and pulled down his grandfathers' toque and carefully walked his way back to the Elsa Bar.

He paid no attention to the usual noise when he walked in. He saw his bag at the door, right where he'd left it. He went up to the bar, ordered a beer.

The secretary from the office handed it to him. "You Smiths' nephew,"

"Yes,"

She smiled as Steve went back to the table he had fallen asleep at. The same one the Hungarians had cornered him at. He took off his coat and laid it on a chair. He didn't take off his new toque. He was aware of being watched by the miners in the bar, but paid no attention. He sipped at his beer and wondered what to do next.

His mind went blank. He couldn't think any thought through. He reached out for something to think about that he could hold on to. He couldn't even do that. He yawned.

The waitress came to his table. "'Nother beer,"

"No, thanks. You know Joe Smith?"

"I know who he is, he's your Uncle, you should know,"

"I just met him,"

She put her tray on the table and sat down. "I was there. He's a weird one. Likes' to be left alone, that's for sure, I've never seen him in the bar, only in the kitchen. Never talks to anyone. People generally leave him alone. I don't know how he gets along at work if he never talks. Gotta talk on the job,"

Steve heard a voice from behind him, "He don't say shit on the job." Steve turned to look at an older man. He spoke without an accent and had a weathered, scarred face.

"Nobody talks to him cause' he don't talk to nobody. Does his job, eats and goes to his room. We call him 'Yappy' on account of he don't talk,"

"What's he do?" Steve said.

"Trammer; runs ore trains in camp. Good job for a guy who don't talk. Don't need to talk."

Steve thought right away to the man he saw in the ore train when he first arrived in Elsa. Was that why he stared like that? He shuddered again.

"Probably do him good to have someone to talk to," said the man.

"So, lemme get this straight," Steve said. "He doesn't talk to anybody and nobody talks to him,"

"That's right,"

"Any idea why,"

"Gotta be some old country stuff, maybe he just got nothing to say, you ask him that. Lot of people here might like an answer to that. Lot of people here would like to kick his ass just to see if he says 'ouch'. If the man wants to keep his mouth shut, this is the right Territory to do it. 'Course on the other hand, one fucken' word a year wouldn't hurt. This guy works hard on sayin' nothing,"

Steve thought on that while he finished his beer. 'Works hard on saying nothing'. It started to run through his head like a broken record. Is this what my uncle does? Or has become?'

"Another?" said the waitress.

"I got it," said the other man as he turned his chair to face Steve. "Name's Kendall, you?"

"Steve Kovacs,"

"Not Smith,"

"No, that was his idea,"

"Ya," said Kendall. "Makes sense,"

"How's that,"

"Anybody works that hard on saying nothing got something to hide,"

"How long have you known him?"

"Known him? I don't think anybody here knows him. He was here when I got here, and I been here close to seven years,"

"Where'd you come from?"

"Long ways from here," glared Kendall.

Steve got the direct idea that any more questions to Kendall would not be about Kendall.

"Thanks," said Steve as the beer arrived.

"No problem," said Kendall. "So, you ask him why he don't talk,"

"No, he talked to me. A lot,"

"Speaks good English?"

"Fine."

Kendall nodded, and then looked over to the corner where the three Hungarians sat.

"Friends of yours," Steve said.

"I know who they are and who they aren't. They aren't friends of your uncle,"

"Had a bit of a run in with them," Steve said.

"I saw, in the kitchen. Gotta watch those D.P.'s, they get mad, they stay mad. For years,"

"Grudges from their war?" Steve said.

"Oh hell, any war. Fuck their sister and they chase you forever just to cut your nuts off,"

"No shit,"

"Well, you could always marry the bitch. But if she looked like them, I'd take my chances with them,"

"I'll try to remember that,"

"Whatever they got going with your uncle is between them. They keep it to themselves. Just as well that way,"

"They said they were glad he had family,"

"Well then, your uncle did something to piss 'em off, or their families."

Steve thought on that for a while. It's the A.V.O. thing. Steve knew they were watching him. He began to regret lying about not speaking Hungarian. He definitely regretted jumping on Wayne in the kitchen.

"The guy you jumped in the cook shack," said Kendall.

"Ya," Steve said.

"Keep clear of him. His friends ain't a problem, but him, you keep clear of,"

"I thought he was going to pull a knife on my uncle,"

"Did you see a knife?"

"No,"

"Well, if you did see it, it'd be too late by then,"

Steve shuddered again. Maybe I should talk to these guys, he thought. Maybe go over to their table, sit down and work it out. He looked over at their table and now they were not ignoring him.

Wayne smiled at Steve and lifted his beer glass in a toast. His friends Peter and Henry did not lift their glasses. They sat there and looked at Steve, then at Wayne.

"Return it," said Kendall.

"Return what,"

"The toast, lift your beer glass and smile,"

Steve wasn't sure what to do, so he took Kendall's' advice and lifted his beer glass and returned the toast. Wayne smiled, took a drink, and put his beer down.

"You wanna jump him, that's one thing; you can get away with that. You wanna turn down his toast, then you're in shit. You can't get away with that; you don't disrespect him in the bar,"

"Disrespect him?"

"You gotta a lot to learn, kid,"

"So this guy wants a piece of me because I jumped him thinking he was going to knife my uncle,"

"Jumping him's forgotten. The family thing, well hell, I don't know. Family's a lot more than that, a lot more. You jumped him thinking he was gonna hurt your uncle.

He knows that, he understands that. But he's got something for your uncle and now you're in the middle of it. You didn't stumble into this; you jumped in feet first,"

"But I just came here to drop off a friend," Steve said.

"Ya, I know Jan. These guys can't understand why anybody would turn down a chance to kill commies. The States is handing out free tickets for commie killing in Vietnam, one-way ticket to join the Viet Cong hunting club. Jan didn't do that in Czechoslovakia; don't matter he escaped, they figured he ran for it. He turned down his country, just like turning down his family. It's all the same to them."

"You think it's that simple,"

"I don't, but they do," Kendall stopped to take a drink of his beer and noticed the flag on Steves' toque.

"Yours?"

Steve took off the toque and fingered the flag. "It was my grandfathers'," he said.

"Look at this," Kendall started."This is the Hungarian flag; and if you see here, no hammer and sickle. Its' from the Second War; before the communists took over. You Hungarian?"

"Canadian,"

"Where were you born?"

"Budapest,"

"And you say you're Canadian,"

"Well, I grew up here,"

"Your family is Hungarian; you pick a fight with a Hungarian over Hungarian history. And you call yourself Canadian,"

"I didn't jump him over history. I thought he was going to hurt my uncle! And I am Canadian,"

"You pick a side in a historical battle. Your side is your uncles' side, and like it or not, that's the side you're on. And being a Canadian means shit. Maybe you should have another look at that toque of yours and think over what it means,"

Steve fingered the toque some more and took some more of Kendall's' advice. He thought it over. Couldn't figure out anything.

"How do you know all of this?"

"Told you, I been here close to seven years. You can't live in Elsa that long without knowing all about these Europeans and their old country shit."

Kendall leaned forward and spoke quietly. "Inquest awhile back for a German. Fell down an ore chute. Or that's what they said happened,"

"You think he was pushed,"

"Wasn't there, don't know, and that's it."

Steve looked over to the Hungarians table and watched them as they drank. They paid no attention to him, chuckled amongst themselves and seemed to be happily enjoying their card game. He knew they hated Germans. After all, they were the same age as his father and had probably fought in the Second War. If they had killed Germans during the war, could they kill Germans after the war? Especially if they knew they could get away with it? Steve gave that some more thought.

They said they couldn't, or was it wouldn't, hurt Smith? They said accidents happen underground. Steve shuddered at those thoughts.

He leaned over to Kendall, quietly said, "Did those Hungarian guys work with the guy who fell down the ore chute,"

"That's one question you should stay the hell away from, kid! A long ways away from,"

Steve sat up straight and thought deeply on those words. That's where I would like to be right now. A long, long ways away. He stared into his beer and saw Sheila staring back out at him.

"Shit," he said as he spilled his beer.

"Ain't that much to worry about," said Kendall.

"No, in my beer, I saw,"

"Bugs in your beer, bugs in your brain,"

Steve chuckled, "Wish it was that simple,"

"You remember this," Kendall said leaning closer again. "These guys never forget anything, not for years, but they can also do fuck all for years,"

"Nothing? For years,"

Kendall snapped his fingers, "Then strike in a second."

Steve jumped in his seat.

Kendall cracked up laughing. "Keep your cool, Kid. Keep your cool."

Steve saw Wayne walk towards them. He walked right beside the table and went to the bar. He leaned beside the till and ordered three beers. The waitress looked to Steve as she passed Wayne the beer. Steve looked to the waitress, and then to Wayne, who smiled at him.

"Evening," Steve said.

Wayne spoke in Hungarian. "You can speak Hungarian,"

"Evening," Steve again said in English.

"You don't like to speak Hungarian," Wayne said in English.

"I speak English," Steve said.

"Yes, I know," Wayne said.

Wayne stood still for a moment and looked Steve over very closely. Something was bothering him and Steve could tell.

Wayne stopped staring at Steve and started staring at his grandfathers' toque. "Let me see hat,"

"Go fuck yourself,"

"Where did you get the hat?"

Steve stood up, leaned over close enough to spit in his face.

He remembered Kendall's' warning, and ignored it. "You want it? Come and get it,"

Wayne leaned back and smiled again. "You are good Hungarian boy! Ready to fight, but not knowing why. Ha, ha, ha. You keep the hat, but show me the flag,"

Steve stood back slightly. He shrugged, took the hat off and holding it tightly, showed Wayne the Hungarian tri-color.

Wayne nodded and smiled. "This is the flag of Hungary before the communists took over. Who does it belong to?"

"This," Steve proudly said, "is mine,"

"Ya, sure. Where did you get it?"

"I got it, that's all that matters to you,"

Steve did not see Kendall wince. He looked away, expecting trouble.

Wayne's eyes narrowed as he smiled again. "What is your fathers' name?"

Steve stood tall as he said, "My fathers' name is Janos Kovacs."

Wayne's eyes popped out in shock. "Janos Kovacs? Brother of Stephan Kovacs?"

Steve felt the wind sucked out of his lungs. He couldn't speak, he could only nod.

Wayne started speaking so fast he was spitting. "You are the son of Janos Kovacs. I know your father! I know your Uncle Stephan!"

Before Steve could react, Wayne took a quick step around the table, leaned over, put his arms around Steve and picked him up in a huge bear hug. "This is the son of Janos Kovacs," he cried out to the entire bar.

Peter and Henry knocked over their table jumping out of their chairs. They ran over to put their arms around Steve, who was now held high in the bear hug of the three Hungarians. Other Hungarians jumped up and joined the cheering. Others, who knew nothing, cheered along just for the fun of it.

Steve was swung around up in the air like a trophy. He still couldn't speak. The three Hungarians danced and spun in circles as Steve held on to their shoulders, desperately trying not to fall off.

"The son of Janos Kovacs," screamed Wayne. "In my arms, the son of Janos Kovacs and he tried to kill me, ha ha ha."

Wayne dropped Steve back in his seat. He put his hands on the arms of the chair, pinning Steve in his seat, while holding himself up. He was breathing so hard he was spitting all over Steve. Peter and Henry were staggering, still trying to stand up.

Wayne was gasping for air, but could not stay quiet. "I know Janos well," he coughed out between gulps of air. "We were together at the Kilian Barracks,"

"Okay," said Steve, struggling for something to say.

Wayne threw his arms up in the air, arched his back and clenched his fists. He roared out, "This is the son of Janos Kovacs," then he collapsed in the seat next to Steve.

Peter and Henry fell into seats, all of them exhausted. The waitress tried to pull her mouth shut, but it hung open.

"Beer," shouted Wayne. "Bring beer for the son of Janos Kovacs." For the longest few seconds Steve ever had in his life he sat totally still and felt himself slipping into a stunned shock. Slowly Wayne regained his breath. He put his arm on Steve's shoulder and said, "I don't care that you jumped me. You are a good Hungarian boy,"

Steve nodded and slowly felt himself catching his breath. Wayne wiped the spit from his mouth, then looked into Steve's eyes and held his stare.

"Janos is good,"

"Yes,"

"Tara is good,"

"Yes,"

"Where are they?"

"Vancouver,"

Wayne leaned over to talk quietly to Steve, "We know Josef and what he did in Budapest. This is not your problem; you have no worry from us. But we talk no more of Josef. Now is the time to celebrate."

Wayne held his beer glass high, all the others picked up theirs and Wayne hollered out,

TO A FREE HUNGARY

He stretched his arm out high over his head, and at arm's length poured beer into his open mouth.

He missed a lot, it went across his shirt and puddled on the floor. He wiped his sleeve across his face and started hollering again.

DEATH TO THE COMMUNISTS

"Your father and me, and Peter and Henry here, we fought for our mother Hungary in 1956, and only one thing keeps us alive, our love for a free Hungary, our Hungary for Hungarians!

No Germans, no Russians, nobody else,"
He raised up his beer glass again and hollered out,

HUNGARY FOR HUNGARIANS

Again he was followed by the others.
"My father, you knew him?" Steve said.
" 'Knew him'? We fought the Russian tanks in Budapest.
We held the Kilian Barracks when the rest of Budapest was in
flames. I know your father well. He is a good man, a
Hungarian patriot. The son of Janos Kovacs jumped me! Ha,
ha, ha! You are good Hungarian boy,"
Peter put his hand on Steve's shoulder. "I spent my first
night at Kilian with your Uncle Stephan. We made petrol
bombs for tanks. I was very young when Stephan showed me
how to fight the Russians,"
Henry put his hand on Steve' other shoulder. "Stephan
showed me how to fill lead pipes with powder from bullets.
We used these on tank treads; we stopped many tanks that
way,"
"Where is Stephan?" Wayne said.
"Yes, where is Stephan," Henry and Peter said.
"You don't know?" Steve said. They all shook their
heads."He died in Austria,"
"When," asked Wayne.
"1956,"
"He took you out of Hungary?" Wayne said.
"Yes," Steve said.
"Stephan was a good man. I saw his stomach bleeding, I
saw him carried away. He still took you to Austria with a
bleeding stomach, when you were a baby?"
"He carried me across his shoulders,"
Wayne, Peter and Henry stopped. They didn't talk, drink or
anything. Wayne went on. "With a stomach wound, that I
myself saw, he carried you through the swamps, on his
shoulders. Is that correct?"
"That's what my father told me. I don't remember,"

"I am not surprised. That is the kind of man your Uncle was. You should be very proud of him. And Janos and Tara, how did they come with you?"

"Dad carried Mom,"

"Yes, he had to. Your mother was taken by the AVO. I saw her after she came back."

STALIN TEXTILE WORKS
BUDAPEST, OCTOBER, 1956

Tara didn't take Josef's advice. She ran a sewing machine at Stalin Textile Works, making warm clothing that went on the trains to Russia. She never saw any of those clothes on the streets of Budapest, and she could never bring any of them home. Everything was counted, everyday they were checked, even if she did manage to smuggle some home, they couldn't wear them in public. They would be seen by informers and that would be theft from the people of Hungary, clothing bound for Russia, and for that Little Stephan would lose him mother.

It was early in the morning and her sewing machine broke down, as it often did, so she lifted her hands to plead to the poorly lit ceiling. "How am I going to make my quota? Every other day this thing breaks down,"

"Ah, Tara Kovacs, you shouldn't complain," her co-worker said. "Be happy we have jobs, that we are fed and the Nazis are gone,"

"I still have to make my quota. This machine must be made in Russia, if it was made in Hungary, it wouldn't break down."

Her co-worker turned away, did not share in Tara's humor, kept her mouth shut. At the end of the day, she reported to their Political Commissar. If she did not inform on Tara, she could be reported on for not informing, and that made her a conspirator. The penalties were the same.

"Tara Kovacs slanders our Russian brothers,"

"What did she say?"

"She said they made poor sewing machines,"

"Thank-you comrade, you will be rewarded for your diligence."

Next morning four AVO were waiting for Tara and she was led away to their waiting car. She sat in the middle of the cramped back seat, with one AVO jammed on each side of her.

As the streets of Budapest went by in the pouring rain, she passed her street, saw the stairs leading into her tenement, saw the lights were out, and wondered of she would ever see them again.

The man doing the talking was tall and thin, with a broad flat forehead, hooked nose, greased back dirty blonde hair, and dark eyes behind thick glasses. His uniform fit poorly. He sat behind a wide desk, cluttered with papers and empty wine bottles, while Tara stood before him. The other three were close behind her

"You think because you are a woman, you can slander our Russian comrades? You think you can commit ideological crimes and have them go unnoticed?"

Tara shook as her small frame closed in on itself. "I meant only,"

"You meant only what?"

"A joke,"

"'A joke'? You think you are a funny person? You think that you can make insults and laugh about them?"

Tara said nothing.

"Where is your brother-in-law?"

"I don't know,"

"Liar, he is your family, you know where he is,"

"He never comes to visit,"

"Who are we talking about, which brother-in-law are we talking about, why are you so sure your don't see your brother-in-law when, in truth, he actually lives with you,"

"I thought you meant,"

"You thought I meant what, who am I talking about?"

"I thought you meant Josef,"

"Why do I mean Josef? Why don't I mean Stephan?"

Tara's mind started to work by itself. She felt that she was just watching it, that if she stayed out of its way, it would tell her what to say. She thought that if she didn't think too much, didn't anger these AVO, maybe she could find her way out of this. She let her mind imagine what she would say if Josef never did come to visit, if she really knew nothing about what he did, that Janos and Stephan really were loyal to the Russians, and then she knew she was thinking too much.

"Your husband is disloyal, your brother-in-law is disloyal, and that makes you disloyal. Is that true? Are you disloyal?"

"I'm not disloyal; I've been a communist since I was a child,"

"Being a communist does not make you loyal. You have many communists who are disloyal. We find them, we always find them,"

Now Tara knew she had to think quickly; if she was loyal, and was accused of being disloyal, what would she say?

"You have no right to question the loyalty of any member of my family. I know for a fact that every member of my family is a loyal Hungarian and devoted communist.

We all fought the fascist Nazis', my father and mother gave their lives fighting fascism. You have no right to question our loyalty, no right what-so-ever,"

He smirked. "Where is your brother-in-law?"

"Stephan is where he is every day at this time, he's at work,"

He smirked again, "No, I mean your other brother-in-law,"

"Josef is in the army, I never see him,"

"What does he do in the army?"

"I don't know, I never see him,"

"What does Janos do?"

"He works hard for the party, he works hard at his job, he is at many meetings, he and Stephan are both at many meetings, they go all the time, they are very loyal."

Tara thought, slow down, don't anger them, make your point clearly, but don't argue.

"Fine," he said. "Have it your way,"

He tied her hands behind her back, and made her face the wall. He took a pencil, put the point on her forehead, pulled her to the wall and forced her to hold the pencil against the wall by leaning on it. Bright lights were turned on her face.

"Don't let it drop,"

Tara was afraid the sweat running off her forehead would make the pencil fall. She stared tightly at the end of the pencil. Her eyes stung, there was a red blur and the drops ran down her nose.

"Lift one foot,"

"Which one?"

"Your feet, your pick, now."

She took her stare from the pencil to her feet. The red blur had made them impossible to see.

She moved her head down, felt the pencil move, and then pushed her forehead against the pencil. It held and the AVO laughed.

"Lift one foot, do it now,"

Her right foot came up, and the pencil dropped. She looked at the pencil on the floor, drops of her blood splattered around it and she waited.

She raised her eyes from the floor and higher still to meet his. His face sagged, with thick creases at the sides and beneath his mouth and eyes; his chin was narrow and pushed back folds of flesh. He smiled, showing broken, crooked teeth. Some were missing, the rest were shades of yellow and brown. One eye was not in line with the other. He stepped forward, brought his face right into hers. His breath stank of rot, of garlic and wine. "We like pretty women, all of us."

He reached out with both hands and grabbed her breasts. She was pulled from behind and pushed down to the floor. She kept her chin close to her chest, hoping to stop the back of her head from hitting the hard wood floor, but she landed on her hands and felt the fingers on her left hand snap. A boot slammed down on her left leg, she heard it crack. They ripped off her blouse and dress, and for the time it took, she prayed for Little Stephan, then it was black.

She awoke to a voice. She was in a dark cell; it was cold
and wet and smelled of urine and feces. There was a sliver of
light coming through a slit in the steel door and a shadow
partially covered a face, peering in at her.

"Are you Tara Kovacs?"

Tara was lying on a mattress, she had a blanket over her,
but she shivered from the cold. Her left leg was numb; her left
hand, numb. She tried to figure out where she was and why,
then the memories came back. She felt the swelling on her leg,
on her fingers. She held her hands up to the sliver of light, saw
the scratched skin where the ropes had bound them, the
twisted fingers. Beside her, in a crumpled pile, were her
clothes.

"How is your leg?" the voice said.

"Numb," she said.

"Your hand?"

"The same,"

"Stay right there, I'll get you a doctor."

Tara couldn't figure out what that supposed to mean. 'Stay
right there'? Where could she go? She thought it was funny.

She couldn't help laughing, and when she started to laugh
the numbness went out of her leg and fingers and they started
to burn. She couldn't stop herself from laughing and the
burning kept increasing. She felt the tears rolling down her
cheeks and now her stomach hurt. She couldn't remember if
they had kicked her in the stomach, but it hurt when she
laughed, but hard as she tried, she couldn't stop laughing.

The light came on in her cell and a man in a shabby
business suit with a black bag walked in. "I'm Doctor
Hadjok." he said. He knelt beside her, examined her leg, then
her hand.

He gave her a needle in the shoulder. "That will help you
relax a little," he gave her a small bottle of juice, then held her
head so she could drink. He kept the blanket snug around her.
"Drink it all down." The pain got less and less until it was just
numb again.

He turned to his black bag, "Bastards," he mumbled.
"Bloody bastards."

He took her temperature, checked her pulse and said, "You're a strong woman, Tara Kovacs, you seem in pretty good shape." He reached into his bag and brought out another can of juice and some pills. "These are for any infections. Swallow them with the juice. Laughing is not good for you in a place like this, did you know that?"

Tara looked closely at the pills, then at the doctor, who smiled at her and said, "They're okay."

And though she tried not to, she couldn't help but to trust the doctor. She put the pills in her mouth and drank the second can, then looked at the doctor.

"I didn't think I would laugh,"

"I want to give you a pelvic exam, are you okay with that?" Tara nodded, so he gently lifted the good knee and let the broken leg lay flat. He pulled up the blanket and Tara winced. "Bastards," he kept mumbling, "Bloody bastards."

He continued with her examination, then said, "All things considered, like I said, you're a strong woman. I'm going to splint this leg of yours, you have to stay off it for awhile, your fingers are going to be okay, the breaks are clean, they'll all heal well. Your forehead only needs a bandage."

Doctor Hadjok stood up, went to the door, looked up and down the hallway. He came back to Tara and whispered in her ear. "Tell them lies," he looked up at the door and continued to whisper.

"You have to tell them something, they have to look like they're doing their jobs," he said while setting the splints. "These people are not smart but very dangerous. I don't think I'll be back, I rarely come back. Remember, give them lies. Can I help you get dressed?"

Tara nodded. He took her clothes, smoothed them out, brushed some dirt off them, then folded them and helped Tara get dressed.

He took great care to protect her injuries and her dignity. "I'm going to get you some soap and warm water." He kept muttering to himself, "Bastards, bloody bastards."

Tara sat quietly and waited for the doctor to return. The shot he gave her took the pain away, and did help her relax. She didn't want to think about the night before, she was grateful things weren't worse.

Doctor Hadjok came back with a wash pan, overflowing with warm, soapy water, comb and hair brush. Over his arm he had a clean towel. He helped Tara wash and never stopped mumbling, "Bastards, bloody bastards."

When he had done the best he could, he gently kissed Tara on her bandaged forehead, "Remember you have to give them something they can write down, but most of them can't read or write. Tell them lies. I have to go now," he said. "May God be with you, Tara Kovacs."

Tara sat on the floor and rubbed the palm of her broken hand. She could still feel the pain, but it didn't bother her too much. She tried not to think about Little Stephan and Janos and Stephan. She knew that to think about them wasn't good; she knew that with one part of her, but the other part wouldn't let them out of her thoughts. What are they going through? She hoped they wouldn't do anything that could hurt them. She wondered if there was any way Josef could help. Why did she have to go to jail because her machine broke down, she told a joke, a simple joke, nobody got hurt?

She couldn't control her thoughts, they just raced on and on, one after another, tightly linked up so that one wouldn't let go of the other.

She couldn't fit herself in between her thoughts, to put a stop to them, to get some kind of control over them, to direct them away from herself. She only wanted to think about Little Stephan and Janos and Stephan and wasn't there some way Josef could help her.

The door opened and another man, in uniform, came in. He smiled at Tara and extended his hand for her, helped her up to her feet, put his arm under hers and half carried her out of the cell.

He had a brief case on a shoulder strap over his arm and he kept pushing it back as he helped Tara to a set of stairs. Tara had no idea where she was. They stood at the bottom of the stairs.

"Well," he said. "There's no point in you climbing up these stairs. I want you to stay off that leg."

He picked her up, cradled her in his arms and carried her up the stairs into an open hallway. It was well lit with many windows and outside the sun was shining, the leaves on the trees had changed color and there were birds singing on the branches.

He carried her into a room and gently placed her in a chair.

All the walls were painted a flat white; there was a couch up against the wall, a desk with a chair, and a chair in front of the desk. Next to the couch was a filing cabinet, and it was painted white.

"My name is Uri Viknikov, you can call me Uri. You must be hungry,"

"A little,"

"Thirsty,"

"The doctor gave me some juice,"

"Yes, he's a good doctor."

He sat behind the desk, opened his briefcase, spread out some papers in front of him, then folded his hands on the papers. "I don't know what to say about the others, they don't treat women with respect. I have my mother and sister to take care of, and my daughters are always loving me. If I knew they hadn't fed you, I would have brought more. I only have my lunch, but I will share it with you."

He reached back into his briefcase, brought out a thermos of warm tea, some chocolates, pastries, fresh bread, some small packages wrapped in waxed brown paper. He helped Tara push her chair up to the desk.

He poured a drink of tea, spread butter thickly on a piece of bread and pushed them forward to her. "You can go home shortly, take some time off work until you heal, these men have been mean to you, they shouldn't be allowed to treat women like they do."

"I'm going to report them for that."

Tara wasn't hungry, but she didn't want to offend this man by refusing to eat, so she politely began eating. "Very good," she said, "The butter reminds me of before the Nazis came and the tea is tasty,"

"Yes, you have to try these pastries, my wife baked them this morning, I only have a few, but I will share them with you,"

Tara saw pastries in the bakers' window, but she could never afford them. She kept eating, though she couldn't taste anything. She knew she should keep eating, do her best to keep her strength up, and not show that she didn't want anything from him.

She couldn't stop thinking about what Stephan had said; that the extras were covered in Hungarian blood.

"Those men are very bad, like I said, I'm going to report them, but unfortunately there is little I can do about them or I would have done it a long time ago. I can keep them away from you, but I only have one small thing to ask of you, it's very simple, will only take a minute and then you can go home. Would you like to take the rest of the pastries home with you? I'm sure Little Stephan would like them,"

"Oh, yes, he would, he has a sweet tooth you know,"

"Oh, yes, just like my daughters, they can never get enough of their mothers' baked pastries. Listen Mrs. Kovacs, do you mind if I call you 'Tara', it's such a pretty name,"

"Oh no, that's fine. You can call me 'Tara' ",

"This one little thing, it would be very helpful to me, and to you, if you could help me with this, you know I have so much work and so little time to do it in, the party keeps me so busy these days, what with the uprising and all, you know,"

Tara said nothing, continued to eat.

"There are many counter-revolutionaries out there, and we have to find them all, root them all out, they are in league with the west, so you can see why I need your help,"

"Comrade Viknikov, I will help you in any way I can,"

"Oh please, Tara, call me 'Uri',"

"Yes, Uri. How can I help you?"

Tara kept putting food in her mouth, using her right hand and keeping her left hand out of sight. She paid attention to her manners, chewing slowly and thoughtfully, sipping her tea, dabbing at the corners of her mouth with a napkin.

"I just have a few papers here; I have so many it's hard to keep track of them all, I'm so busy, you know."

He kept shuffling the papers back and forth across his desk, sorting them and un-sorting them, putting them into little piles and then taking the piles apart and starting all over again.

"You know I have such trouble with all these papers, I have so many of them and mostly they are all just the usual stuff, you know, documents for this, documents for that, just lots of the usual stuff. Oh, here we are."

He pushed one forward to Tara. "Could you just sign this one and we'll be out of here and on the way home with some fresh pastries for Little Stephan. Here, let me pour you another cup of tea." He handed her the fresh cup of tea and a pen.

Tara took her napkin, folded it neatly, then refolded it with her good hand, then dabbed at the corner of her mouth and took another sip of tea. She picked up the paper, left the pen on the desk and began to read.

Viknikov smiled and chuckled. "Oh, you don't have to read all that, it's just the usual stuff,"

Tara nodded politely and kept reading. It said that she was visited by Josef, that he had brought cheese and sausage and a new sweater for Little Stephan. How much trouble could that be?

Stephan's voice ran around inside her head, 'don't sign anything'. She wondered, when did he tell her that?

How did she know that, did somebody else tell her? Or was it something that everybody 'just knew'? No, she was sure it was Stephan because that's the kind of thing he would say.

He was always watching out, handing out advice, making sure things didn't go wrong and there was something terribly wrong with signing papers for the government.

Especially if they had somebody's name on them and that somebody was over two days before and said 'they're watching me, they're following me'.

Josef stole those things and that was theft from the people of Hungary and that was very serious trouble and these days everything was serious trouble.

"I can't sign that," she said.

"Oh, don't worry about that, it's nothing, just some simple paperwork, you see how much paperwork I have, it's all just pieces of paper, nothing serious, don't worry about it."

Tara chewed on her bread. What would she say? Was Josef really being followed? How did they know what was in his duffel bag? If she knew what they knew, she'd know what to say.

She was terribly afraid that if she said the wrong thing, something that seemed quite small but wasn't, she could get Josef in a lot of trouble. She heard Stephan's voice again, 'don't get caught in a lie,' and Josef said he played dumb and that it seemed to work for him. Then she heard Doctor Hadjok, "Tell them lies."

"We haven't seen Josef in a long time, he works so hard, and he spends so much time out of town and we don't know what he's doing, but it's very important, Janos told me that what he does is very important work, he's in the army.

He protects us from fascists sneaking into the country to do us harm, it's very important work he does, but we rarely see him,"

"Yes, but did he come to your flat two nights ago,"

"I was out, I was walking in the park, I go out for walks for my ankles, they get stiff so I walk them a lot. I haven't seen Josef in a long time,"

"What did you have for breakfast yesterday?"

"We had potatoes and porridge yesterday, like we do every morning."

There was a knock at the door, Viknikov looked surprised. "Who would that be? I left instructions not to be disturbed."

He got up, went to the door, opened it, the person at the door whispered in his ear and Viknikov turned to look at Tara. He whispered back. "Very well, then." he said to the man at the door.

Still looking at Tara, he closed the door and stood there. He shrugged his shoulders and returned to his desk. "Now, where were we, oh yes, and Little Stephan, how is his cold?"

"Oh, it's fine, just a runny nose, it'll pass,"

Viknikov looked puzzled by something. "Do you need anything," he said.

"No thank you, we are well supplied with Janos and Stephan's wages, we don't need extras,"

Viknikov stared at Tara, then he smiled and stood up. "Well, Tara Kovacs, I think everything is in order here. I still have this piece of paper, but you don't have to sign it now, you can sign it later,"

"Well, that's fine then. But I must be getting home, Little Stephan will be worrying, you know how the young ones are,"

"Yes, I do," Viknikov was puzzled. He was thinking about something else. "Yes I do,"

"Well, okay then, I'll be on my way," Tara put down her napkin.

Viknikov gave her a strange look, again shrugged his shoulders, then said, "I'll be right back." He walked out of the room and Tara waited for the AVO to come back.

Doctor Hadjok came in carrying a pair of crutches. He looked straight at Tara, his eyes boring into hers and said, "Those are very slippery stairs. These crutches will help you." He kept digging his eyes into hers, telling her to be quiet, to say only what she should say, and nothing else.

"Oh, yes, slippery stairs. These crutches should be quite helpful, thank you, Doctor."

He helped Tara along the hallway to the door, his eyes still digging into hers. "Yes, very slippery stairs. The next trolley will be here right away. It will take you straight home,"

"Yes, Doctor, straight home," Tara kept looking around for the AVO.

Viknikov reappeared in the hallway "Oh, Mrs. Kovacs," Tara felt her heart drop, "one more thing,"

"Yes, Mr. Viknikov,"

"I can't keep the AVO away forever. If I should ask you for some help, in the future sometime, do you think you will be able to help me then?"

"Oh, yes, Mr. Viknikov,"

"Thank you, Mrs. Kovacs."

Doctor Hadjok put his arm under Tara's shoulder and began walking her to the front door.

There was a sudden slamming of doors and shouting and the sound of heavy boots running down the hallway. The group of AVO from last night ran full speed at Tara.

She shook and her knees gave out, slumping away from her crutches. Doctor Hadjok wrapped his arms around her, pulled her head into his shoulder, her body into his, turned his back to the attack, and shielded her.

The stampeding AVO changed directions, kept running full speed
down the back stairs, out the door and gone.

Tara looked up at Doctor Hadjok, he looked down at her, neither let go. They both turned and looked at the back door, left swinging open. They didn't know what to do, so they laughed.

"Quiet," he said. "Laughing is not good here."

He helped her out the door and down the stairs to the trolley stop. "You take it easy on your leg, here's some money for the trolley," he said. Under his breath he added, "How are you so lucky? Go home and clean your flat,"

Tara nodded, "Thank you Doctor, thank you for everything,"

"Clean your flat, Tara Kovacs, clean your flat."

The trolley arrived immediately and Tara got on. She didn't expect to make it home, somebody on the trolley was AVO, or the trolley would be boarded by AVO. Every time the trolley stopped, she expected somebody to get on and take her off.

When it came to her stop, she got up, struggled on the crutches, and got off. She leaned on her crutches on the sidewalk, looking around, wondering where the AVO were.

Did they forget her? Did they lose their way? Were they just late? Were they waiting in the flat for her?

When would they be back?

Tara couldn't stop thinking about what Josef said, how the AVO made women spy on their husbands. Was he telling the truth?

Was Viknikov going to ask her to spy on Janos and Stephan and if she didn't would she be raped again?

Tara started shaking. She sat down on the trolley stop bench and watched the fingers on her good hand quiver.

She wondered what to say to Janos and Stephan. She hadn't given any thought to telling or not telling anybody about her rape.

She couldn't hide the crutches or her hand or her forehead. It was then that she decided not to tell Janos or Stephan or anybody else what really happened. There was too much on her mind with everything else happening to her to think about how she was going to tell her husband and brother-in-law that she was raped.

Tara struggled to get up the stairs to her flat. She was quietly working her way down the hallway, hoping the AVO wouldn't hear her, when Stephan opened the door and peeked out. He rushed down the hallway, grabbed her, put his arms around her and hugged.

Janos came out, followed by Little Stephan, and together they held each other so tightly it hurt Tara's hand.

"My hand, my hand, it's hurting," she whimpered. They carried her into the flat, put her on the couch, supported her leg with a stool and sat all around her. Janos looked at her crutches and her hand and her forehead, and started crying. He knelt beside her and held her good hand.

"I didn't sign anything," Tara began, "they asked me about Josef and I said I hadn't seen him in a long time and they said you weren't loyal and I said you were loyal. They asked me what we had for breakfast and I told them we had potatoes and porridge, and the doctor set my leg and my hand and gave me a bandage."

Tara was struggling to get her breath. "Then he gave me some juice and he was nice to me, and they said that one day they would ask me for a favor. I said I would, but I never will and I didn't sign anything but they asked me to and I said I wouldn't sign it."

She stopped now that she had caught her breath. "We have to clean the flat right away, the AVO are coming."

Janos put his hand on Tara's forehead, Stephan went to the sink and got a face cloth, wiped the sweat from around her bandage and Tara started crying. Little Stephan wrapped his arms around his mother and wouldn't let go.

Tara started shaking again, she felt hollow inside, like she was a cold shell and when she shook she felt her bones rattle. Now, at home, she had wave after wave of tears pour out of her, but with the AVO, her dam held. She was safe now, at home, where Janos and Stephan could protect her, but for how long.

"Do you know when they're going to be here," Stephan said.

The shivering went from her finger tips, up her arms, across her shoulders and down her back. "I don't know, we have to be ready,"

"Janos," Stephan said, "go to the fridge and get the cheese and sausage Josef brought, then get the sweater for Little Stephan and put them all in a bag,"

"You do it, Stephan. I'm staying with Tara,"

Stephan jumped up, "Right,"

Stephan grabbed the cheese and sausage, cut them into pieces, handed the pieces out and said, "Eat, eat it all now."

Stephan went into the bedroom, stuffed the sweater into the sleeve of his coat and threw it over his shoulder.

Tara held the tears in and put a piece of cheese in her mouth, then spat it out. Janos picked it up, put it in his mouth and swallowed it.

"Mommy, I missed you. Daddy and I couldn't sleep without you home, are you staying home now? Why are you crying so much, Mommy?"

"Because I missed you my little sweetheart, because I missed you,"

"Uncle Stephan is going to be happy to say he's sorry,"

Tara wiped the tears from her eyes and cheeks, "Sorry," she said. "Why would Uncle Stephan say he's 'sorry',"

"Because he spent all night walking back and forth on the carpet and Daddy said he was going to wear a hole in it if he didn't sit down, and Uncle Stephan said that when you came home he would be happy to say he's sorry,"

"Well, my little sweetheart, when Uncle Stephan comes home, you can remind him to say he's sorry."

Janos sat next to Tara, held her hand and said, "You can tell me, did they, you know, did they...?"

Tara shook her head, it was the only time she ever lied to Janos, she thought the truth was more dangerous than what it was worth. She feared that Janos' hot temper would get them all in trouble. What was done, was done, she thought, there was nothing she could do about that, best to put it behind her and carry on.

HOW IT HAPPENED

Again Steve had the wind sucked out of him. "So that's how it happened,"

"Your mother never told you?"

"No,"

"I understand. Tara would not speak of it."

Wayne picked up his glass, "For Stephan Kovacs, I know our Good Lord will welcome him into heaven."

They picked up their glasses, drank them down, and Steve realized that he had never drank a toast to his dead uncle.

The waitress returned with another tray of beer. Everybody poured their beers down again and within a few rounds the floor and everybody's shirts were soaked. The waitress had trouble keeping up with Wayne's demands for more beer, while Steve wondered what had happened in the last few minutes. Wayne and the others were getting drunk in a hurry. Steve had a hard time keeping up. They told Steve more about the war with the Nazis, the revolution with Russia; they made it all sound like fun. They were laughing a lot and sounded like they missed it all and would like to have it happen again. They talked of the killing they had done, but not of the friends' dying they had witnessed. Steve thought it strange that they could talk about a subject like that, when his father never spoke a word about it.

"My father never talks about it," he said.

They all stopped talking, stopped laughing. Wayne said, "We hope someday the communists will be gone from Hungary, then we can go home. Tonight we talk of good times, happy times.

But there were bad times, very many bad times. But we don't talk about that," Peter and Henry nodded.

"I fought the commies in Korea," Kendall said. "Princess Patricia's Canadian Light Infantry." He held his glass up and hollered out,

KOREA

Then they all lifted their glasses again in a toast to Korea.

"Korea was a nasty piece of work," Kendall said. "Lotta us in Keno Hill been 'round the commie block. We can laugh when we want to, cause we know which end of life's stick has the shit on it. We cry alone." He paused to take a breath, then leaned closer to Steve. "You just consider yourself damn fortunate to be Canadian," he said as he pointed his finger into Steve's face. "You can't get drafted for Vietnam, you can stay home."

Steve nodded. He stood up on shaky legs and headed for the washroom. When he got there he leaned against the wall over the urinal. He tried to piss, knew he had to, but couldn't. He listened to the noise of the drinking and yelling of old anti-communist soldiers and wondered about his father. How would things be if he was here, if he met these men who knew him from the Revolution? If he was with him, things would be simple. He would know what to say, what to do. He would take care of everything. He would tell him why he never heard of Uncle Joe.

Steve felt young and lonely. He wanted to cry, but instead started chuckling. He was getting tired of trying to cry, of having a good reason to cry, and not being able to.

What the hell is going on here, he thought. He heard the words running through his head, 'you've got a lot to learn kid, a lot to learn', and he tried to think about what he had to learn.

A rush surged through his body and the lights went out. He woke up on the floor, couldn't focus his eyes; they hurt too much. There were sounds in the distance, but couldn't make them out. His legs and arms were tingling and hot.

Buzzing in his ears grew into a dull roar, like a waterfall pounding down on his skull. He struggled to stand, but couldn't find his legs.

Tried to stretch his arms, to push off the floor, couldn't find his arms. It was quiet and he waited. He wondered what he was waiting for. Arms around him; soft voices, cold face, something soft and warm. Boots taken off, something warm being tugged over his ears.

Steve woke up very slowly and very painfully. His throat was
dry and his head was thick. Scratched his nose, wiggled his
toes; moved his arms and legs. He became acutely aware of a
pounding head, and a serious need to piss and drink. His eyes
didn't seem to hurt, so he opened them. Looking around him
he lay in an empty room, bag and boots on the floor.
Scratching his scalp, an old gray toque fell into his hands. He
looked at it, wondered where it came from, put it back on. As
he sat up on the side of the bed, he rested his head in his hands
and thought about his thirst and swollen tongue.

The door was only feet away but seemed like a long
journey. Standing up, he wavered, and then fell on his knees.
On the floor her caught his breath, and leaned on the bed.
Pulling himself up to the bed, he stretched his legs, then stood
up and stayed up. One step at a time and he was at the door.

He turned the handle and looked out into the hallway.
Up and down the hallway, more doors, only one open. In it he
saw sinks, went in and started drinking, then washed his face
with cold, cold water; looked in the mirror and saw someone
he didn't recognize. Bags under sunken eyes; drawn and
sagging face. Long strands of dirty matted hair hung limply
out of an old gray toque. He drank more, had a long piss.
Walked into the hallway and back to the room where his boots
and bag were. He lay back down, pulled the blanket up to his
face and closed his eyes. He wondered about the toque.

He didn't know how long he'd slept when he heard, "Hey,
wake up! Wake up!"

He didn't recognize the voice, it sounded familiar. He
opened his eyes and his head started pounding again.

"You awake yet?"

"Ya,"

"Wanna sleep some more?"

"Ya,"

He heard footsteps, loud and heavy as they walked away.
He felt the toque. He looked at it and tried to remember
something about it, but his head hurt too much to think.

There is a Season   J. Harding Montgomery

Sometime later he heard the voice again, "You still sleeping?"

"Not anymore."

He opened his eyes and recognized the face, but didn't know who it was.

"Remember me?"

"No,"

"Name's Kendall, we met in the bar last night,"

"Now I remember. Korea, right?"

Kendall nodded, "Found you on the deck in the head. How you feeling?"

"Rotten,"

"No surprise; brought you some juice." Kendall handed him some cans of juice.

Steve took one and drank it in a mouthful.

"Hungry?"

"Not really,"

He sat up and put his feet on the floor. His head was spinning and pounding. "What now," Steve said.

"That's up to you,"

"I need to,"

"See your uncle is a good idea,"

"Uncle?"

"Joe Smith."

Steve's memory came back to him like he was thrown through a plate glass window. He held the toque, ran his fingers across the flag. Vague fears started to float about and arrange and rearrange themselves. He knew he had decisions to make, and soon.

"Can I get that taxi to Keno City?"

"I'll take you." Kendall grabbed Steve's bag and threw them up to his shoulder. "Truck's warm. Let's go,"

"What time is it?"

" 'bout five o'clock."

They walked out of the bunkhouse and down the slippery steps to Kendall's truck. Steve looked around in the darkness, watched Kendall throw his bag in the back of his truck and climb in.

He leaned across the seats and opened the passenger door. "God
damn it, its cold! Get in,"
Steve climbed in and Kendall started driving.
"Five o'clock," Steve said. "Day or night?"
"I just finished day shift. You had a good sleep. Drank your
share of beer last night,"
"Had some, ahh, Palinka, too,"
"Pa-fucken-linka! No wonder you keeled over in the head.
What the hell you doin' drinking that rot gut,"
"My uncle gave it to me."
Steve stared out the window into the darkness as Kendall
drove on quietly. The truck wound its way through some hills,
and then came out to a small plateau. Scattered about on the
plateau were some small log cabins and old houses. In the
middle of them all was a large barn.
On the side of the barn, in large and faded white lettering,
was written

KENO CITY HOTEL

Steve thought it was something out of an old western
movie. Crowded around it were a few more small cabins. One
house had two floors and was covered in faded wood
planking. Next to it were two cabins joined at the side by a
planked in walkway.
Outside of the hotel were five pickup trucks all running and
all pouring exhaust clouds high into the dark night air. Steve
climbed out of the truck, grabbed his bag and walked in.
The bar was quiet. There was a crib game going on, and a
few others sitting at tables. Steve walked up to the till. The
same old man with long gray hair and beard from the Elsa Bar
sat there, reading a newspaper.
"Got a room," Steve said.
"Ya, ten bucks."

Steve headed up the stairs and threw his bag on the floor of the small room. He looked around at a single bunk, one chair at a small table, and a dented and scraped mirror over the table. He lay on the bunk and was snoring as soon as his head hit the pillow.

When he woke up he was wide-awake immediately. He stretched all over, then lay on the floor and did push-ups. Then he rolled over and did sit ups. Then he stretched everything he could stretch, once again. He went to the mirror and examined the blisters from his frostbite. They had gone down a little, but he still put some more cream on them. He looked out the window and saw the sun rising on the southern horizon. He looked at his watch. Twelve O'clock.

Nothing like getting up at the crack of noon, he chuckled. Now what? Dads at work, Uncle Joe's at work. (Uncle Joe's at work? Never said that before!) Mom's at home, or is she working? Sheila's in class, Rolly's in the bush. Shit, gotta phone somebody. Who's first? Eat first.

Steve dug out the bags of fruit and cake and cookies that uncle Joe had stuffed in his bag. He laid them out on the small table. Not bad, not bad at all, he said.

There were apples and oranges, plums and pears, cherries and grapes. The cookies were thick and filled with chocolate chips and raisins. Some were peanut butter, others coconut, still others that Steve didn't recognize. He started eating. Thank you, Uncle Joe, thank you very much. Steve munched away happily, filling his face with mouthful after mouthful. Cookies were followed by apples, apples by cakes, cakes by plums, plums by more cakes, then back to cookies.

He followed all that with oranges. He ate like a pig, and then burped. It felt so good; he ate more and burped again. When he was stuffed he scratched his bloated belly, and then let out his best burp yet. He grabbed his toothpaste, brush, soap and a towel and headed down the hall for a long hot shower. There was no hot water, so he showered in cold water and didn't care. He actually enjoyed it. When he was finished he put on clean clothes and went looking for a telephone.

Across the road from the hotel, in a two-floored planked building, was a small cafe'; the one Jan said had such good food. The café' that Steve had promised to buy dinner for Rolly and Rosie. An Italian family, who also ran the only taxi for fifty miles, owned and operated it.

They cooked for miners tired of cook shack food, and drove them back and forth from Elsa to Keno City, sometimes further.

Steve found the phone on the front porch. He called his mother.

"Hi, Mom,"

"Stephan, Stephan, so good to hear from you. How are you? How's the new job? Do you get enough to eat?"

"I'm fine. Haven't started the new job, yet, and I'm eating fine," Steve held his breath. "Mom,"

"What's wrong? I can tell if something is wrong, and something is wrong,"

Steve let his breath out. "Mom, I met my Uncle Josef,"

"............."

"Mom?"

"Yes, Stephan,"

"I met my Uncle Josef. He lives here in Elsa,"

"He is there? With you?"

"Yes,"

"Let me talk with him,"

"He's not with me now. But he lives here, I met him. I had dinner with him,"

"Are you sure it's him?"

"He showed me a picture of you and Dad and Uncle Stephan and him and me, when I was a baby,"

"You can get him to talk with me?"

"Mom, I drank Palinka with him,"

"You don't drink that! Rotten plums! Bad for your stomach,"

"Wasn't that bad. Had an after burn, though,"

"Of course it had an after burn. Don't drink anymore,"

"Mom, why wasn't I told about him?"

"I have to talk to your father,"

"What shift is he working today?"

"He's on day shift, home by five,"

"Uncle Joe should be back from work by five. Him and Dad can talk,"

"You call him Uncle Joe? He's with you at five o'clock?"

"Six o'clock,"

"Why not five o'clock?"

"Give them an hour to get ready,"

"They don't need another hour,"

"Mom, what do you think Dad will say?"

"Your father never talks about him, but I know he will want to talk with him,"

"Why wasn't I told?"

"We were so young, so afraid when we escaped. Stephan got us out,"

"He said Uncle Stephan banned him from the family,"

"I have to talk with your father; this is so much right now. I have to be careful with your father. He is very upset over you leaving university. This will be hard for him, for his heart,"

"His heart? Is he okay,"

"Well yes, he's okay. But it's been a difficult week for him. And me,"

"You know what Uncle Joe said,"

"No, I don't know what your Uncle Joe said; I haven't talked to him in sixteen years,"

"He said I should go back to university,"

"Well, he's right. When are you going back?"

"Got work to do,"

"What work is it that is more important than university?"

"You know, my job, gotta take care of myself for awhile,"

"I'll wait for your father, try to find a way to tell him, make him a drink,"

"Why, Mom? Why wasn't I told?"

"We read a list; his name was on it, so was ours. You call tonight,"

"Good bye, Mom. Talk with you later."

HOME OF JANOS AND TARA KOVACS, VANCOUVER, B.C.

Tara put the phone down. She exhaled deeply, then walked across her living room to her kitchen. She looked at her new electric stove, next to it a new extra large fridge and freezer; both stocked full. Janos bought them for her birthday. She had two walls full of cupboards, and two sets of cupboards under her double sink. All full of boxes and bags of food and complete sets of pots and pans and assorted cookware. The breakfast dishes were in the sink, waiting to be washed; she never ran out of hot water.

There were two floors in her home; both floors fully furnished with nice furniture from a reputable second hand store. On the main floor she had an L-shaped living room, a dining room with a table set for six; two bedrooms, one for her and Janos and one for Little Stephan. There was a wood burning fireplace in the living room; Janos always worried about being cold, it was bad for Tara's hand and leg. Under the back porch there was enough firewood for weeks. Janos also had a full supply of candles, batteries, and everything else they would need if the electricity went out. It amused the neighbors, Janos being prepared for the cold. It didn't amuse Janos.

In the basement, a washer and drier, a play area for Little Stephan, full of toys, and one extra bedroom. Tara never forgot the promise she made to Stephan: a room of his own. At times she would sit in the extra bedroom and dream of Stephan and his Canadian wife, and their lots of Canadian children, cousins for Little Stephan.

She knew he was gone, but she could never break her promise.

Every room in the house was full of nice furniture, everybody had more clothes than they needed and she always had electricity. In Budapest she had a small one-bedroom for four people, broken furniture, not enough food, not enough clothes and it was always cold.

On the mantle, over the fireplace, were the pictures she carried through the frozen swamps to Andau: pictures of her mother and father, of Janos and his older brother Stephan, and their mother and father. More pictures of Little Stephan as a baby.

Next to them, spread about and neatly arranged; her favorite pictures taken since the family's arrival in Canada. She looked carefully and caringly how the family had aged. How Little Stephan had grown up. His first birthday in Canada, he was three. His first two-wheeled bicycle, first day of school, bright eyed and smiling, missing his two front teeth. Little Stephan's first soccer team, coached by Janos. She chuckled at the problems Janos had coaching the Canadian children when he spoke so little English. It was how he learned to speak English. She proudly wiped a tear at the soccer pictures.

Hockey pictures, when Little Stephan had learned to ice skate. Janos didn't coach hockey because he couldn't skate. Even after Little Stephan quit soccer for hockey, Janos still coached soccer. Tara had many pictures of Janos' championship soccer teams. It was what he did for his community, he was good at it and he enjoyed it. As she looked through her pictures, she kept seeing a picture that wasn't there. The one other member of the family who should be on the mantle, who wasn't on the mantle, and again now, she began to wonder why.

She went into the bedroom closet and spread out her arms to touch the walls. She used to do that in her bedroom in Budapest. She took out her shoeboxes and looked at them.

She remembered a time when she only had three pairs of shoes; one for work, one for the cold, and one for wearing with her one nice dress. All three of those pairs could fit into one box. Now she had shoes for every occasion, even spares and extras. She put the boxes aside and went deeper into the closet. Under a neat pile of Little Stephan's old coats, ones she couldn't bear to throw out because they were still in good shape and had too many good memories, she had hidden an old brown envelope.

There is a Season   J. Harding Montgomery

She reached into the envelope and pulled out a picture and stared at it. It was of her and Janos holding Little Stephan, just after he was born. Next to Janos were his two brothers, Stephan and Josef. She reached further into the old envelope and pulled out a piece of paper.

She carefully unfolded it. It was very weak at the folds. Her hands shook slightly. She hadn't opened the envelope since....

AVO COMING TONIGHT
NO GUARDS AT ANDAU
GET OUT OF HUNGARY

He's alive, she whispered. He's alive. She worried about what to say to Janos, how to say it. But no matter how much she thought about it, or worried about it, all that came to her mind were the blurred memories of a frozen swamp on the Hungarian border. The one memory that wasn't blurred was her lying across Janos' shoulders while he held her tight with one arm and broke ice with the other.

That much she clearly remembered. He carried me through that frozen hell to this country, where I have more shoes that I can count.   Tara put the picture and the piece of paper back into the envelope, into her pocket, then went down to her basement, to her extra bedroom. She sat on the made and unused bed, thought of Josef.

And she thought of maybe Josef's Canadian wife and lots of cousins for Little Stephan, who wasn't so little anymore.

She went back upstairs, filled a suitcase with clothes for herself and for Janos, and called a taxi. When the taxi came she told the driver to take her to the machine shop where Janos worked. She told the driver to wait as she walked in, with the envelope under her arm. She went to the front desk and told the secretary, her friend Cathy, that she wanted to see Janos.

Janos came out in a panic. "What's wrong? How is Little Stephan?"

"Janos, sit down,"

"What do you mean 'sit down'? What's wrong? Tell me, tell me,"

Tara handed him the envelope. He looked at it, then her.

"Open it," she said.

Janos opened it. He took out the picture of himself, his brothers and his wife and new baby. He stared at it, stared at Josef. He looked up at Tara. "What does this mean?"

"He's alive, with Little Stephan, in the Yukon,"

"Alive? With Little Stephan? In the Yukon?"

"That's what I said,"

"My little brother is alive? He's alive,"

"Little Stephan phoned. He met him,"

"How do you know this is true?"

"He showed Little Stephan this same picture. He's quite upset,"

"Who's upset?"

"Little Stephan,"

"Why,"

"We never told him about Josef,"

"Now what do we tell him,"

"We? He's your brother, you tell your son,"

"How,"

"Taxi's waiting,"

Janos turned to Cathy. "I'm taking some days off,"

"How many," she asked.

"Tell you when I get back,"

Janos took Tara by the arm and led her out of the machine shop office and into the waiting taxi.

"Airport," Tara said.

"What am I going to say to him," Janos said.

"To which 'him',"

"Oh shit,"

"Do you know what your little brother fed your son? Palinka,"

"Rotten plums," Janos snorted. "Bad for your stomach, I'm going to have to talk to Josef, about being an uncle,"

"You do that,"

"Did you tell Little Stephan not to drink Palinka?"

"I told him,"
"Did he listen?"
"He's your son. What do you think?"
"Oh, shit."

PARLIAMENT SQUARE,
BUDAPEST
OCTOBER, 1956

After work the next day, instead of going to their mandatory political meeting, Janos and Stephan snuck out to a demonstration at the Technological University in Budapest. Students in Warsaw had presented a list of demands to their Russian authorities. Their demands were rejected; the students rioted, and were now surrounded by Russian tanks. The Budapest demonstration, in support of the Polish students, was not initiated by Hungarian authorities and had no permit; it was illegal and a dangerous place for Janos and Stephan. Stephan was a leader in the Worker's Association and his presence was good for the workers, but bad for Stephan. He knew he would be reported for being there.

Stephan gripped Janos by the collar with both hands and stared him straight in the eye. "You keep your mouth shut. You know what happened last time,"
"I won't forget,"
Janos and Stephan wore hats and turned up their collars when they walked into the University meeting hall, but were still recognized by many members of their association. Hundreds of their poorly dressed co-workers mixed with hundreds of not so poorly dressed professors and students.
A student jumped to the podium, took off his coat, threw it to the floor, yelled into the microphone, "Just like Polish students, we too, have a list of demands!"
His first demand brought on roars of approval. "Academic freedom, we want the right to read books from the west. No more forced teaching of Russian."
The students jumped up and clenched their fists in the air. "An improvement in working conditions for all Hungarians," now the workers were clenching their fists in the air. "The right to check the books on our exports, to know how much we produce, and why our own products are rationed; an end to five-year plans for production and still no decent housing,"

The cheering flowed out of the meeting hall and across the campus as more students and workers flooded into the already over-crowded meeting hall. Loud speakers were set up at the doors.

"Most important for all Hungarians," the student took a deep breath, held the microphone high and sang out their last demands.

"We want an independent Hungary, the removal of Russian troops from Hungarian soil and out of the Warsaw Pact."

Now the cheering was foot stomping as the crowd marched out of the meeting hall and onto the campus grounds.

The demonstration headed to Parliament square, all singing the Hungarian National Anthem, now banned by the communists. They filled the streets, covered both sidewalks as shops and factories closed and everyone joined in the demonstration. Janos and Stephan followed close behind a group of their co-workers holding a banner from the Csepel Metal Works. They still tried to stay out of sight, hiding behind the banner.

Two hundred thousand people crowded into Parliament Square with more signs and banners, all proclaiming solidarity with Polish students, and more rights for all Hungarians.

The ground thumped in rhythm with the chanting and singing crowd and then the lights on the top floor of Parliament went out.

From floor to floor, down to the ground, every light went out. Every building, every Ministry up and down the boulevards, turned their lights off. Parliament Square was dark and the demonstration went silent. Pravda newspapers were rolled up and lit as torches. Burning them was a crime against the state.

One single spotlight lit up the Parliament podium and Erno Gero, leader of the Hungarian Communist Party started screaming into the microphone."There are people who want to create a conflict between proletarian internationalism and Hungarian nationalism." He was arrogant and angry and his anger spread to the demonstrators.

Stephan turned to Janos, "There's going to be trouble, stay in the crowd and keep your head down,"

Through-out the demonstration went a cry, "Onto Radio Budapest," and the angry demonstration found a direction.

Stephan and Janos followed their co-workers and students, and lit by burning communist party newspapers they went with thousands of demonstrators across Parliament Square to Radio Budapest.

The demonstration marched past the Communist Party headquarters, where the students screamed out insults; the civilian Hungarian Police Headquarters, where police leaned out windows and cheered them on.

Radio Budapest was a brick building, five floors high, guarded by a ring of sand bags and barbed wire. Behind the sandbags, a full company of one hundred AVO, manning machine guns; on the roof-top, another full company with more machine guns

Janos peered over the sandbags and studied the faces of the AVO.

"He's not there." Stephan said.

In a side street, a full convoy of twelve truckloads of Hungarian Army regulars sat nervously quiet. Leaning on the lead truck was an army Major, an old friend of Stephan. They had been in the Mokan together. Stephan walked out of the crowd, collar up, hat brim down, and spoke with him.

"Major Malater, how are you,"

"Stephan Kovacs, good to see you. I'm not so good,"

"The students want to broadcast their demands. Somebody has to give the list to the AVO," Stephan said.

"That's why I'm not so good; this is going to be trouble. My orders are to stay here. You give the list to the AVO," the Major said.

"I can't,"

The Major nodded, "So much for my orders. Okay, I'll do it."

The AVO Captain shook his head, "They can tape their demands, we'll broadcast them later," he said. "We won't edit the tape."

The Major came back to Stephan and Janos. "Not good, not good at all," he said.

Janos paced nervously, then walked into the side street to talk with the Hungarian Army soldiers.

"Martin, Martin Floris," Janos said. "I've known you since grade school,"

"Yes, Janos Kovacs, how are you?" Martin said quietly.

"How am I? What kind of a question is that? We are here to have the demands broadcast,"

"I know, we're ordered here to put a stop to..., listen, Janos, we're under orders. It's not our choice to be here," Martin looked to the floor.

Janos turned to the other soldiers. "This is our country, all of ours."

He started pointing at different soldiers. "I know you, and you and you."

The soldiers all sat quietly, hands between knees, and stared at the floor. Janos left the truck and headed back to Stephan and the Major. Martin dropped his rifle and ran up to them.

"Janos, listen to me," he said. "They expect trouble, that's why we're here. You have to be careful,"

"We're not looking for trouble," Janos said.

"Trouble is looking for us," Stephan said.

"Major, what are we to do," Martin said.

"Stand by until further orders,"

Janos looked across the sea of burning newspapers that lit the darkened square, shook his head slowly from side to side, and softly said to Stephan, "What do you think,"

"Good for Hungary, not good for us. Keep your head down."

The Major climbed onto a garbage can and yelled out, "The AVO says they will let you tape your demands and broadcast them later. They said we could trust them,"

"You want us to trust the AVO," the student said.

The Major shrugged.

The student went back into the crowd and the students replied as one.

BROADCAST NOW BROADCAST NOW

Martin whispered into Stephan's ear. "We can't give you our rifles,"

Stephan thought about that and said nothing.

"They will shoot us if we give them to you," Martin said.

Stephan turned to Martin; put his hand on his shoulder, "You shoot first."

The student came out of the crowd and handed the list of demands to Stephan, who turned them over to the Major.

"For Hungary," the Major said, then took the list to main entrance. A single shot rang out.

The Major stopped, turned to look at the pavement where the bullet hit, looked into the crowd to see if anyone was hit, then yelled at the roof-top. "If you intend to shoot me for this, then shoot now!" He stood his ground and stared up at them. He took a step forward, another shot and the Major fell.

Tear gas canisters rained from the rooftop and quick bursts of automatic weapons fire tore up the crowd. The sea of torches fell as thousands panicked and scrambled away in every direction.

The shooting stopped. Stephan ran out, grabbed the Major and pulled him out of the line of fire.

Students; men, women, the innocent and the curious, fell where they once stood. Two anti-aircraft searchlights scanned the square. The wounded lay crying; while some made no sound at all. Two men ran out and picked up a young woman whose white blouse ran red.

They picked her up and the three went down in another burst from the automatics. No one tried another rescue.

Stephan and Janos, followed by dozens of their co-workers, sprinted into the side street, to the convoy of soldiers.

"If you won't do anything, give us your rifles," they screamed.

The soldiers gasped in panicked confusion.

"They've shot our Major, do it," ordered Martin Floris.

In a slight and hesitant trickle, then a flood, from the back of every Hungarian Army truck in the convoy; rifles, ammo belts and then the soldiers themselves.

Stephan threw an ammo belt across one shoulder, a rifle across the other, handed one to Janos. "Take it; this is our chance, now we fight the AVO."

Janos' mind flashed at him. Pictures of Tara coming home, her wounds and her tears, his beating at AVO headquarters, Sandor and his demotion, Tara's leg, her hand, her forehead, her shaking fingers, Little Stephan's cold and hungry face, fighting the Nazis', Russian tanks in Budapest, pictures of his mother and father, cheese and sausage and warm clothes for little Stephan, and Stephan yelling at Josef.

Was Josef on the roof-top? He took the rifle and slung an ammo belt over his shoulder.

Stephan slammed home a clip in his rifle and loaded the chamber.

"Listen up," he yelled out to his armed co-workers. "What's our count?"

"Half a company, maybe more," one yelled back. "We need more rifles,"

"On me, Mokan," Stephan yelled out again. Men from his job, from the Mokan, gathered around him. "Don't let them catch us in a crossfire, we have to get those searchlights," he pointed to a clearing in the next alley, out of fire from the roof-top.

Then he pointed out five men, "Wait 'till we get the lights, then gather our wounded, find some medics, cover them and get them in there. The rest of you, come with me."

Two blocks away, another full convoy of twelve trucks, filled with Hungarian Army soldiers, roared into the square and slammed on their brakes, just out of line from the rooftop.

The soldiers from the first convoy, who had just handed over their rifles to rebels, stood in fear of the second convoy. What would they do? Remain loyal to the Russians, or would they too, go over to the rebels?

"I'll talk to them," Martin said, then ran up to the first truck.

"The AVO shot Major Malater. Are you with us for Hungary, or do you remain loyal to our Russian masters."

The second convoy, to a man, was quicker than the first. They jumped out of the trucks, screaming, "Hungary for Hungarians."

Rifles and ammo belts flew out of the truck and rapidly found gripping hands.

Throughout the square, armed men and women spread out and with single shot accuracy opened fire on the rooftop. Automatics returned hails of bullets in all directions as pavement, walls, and windows erupted in thousands of little clouds of smoke and dust. The shooting stopped as fast as it started, cheers followed the sudden quiet.

Five trucks from the armories in Csepel, filled with men armed with automatics, braked to a sudden stop in a side street and slammed doors as they jumped out and ran into the square. One truck spun about to back slowly to the side of the square.

The tarps flew off and an anti-tank gun opened fire on the rooftop. One searchlight blinked, fluttered, and then went out. The truck moved a little for aim, fired, and the other searchlight went out.

With the search lights out, the automatics, rifles and anti-tank gun all opened up on the rooftop.

The AVO ducked for their lives, and unarmed students, under the cover of the armed workers got to their wounded.

Sirens wailed as the first ambulance arrived at the square. Janos waved it over to the alley where the wounded had been gathered. It didn't stop, but kept pushing through the crowd, knocking people over, headed for the radio building.

He took his rifle butt, smashed in the window and put the barrel in the drivers face.

"Out," he screamed.

Martin yanked the ambulance door open, grabbed the driver, hauled him out and pinned him to the side of the ambulance.

Janos opened the back door and grabbed a box of medical supplies. "Get these to our wounded, we need them, they're not for those bastards." He pried open the first box and looked in. "Oh, Jesus, Mother of Mary. Martin, look at this,"

Martin still held the driver, looked in, and then gave himself the cross of Jesus. "These belong to us now; the AVO shall reap what they sown."

From large wooden boxes, marked with the Red Cross, Janos started passing out hand grenades.

Stephan ran up, shouldered his rifle, and looked in the box. "This is the driver?"

"This is him," Martin said. "He's AVO."

Stephan grabbed the driver by the throat, pointed his rifle into his chest. "Come with me," he took him behind some bushes. "You have five seconds to pray,"

"I didn't know, I didn't know," cried the driver.

"Liar." Stephan said.

The driver fell to his knees; Stephan counted to five, shot him, then returned to Janos and Peter.

"Did you have to do that," Janos said.

"Yes," Stephan said. "He'd have done it to us."

With weapons from the Csepel armories, and the rebel soldiers, and hand grenades from the AVO, the battle for the radio station was no longer one-sided. The AVO at the perimeter retreated into the building and took up positions on the first and second floors.

Stephan and his friends for the Mokan, under heavy fire, fought their way up to the building and tossed grenades in windows.

Glass and plaster exploded over their heads into the air and the AVO retreated to the upper floors. The front doors of the radio station were blown out and the rebels stormed in. Stephan and Janos were with the first wave through the door, while Peter and the rebel soldiers lay on the sandbags, still giving covering fire.

They stopped firing as soon there was no return fire; then sprinted across the open courtyard and jammed in the front doors.

Stephan and Janos got separated in the confusion of battle throughout the rooms on the first floor.

Janos jumped over the sprawled bodies of two AVO and ran up the first stair, saw the pistol barrel aimed at his head and ducked as the bullet crashed into the wall beside him.

He fired back and the AVO man stopped. He watched as the man dropped to his knees, gripping at the blood stain spreading across his chest.

His mouth opened wide gasping for air as he flipped over and slid down the last few steps. He lay upside down, with his head resting on the floor, still gripping the spreading stain.

Janos stood over the man as the blood still flowed from his chest, turning his black shirt brown. He knelt down and watched as the light in his eyes went out, then puked on the floor. He stepped over the AVO he killed and ran up the remaining stairs.

It became a floor-by-floor battle to dislodge the AVO. He saw fellow workers from Csepel lying wounded and bleeding, being tended to by students. The wounded AVO were stripped of their weapons and left to die.

"STEPHAN!" Janos climbed up and down stairs, through rooms and hallways, stepping over the wounded and dead that lay everywhere in the broken and shattered building. He was looking for his brothers and the smell of piss, shit, puke, blood and spent gunpowder turned his empty stomach. He stumbled out the back door of the building, where a squad of AVO lay in a grotesque pile; arms and legs tangled into a bleeding heap where they had all been shot in the back, trampling each other while trying to escape.

At the side of the pile, looking over the bodies, checking their identification, in a crowd with many others, was Stephan.

"We're the lucky ones," Stephan said, hugging Janos who didn't want to let go.

"Look at this," Stephan held a piece of paper. "It's his pay slip. He makes ten times what we do," Stephan crushed the piece of paper and threw it on the body. "That's what you get for being a traitor."

Janos looked around him, struggled to hold the bile down and keep the tears in.

"We chased them out," Stephan said. "We won this one. We need more ammo; more men. They'll be back."

Janos looked at the pile. He pulled over a body, looked at the face, then another and another.

"He's not there," Stephan said.

"Are you sure?"

"I'm sure." He pointed at one of the bodies. "Look what he gave me." He held a package of rolled cigarettes, lit one; let it dangle from the corner of his mouth, offered one to Janos.

"No, I don't want it,"

"Suit yourself," Stephan shrugged.

"Sweet Mary, Mother of Jesus. Are we fighting the Russians, or each other?"

Stephan shrugged again. "We fight for Hungary,"

"I have to go home," Janos said. "I have to check on Tara,"

"I'll come with you," Stephan said. "But I have to come back."

Tara cradled Little Stephan in her arms and rocked him slowly as she bit her lip."What now," she said.

"They'll be back," Stephan said.

"What then?" Tara never let Stephan have his way without her acceptance.

"What we've started, well, I don't know," was all Janos could say.

"Our army is ready," said Stephan. "The AVO is on the run, and the Russians have left the country. It's time to rebuild."

"What about Josef?" Tara asked.

"I don't know," Stephan said. "For his own benefit, I hope he's left the country,"

"You know," Janos said. "Josef...he may not have fought. He may have..."

"'May have' what?" Stephan said.

"We don't have to condemn him," Tara said.

"Doesn't matter what 'we' do, every other Hungarian will," Stephan said.

"It's going to take a lot more than that before I ever condemn him," Janos said.

Tara cuddled Little Stephan, then looked up to Janos and Stephan and sighed. "I will pray for Josef; but if it's a revolution you've started, you'll have to win a civil war. The Russians made the AVO; they turned our own against us. You have to deal with them first." Tara rubbed her crippled left hand, "My mother, may she rest in peace, used to say, 'It's not how many Nazis you kill that counts, its how many Hungarians you set free.' Remember that, both of you."

ETHEL LAKE, YUKON TERRITORY

Rolly McGarret loved his cabin on the North Shore of Ethel Lake. It faced south and he could watch the sun come up in March and go down in November. Ethel Lake gave him all the fish he could catch, and the surrounding hills and mountains were full of wild game. Hunting was good, and they didn't shoot back.

While tracking a moose through a forest fire swept plateau he had stumbled into a clearing. There were tall straight trees all around the clearing and Rolly knew they would make excellent building logs. He went directly back to Whitehorse and laid claim to the area for woodcutting, and started calling Ethel Lake home.

Rolly became a woodcutter because he'd had enough of giving and taking orders in the Marines, so he either couldn't or wouldn't give or take orders from anyone in a regular job. He found that out during his short stay at Yukon General Warehouse. It was his first job after leaving the Marines and the last job where he gave or took any orders.

He decided that the quickest way to feed himself and to work for himself would be as a woodcutter. All he had to do was keep his truck and his chain saws running and work his ass off. He had a small propane tank and tiger torch to thaw out the truck when it froze up, and his saws he kept in the cabin.

For hundreds of acres around the cabin all the trees' branches were burnt off and the bark had fallen off.

The fire had killed the trees and they were now were dry and light which made them easy to cut and stack.

Rolly cut them down to sell for firewood, and the bigger, straighter logs he sold as building logs for cabins.

All around the old dead trees was new strong growth of Willow, Alder, Birch and Maple, and lots of wild berries. They were young, strong and healthy trees and in the spring the leaves covered the entire north shore in a soft blanket of multi-colored green. In the fall the blanket turned from light green to golden orange and yellow.

And everywhere, the fireweed flower, tall with thin shoots covered in white and pink buds, so named because of its' rapid growth in ground once burnt.

Rolly thought it was the most beautiful flower and place he had ever seen, and he regarded his woodcutting as cleaning up the mess the forest fire left behind. He liked his job and where he worked. No one asked him questions about where he came from or what brought him to the Yukon. He dealt with people when he wanted, and how he wanted. He kept no records and paid no taxes. He liked it that way.

He built his cabin from logs he cut only feet from where the cabin stood. He hired two local trappers and they built a 12 by 20 foot cabin in one week. The walls were 6 feet tall, but the high peaked roof went to 12 feet, which gave him a large warm loft to sleep in. The main floor of the cabin was a kitchen with one old wood stove for heat and cooking, and some shelves full of canned goods; it was also his living room, with one beat up couch with matching beat up chair; a library with a twelve foot wide floor to ceiling shelf overflowing with paperbacks; and a work shop with one bench covered in tools, chain saws and assorted spare parts.

The first winter his cabin had only a dirt floor, which didn't bother Rolly too much, until the dirt turned to fine dust and covered everything, including the meals he cooked.

In the spring he bought planking and plywood and gave it gave it a proper floor. He also threw down some old rugs so he could walk barefoot without getting his feet frozen. There was no radio, no news, and no war. On a wood hauling trip to Whitehorse he met Rosie, took a liking to her, and hired her on as cook for his crew of one. She brought a tent, but one thing led to another and she moved into the cabin with him. She was not shy of hard work and was also damn handy with a chain saw. By the following winter life seemed to be moving along somewhat okay.

Rolly still had mortar rounds falling in his nightmares; still suffered night attacks of the Viet Cong. Rosie managed to deal with them, and with Rolly.

There is a Season   J. Harding Montgomery

She never complained, or asked difficult questions, until Rolly let it slip one day that he had a kid brother. Rolly said no more about Peter, but Rosie knew that there was a lot more to it than Rolly was letting on.

So she wrote a letter to Peter and gave it to Larry to address and mail. She knew that a reply would be quick, because if Peter was anything like his brother, he wouldn't waste time. He didn't and Rosie had no need, for the time being, for more questions.

"I have something for you, Rolly," Rosie said, back in the cabin at Ethel Lake.

Rolly looked at the letter, the postmark and looked up at Rosie.

"How'd you do it?"

"I did it, that's all that matters. Read it,"

Rolly put the letter on the table and poured himself a stiff drink of whiskey, went over to the window and leaned on the sill, stared out the window and didn't move.

"There's a lot more here than you know about, Rosie,"

"I know there's a lot I don't know, but whatever it is; the weight you're carrying is going to kill you,"

"You can see that?"

"Always."

Rolly turned from staring out the window, to staring at the letter on the table. He finished his drink and poured another.

"It's not going to open itself," Rosie said. "I'll open it and I'll read it to you, but you can't leave it on the table forever,"

"You better read it for me,"

Rosie picked up the letter. She sat down and poured herself a drink. "Its post marked last week." She took a deep breath and started reading.

Dear Rolly: I won't tell you where I got your address. It would just get you mad at your friend. We knew you went to Canada when you applied for Political Asylum. The Marines told Dad, and he told us. I don't know if you know about grandma, but her heart gave out. The past few years have been hard on everybody.

The war has been hard on the whole country, but I guess even in Canada you get the news. I looked on the map for where you are. I had to go to the library to get the map. Is there any gold left in the Yukon? I guess Alaska is no good; the Marines will get you there.

Dad hasn't mentioned your name since you left, but Mom still stares at your picture. Actually, I don't think anybody mentions your name. I think everybody is scared, but I don't know what they're scared of. This whole country has changed so much since you've been gone.

More and more Vietnam Vets are marching against the war. The F.B.I. watches them closely, but what can they do? So many are decorated, who can argue? In Washington a bunch of vets threw their medals over the White House fence; gave them all back to Nixon. Guess they didn't want them anymore. What did you do with your medals? For what it's worth, I hope you kept them. Don't give them back, don't throw them away. If you don't want them, give them to me.

I took a break and read over what I've written so far. I didn't change anything.

I walk okay now. Not much pain in my foot. I know it's almost funny sometimes, but when I use my cane, sometimes people think I'm a vet. I can see it in their eyes. I'll never forget that bitch in the airport that spat on you. I didn't understand her then, and I don't understand her now, but sometimes people look at me the same way she looked at you and I get a feeling for how you must have felt that day. I see the vets come home now; they're so, well, I can't explain it. I know you lost friends in Vietnam, and now I've lost friends in Vietnam. The war just keeps on going, and still the government can't tell us why. I still remember from before the war, you throwing the football to me and showing me how to run a pass pattern. Every time I see a football game on T.V. I think of that. For some reason now, when I see a pass being thrown, I hear guns and bombs. I don't watch much football anymore. Still can't catch very well, you never finished showing me. I did what you told me to do. I finished one year at Berkeley, but all the demonstrations got to me.

I don't know whether to join them or fight them. Last summer I started working at a fish cannery here in the bay. It's a desk job. Been at it since then and saved some money.

I asked Dad if he thought I should go to the Yukon. He didn't answer, so I asked Mom. She just started crying.   I know she worries about you; I can see it in her eyes. I have this to tell you. I went down to the travel agency and booked a flight for Whitehorse. I'll be there on Feb. 27, until the 30th. I'll be staying at the Miners' Inn. If you don't show up, I'll understand,

Peter.

Rosie looked up from the letter to Rolly. He drank his drink, and poured another.

"Tell me about Peter,"

"He's my kid brother,"

"What is he talking about, about your medals?"

"He said 'don't throw them away',"

"Where's yours?"

Rolly pointed to a green metal box under his workbench.

"Can I see them?"

"Leave them alone,"

"I leave them alone every night when you have nightmares, and every morning when the sheets are soaked in your sweat. I don't want to leave them alone anymore,"

Rolly shrugged. "Fair enough. What part of February is it?"

She looked at the back of Rolly's cigarette package. It had a small calendar on it. "It's February 26,"

"When did he say he was going to be in Whitehorse?"

"Tomorrow, 'till Monday. What's this he mentioned about his foot? That it doesn't hurt anymore? And football, he doesn't watch it anymore. What's that all about?"

"We played a lot of football when we were kids,"

"Football and gun shots? What's that all about?"

"Beats the shit outta me,"

"Bullshit. What's your business is your business, but some part of your bullshit is my business,"

Rolly looked at the green metal box under his workbench and nodded to himself. He reached into his pocket for his truck keys and handed them to Rosie.

"Little silver one," he said.

She took the keys and stood still for a few long seconds. Then she pulled out the box, sat on the floor and opened it.

Rolly poured another drink, "I haven't been into that thing since I loaded it,"

Rosie looked up from the open box. "Why not,"

"I know what's in it,"

She took out a large brown envelope. It was filled with pictures. The first one was a picture of Rolly standing in a group of Marines. They stood in a small semi-circle, arms around each other on a sandy beach. Behind them were tall palm trees.

"Where's this,"

Rolly grabbed the bottle and sat on the floor next to Rosie. "This is China Beach. We used to go there during stand-downs,"

"What's a 'stand down'?"

"Outta the bush for a few days,"

"Who are these guys?"

"My squad," Rolly leaned over Rosie's shoulder and started pointing at the men in the picture. "This is... this is Ernie something-or-other... he's from someplace in Kentucky. This is... Piss-Head we used to call him, hell of a nice guy, do anything for you, damn good with a sixty, lost him in the I Drang Valley,"

"Lost him? You mean killed?"

"Ya, that's what I mean, he was there, then he was in pieces."

Rosie put the picture down. She crossed her legs and folded her hands on her lap. She closed her eyes and was silent for a moment.

"Then what," she said.

"Picked up the pieces, put them in a bag and sent him home."

Rosie picked up Rolly's drink and finished it for him. She put the picture back in the envelope, and pulled out a small cloth bag and opened it. "These are your medals,"

"Yes, ma'am. That's a Silver Star, a Bronze Star, two Purple Hearts; and these here are all the usual you get for service in 'Nam,"

"What do they mean?"

"You get them for doing what we were there to do, what we were trained to do. Mostly just for staying alive. The Silver and Bronze I got for, well shit, I don't remember what I got those for. The purple hearts you get for bleeding."

"Bleeding? You mean like wounded?"

"Exactly,"

"On your shoulder and stomach,"

"That's it. See this here," Rolly picked up a small piece of shredded metal.

"Medic pulled that outta my shoulder, from a mortar barrage in the I Drang, same place Piss-Head got it. Now this here," Rolly lifted up a dented bullet, "came outta my stomach,"

"Same time,"

"No, a few months later. Place called Khe Shan. Not far from the I Drang,"

"These wounds, is that why you grunt so loud when you're lifting logs?'Cause of the pain,"

"No, that's 'cause it feels good to grunt when I'm working hard. No pain in the holes in me, 'cause they weren't deep. No muscle damage, just flesh wounds,"

"Are you going to keep your medals? Like your kid brother asked you too,"

"Keep 'em? Hell, if he wants 'em, he can have 'em. Start packing."

SAN FRANSISCO AIRPORT

Peter McGarret wiggled his toes to get the blood flowing into his foot, then climbed out of the taxi cab, lifted his duffel bag out of the cab trunk, easily heaved it up onto his left shoulder, leaned on his cane with his right hand, then limped into the San Francisco airport.

He quietly checked his bag as he fought back the urge to puke. Taking a seat, he waited for the announcement of his flights' departure. He gripped his cane handle in both hands and rested his chin on his knuckles. He tried to still his mind by watching the people at the airport. He looked to the arrivals from Hawaii, as he had done only a few short years before. Another group of veterans had arrived home. It was their eyes that held Peters' gaze.

Some walked straight and steady, spread their arms to hold friends and family. Peter watched as small mobs competed to hug and hold their own. The vets' eyes were tired and sagging. Others stood around as though they didn't know where to go. They set their bags on the floor and formed into small groups, lit smokes and stood around, waiting for something or someone. They stared into the distance, when there was no distance to stare into, just the wall a few feet from their faces.

Some knew exactly what they wanted to do. They went into the washroom, changed out of their uniforms and into their civilian clothes. Their eyes were fixed and firm and they marched straight out of the airport without a glance to anything or anyone. Peter gripped his cane and readied himself for a woman he remembered from the day he met Rolly at this airport.

He looked around carefully, but couldn't see the woman that spit on his brother. She wouldn't get away with it this time, that's for sure. He wanted to see her, catch her, take his cane, but he didn't see her and he felt strangely relieved by that.

He watched as all the vets left. No flags, no bands, no welcoming home ceremonies; the same way it was for his brother. Nothing had changed, the war just got longer and everybody got older.

The public address system announced his flight; he stood up and limped the long hallways to his flight. He was used to people staring at him and his cane as he kept close to the wall and out of their way.

They quickly walked around him as though he were no more than a minor obstacle. He didn't pay them any attention, it didn't bother him anymore. He heard the whispers he'd heard so many times before;

'Probably shot in Vietnam.'

'Land mine in Vietnam.'

'Another wounded Vietnam Vet'.

He used to deny he was a vet, thought it was an insult to all the real Vietnam Vets, but after awhile he just ignored them. It was too much work to fight them all, to set the record straight, to tell them that he wasn't shot in Vietnam; that he was shot..., but that part was too much.

He was the last to board, the last to be shown to his seat. He looked around him. There were other young men on the plane, maybe eighteen or nineteen. Two were busy in their bible study. Behind them were two hippie types too nervous to be stoned.

More surfer types, their California suntans drained away to show white fear, all of them taking the direct flight to Vancouver, Canada.

Peter had given a lot of thought about those who chose Canada over their military obligations. He used to have strong opinions about the war and those who turned their backs on their country, and strong conclusions about them. He used to understand, back when things were simple. Now, he had no conclusions, no opinions. He'd even run out of questions. After losing so many friends and not knowing why, after Rolly lost so many friends and couldn't tell him why, he didn't understand anything anymore..

So many people seemed so sure of so many things, and now he wasn't sure of anything.

Sometimes he wondered if everybody knew something he didn't know. Maybe there was a big secret out there, and nobody would let him in on it. Since he had made the decision to find Rolly, to see how he was doing in this country called Canada, he didn't think much about the other stuff. He wanted a reason, any reason, to be able to look forward to something again.

He wanted to talk to one of the draft dodgers; he knew they were all draft dodgers. Anyone of them would do. He didn't care about their bibles, long hair, or surfer attitudes.

He just wanted to know how they felt, why they were doing what they were doing. Could they tell him something he didn't know? Could they help him understand? But he had to think about himself for a moment. What if Rolly hadn't shot him? Would he have gone ahead and volunteered for Vietnam, or would he, after all he had seen and heard about the war, leave his home and family for Canada? Just like his Vietnam Vet brother who knew more about the war than he could ever imagine.

He shook his head and threw away the question. All it had ever given him was a headache.

The plane took off and Peter stared out the window and watched the skyline of his hometown slip off into the distance. It came to him that he had never left the coast before. All his life had been spent within sight, or at least a short drive, of the ocean. Now he was flying over the ocean and he couldn't see the land.

He was going to a country he had never been to before and knew nothing about, and that made him feel good. The muscles in his back and legs loosened up, the constant nagging pain in his foot went away, so he stretched out to get more comfortable, and was surprised to discover that he could get comfortable.

He realized that for the first time since he'd been shot, he wasn't seriously tight on the inside.

VANCOUVER AIRPORT

Janos and Tara made the Vancouver Airport just in time. They checked their bags and Janos half carried Tara to the flight. They had the two aisle seats and a young man with a cane sat in the third seat, by the window. He held the handle of his cane in his hands and rested his chin on his knuckles. He was staring intently out the window, watching the other planes at the Vancouver airport and didn't notice Janos and Tara taking the seats next to him.

Janos helped Tara into her seat, as her leg was stiff and sore from the run to the flight. She held onto Janos' arm with her left hand while her right hand held onto the seat in front of her. As she lowered herself into her seat she accidentally hit the young man's cane with her cane. He looked up, unaware that they had sat next to him. He stared at Tara's' cane, then at her. Tara stared at his cane, and then she smiled at him.

She's old, he thought. Not surprising for an old woman to need a cane.

He's too young, Tara thought, to need a cane.

She smiled again at him, "Why do you have a cane," she said.

He gave her the same answer he gave to everyone, the same way. "Car accident,"

Tara nodded. She didn't believe him.

The young man heard her accent, paid little attention to it, then said, "How'd you get your cane,"

"Oh," Tara said, as she massaged her leg. "That was a long time ago,"

Janos leaned over to the young man. "You are going to Whitehorse,"

He turned to Janos, without showing any emotion. "That's where the plane goes." He thought he might have been rude, and he saw no reason to be rude to these old folks. Maybe her question about his cane was just that, an innocent question. She didn't have that look in her eyes, that knowing look that was in the eyes of all the others who asked about his cane. After all, these old folks had accents.

They were probably from some distant country and didn't even know there was a war going on.

"You're going to Whitehorse, too," Peter said.

"We're going to Elsa,"

This got Peters' attention. "Elsa?" He'd seen it on the map.

"Yes," said Janos. "My brother and our son are there,"

"I have a brother not far from Elsa," he said.

"You're going to visit him," asked Tara.

The question stunned him. What's a visit? A visit was something you did after church on Sundays.

Janos saw the look on the young man's face and turned away, because he knew the sickness in his eyes.

The young man turned away and stared out the window again, absorbed by this question of just what a 'visit' was. He wasn't sure what it was that he was doing, but whatever it was, it wasn't just a 'visit'. He turned back to Janos and said the only thing he could say, "Yes, a visit,"

The stewardess came by, told them to fasten their seat belts, asked them if they wanted a drink. They all ordered beer.

As they fastened their seat belts Peter slipped back into himself, to picking up Rolly at the airport when he returned home from Vietnam, Rolly fighting with their father, their mother crying, Rolly not even staying home for dinner, and when Rolly came back to the house and...

Looking at his cane he had to ask, is this whole thing just a 'visit'? He hated having these questions again, these questions that didn't have answers. He wanted to go back to when questions had answers, but by now too much had changed to have questions and answers that came in pairs. Now he loosely gripped his cane, rested his chin on his knuckles and stared into the clouds.

Tara stretched her leg, carefully placed her cane between Janos and herself, and then settled into her seat. She didn't look at Peter; felt that it was best to leave him alone. She felt his presence, and she knew he felt hers.

Peter squirmed in his seat. It was too hard. The seat in front of him was too close, he couldn't stretch his legs, the seat behind him was too close, he couldn't lean back.

He looked around for the stewardess.

"Where's the beer," Peter said.

"Wait 'till the plane takes off," Tara said to Peter.

The stewardess walked by checking seat belts.

"Where's my beer," Janos asked the stewardess.

"Wait 'till the plane takes off," she said.

Janos began to fidget. He turned to Tara. "What do you think Josef will say?"

"I don't know. Perhaps 'hello',"

"Ahh, it's been so long,"

"Too long," said Tara.

"Do you think he will be angry with me?"

"Better he be angry with you, than angry without you,"

Peter snapped his head around to Tara. His eyes were tight and focused. "What did you say," he demanded.

Tara was taken aback by his abruptness. "Excuse me,"

Peter softened. "I'm sorry. You mentioned something about being angry,"

Tara looked back at Peter. His eyes were too deep for such a young man. She wished the beer would arrive soon. "Better to be angry with someone," she said, "than angry without them. If two people are angry with each other, and they are together, then they can work it out. If they're apart, their anger will never leave them,"

Peter thought about that. He nodded slowly as the plane rumbled into the air.

"Where are you from," he asked.

"Vancouver,"

"No, I mean your accent,"

"Hungary,"

He nodded again.

"Where are you from," Tara asked.

"California. When did you leave Hungary?"

"1956. When did you leave California?"

"I haven't left. I'm just... visiting,"

"Your brother,"

"Yes," Peter reached out his hand, "I'm Peter McGarret,"

"My name is Tara Kovacs, and this is my husband, Janos,"

Janos leaned over to shake Peters' hand.

"Listen,'" Peter went on, "when I was in University, I took a course in European History. We covered the Hungarian Revolution in 1956. Were you part of that?"

Janos turned to look up and down the aisle. He kept looking, and then turned to stare at Peter. "That's when we left,"

Tara took a deep breath and spoke. "It was... many years ago. We... had to leave. Canada was very good in taking us in from the war," she smiled at Peter.

This time Peter smiled back. "Canada seems to be very good at taking people in, people from wars,"

"Are you leaving the war?" Janos said.

"You mean Vietnam,"

"Yes, are you leaving your home because of that war?" Janos waited quietly for an answer.

"No, no. I don't have to; the military doesn't want me,"

"Doesn't want you? What army doesn't want a young man?"

"My foot, my cane,"

Janos looked at Peters' cane and nodded. "Your foot made you a lucky young man. It saved you,"

"Saved me?"

"Saved you from Vietnam, I read in the papers that many young men come to Canada. Many young men die in Vietnam, brave young men. Wars take too many young men,"

The stewardess came with their beers. Janos took them and handed one to Tara and one to Peter.

"We will have a toast," Janos said. "To all the brave young men," Peter looked at his beer, then Janos, then Tara, then the window. He stared out and watched the clouds drift away and leave an open clear blue sky, above a land called Canada. He turned back to Janos.

"To all the brave young men," said Peter and they tapped their beers and drank.

"My brother fought in Vietnam," said Peter.

"This is the brother you are to visit?" said Janos.

"Yes,"

"He came home from his war," Tara smiled. "I am happy for your mother,"

Peter nodded, "Thank you,"

"He will meet you at the airport?" Tara said.

"I wrote him a letter, I don't know if he got it. I'll wait and see if he shows up,"

"And if he doesn't show up?"

"Just go home,"

Janos leaned across Tara and tapped Peter firmly on the knee. "You say your brother is near Elsa?"

"Somewhere around there,"

"Then you come with us, we find him. You don't go home without your brother."

KILIAN BARRACKS,
BUDAPEST
NOVEMBER, 1956

Stephan watched carefully from the roof top as the tank cautiously approached the Kilian Barracks. He'd lost count of the shells Janos fired and didn't know if he was out, or leading the tank into a trap. There was only one answer when Janos didn't fire at the tank, when it aimed its' barrel to a point ten feet above Janos' head, then fired.

Stephan gave himself the cross of Jesus as the barracks shuddered and belched out clouds of smoke and dust. Stephan gave the order and the tank was covered in Molotov cocktails. The flames drove the crew from the tank, right into rifle fire. Seconds later, Stephan was running to find his brother.

Janos lay on the ground floor of the barracks and shook his head clear of dust. He heard footsteps crunching across the broken pavement and someone calling out,

"Janos... Janos..."

"Here, I'm here," Janos said.

Stephan peeked through the blown out window and smiled down at Janos.

"Ahh, you look good little brother, you look very good,"

Stephan crawled through the window, slid down the anti-tank barrel, and lay across the bricks next to Janos.

"Stinks in here," he said.

"That's 'cause you're here," Janos said.

"You had me scared. When I saw that last round hit the building, I thought,"

"Well you thought wrong, didn't you?"

"Your leg's bleeding," Stephan said.

"How'd you see that in this mess?"

"Shut up," Stephan said as he felt Janos' wounded leg. "Does this hurt?"

"No," Janos cringed.

"Well, let me try again," Stephan said as he felt again. "Does this hurt?"

Janos cringed again. "Well, if you quit grabbing it, it wouldn't hurt,"

Stephan reached into his medics' bag, took out a pocketknife, cut away Janos' pant leg to expose the wound, pulled out a bandage and wrapped the wound.

"Just a cut, not so bad," Stephan said.

"Doc Stephan, on the job," Janos chuckled.

Stephan shook his head, rolled his eyes upward, then looked down at his little brother, "That'll be enough of that."

Janos winked at Stephan. "Enough of what,"

"Get up," Stephan put his arm under Janos and lifted him to his feet.

"What now," Janos said.

"Look-out says the tanks have gone back east, probably all the way to the border. Major Malater says we should go home and check on our families. Can you walk to my new car?"

"Your new car?"

Stephan smiled and winked at Janos. "Found it,"

Janos went out the window first, pushed up by Stephan, then took a position watching, waiting, listening. He waved for Stephan to follow, but didn't see how Stephan climbed out the window, how he rolled onto his side, the pained difficulty he had standing up.

Janos and Stephan leaned on each other and looked around them.

"Remember the last time it was like this," Janos said.

"We were hardly children,"

"Who's worse; the Nazis or the Russians?"

"Good question," Stephan said. "Come on and I'll show you our new car, then we have to check on Tara."

KENO CITY

Steve went back to his room and sat on the bed. Now what? He'd told him Mom about Uncle Joe, she would tell Dad, Dad would shit. What about his heart? Maybe he shouldn't have told them. Maybe he should have got on a plane and brought Uncle Joe home, and then? What if they couldn't solve this problem of theirs? Well, at least he would be there if his Dad had a heart attack, then he could, could do what? Maybe he should have just had a drink with the crazy old bugger and left him alone, but it was too late for all that, he'd done what he'd done and now it was time to get on with it.

He packed his duffel bag. Slinging it over his shoulder, he opened the door, stopped, turned to see if he'd left anything behind. He couldn't see anything, so he started looking.

Under the bed, nothing; opened the drawers that he never opened in the first place, nothing; behind the door, in the corners; nothing. Then he went back to his bed and sat down.

He reopened his duffel bag, took everything out and spread it all over the bed. Everything that was supposed to be there, was there. He checked one more time and even checked to see if there was anything there, that wasn't supposed to be there. Nothing.

He quickly repacked his duffel bag, threw it up on his shoulder and left the room. He went across the road to make reservations for Rolly and Rosie. He looked through the window and saw a short stocky man in an old ragged bathrobe. He had his back to Steve, and he was making coffee. Steve banged on the door.

The man looked up and came to the door.

"Not open," he said in a thick Italian accent. "Come back later,"

"When,"

The man sighed, and then opened the door. "Coffee in minute,"

"You take reservations here," Steve said.

"Yes, reservations. When,"

"Saturday,"

"How many you have,"

How many, thought Steve. Rolly and Rosie, me and Uncle Joe? Jan?

"Four, maybe five,"

"What you want?"

"What's your best?"

"No get smart. What you want?"

"Spaghetti, meat balls, the works,"

"Every Saturday night I cook spaghetti, meat balls. I don't cook 'works'. What are works?"

"Well, whatever you cook with spaghetti and meat balls,"

"Many people come from Elsa, Mayo, even Whitehorse for my spaghetti and meat balls. I cook chicken; I cook lasagna, what else you want,"

"That'll be fine. Thanks,"

"What name for reservation?"

"Kovacs,"

"You Hungarian,"

Steve thought that over. "Not so simple, now I am,"

"Now? What were you before?"

"Used to be Canadian,"

"Where you born,"

"Budapest,"

"Once you are Hungarian, you are always Hungarian. Just like I am always Italian. I am Luigi from Naples," Luigi put out his hand. "Don't matter where you live now, matters where you come from, who you come from, family before country. Canada is place on map, no history for you or me,"

Steve sipped on his coffee and thought about that. Was Canada just a place on the map because it had no family history?

"What was that you said about Canada and a map?"

Luigi sat down and motioned for Steve to join him. He poured them both a cup of coffee. "I said Canada is a place on the map,"

"Yes,"

"Canada has a little history for me, a little more for you, more for our children. You and I, we are like a door hinges; we swing back and forth in the wind until we get rusty and are stuck in place. Then we are too old to make a difference. Or, at least, I am. You still have to find out which way your wind takes you,"

Steve sipped on his coffee and couldn't make any sense of what Luigi was saying. But he knew that somewhere, there was something he should listen to.

"So just being in Canada, being a resident or landed immigrant or whatever, doesn't make you Canadian,"

"Oh no, not at all. You and me we live here, we haven't fought a war for Canada; Canada has none of our blood. Maybe some day it will take the blood of our children, I hope not because I have seen war, but, it might happen. That will make them Canadian,"

"You have to fight for a country to make it home?"

"No," Luigi laughed as he sipped his coffee, "but it helps,"

Luigi looked at Steve very intently. "I know some Canadians who are more Italian that they are Canadian. You know why,"

Steve shook his head, "No,"

"During the war, the Canadian army invades Italy. We Italians kick out Mussolini, kick out Hitler. Canadians die on Italian soil to help us do this. They bleed for Italy. You ask me; maybe they're born in Canada, but they're more Italian than Canadian."

Lord, Steve thought, now what? As if I don't have enough to worry about with Americans, Hungarians, and Czechoslovakians, all telling me things they think are so god damn important; whether or not I'm Canadian or Hungarian. I can't get an answer out of them without a god damn history lesson and somebody else's god damn war and now I got an Italian with an obsession with god damn rusty hinges. What's with this Yukon? When is somebody going to give me a straight answer to a straight question? The only guy I met in this territory that can give me a straight answer to a straight question is Rolly, and where the hell is he?

There is a Season   **J. Harding Montgomery**

What would he say, how would he explain all this shit?

A truck rumbled up to the cafe' and ground to a stop. The driver came in with a metal thermos and filled it with coffee. As Steve thought over what Luigi was talking about and where the hell was Rolly and what would he say, the driver walked out and said, "Going down to Pelly, Luigi, see you later,"

Steve jumped up. "Can I get a ride?"

It was a quiet ride to Pelly Crossing. The driver said little while Steve thought a lot.

He gazed out the window, but the snow and the trees and the hills and the valleys all ran in and out of each other in a blurry mesh of colors and images of blood stained maps, rusty door hinges, and faded black and white photographs.

Rolly would explain it all, he would have the answers.

In three hours Steve was walking into the Pelly Crossing Lodge. Eleanor picked up her book, and without taking her eyes off it, poured him a coffee. "It's too early for beer. I'll make you a sandwich,"

Steve stood still, feeling somehow humbled by Eleanor. He very gently lowered his bag into a chair. Then he sat next to it.

Eleanor glared at his bag, and then glanced at the corner by the door. Steve picked up his bag and put it in the corner by the door. Eleanor nodded, then handed him his coffee and sandwich and went back into her book.

"Listen Eleanor, can I ask you a question," Steve said between mouthfuls. She put down her book and looked at Steve and let out a sigh. "What?"

"A guy in Keno City told me that you have to bleed for Canada before you're Canadian,"

"Luigi got lots of opinions,"

"What do you think?"

"You named Canada,"

"What?"

"You white people named Canada, then you got lots of opinions on what to do with it, what to do with us. You never ask us anything. Just ask us if bleeding for a country makes it yours. My people done one hell of a lot more bleeding for this country that yours ever did. Let me ask you a question,"

"Sure,"

"What makes you think this place you call Canada is yours to have opinions about?"

"Oh Jesus, Eleanor, I'm just trying to sort out what Luigi said,"

"You got questions about this country? You should ask the people who were here long before you got here,"

He knew that was more than he could handle. But like what Luigi had to say, he knew there was something in there he should listen to.

"Rolly been here yet," he said, ducking as Eleanor gave him a nasty glance for changing the subject.

"He'll be here soon," she sighed.

"How do you know?"

"Rosie said so. You gotta call Vancouver again,"

"Oh, shit,"

"Told you so,"

"What do you mean 'told you so',"

"What did you forget?"

"Holy shit, I forgot my Uncle Josef. I've got to get him on the phone to my folks,"

"I knew you forgot something. It always happens. You should pay more attention to what you do and not to what you want to do,"

"What?"

"What you do and what you want to do are two different things. That's why you forgot your uncle. You weren't watching yourself,"

"What are you? Some kind of philosopher?"

"No, I'm a bartender. It's my job,"

Steve sipped his coffee, then the door opened and he looked up to see Rosie.

She stopped, placed her hands squarely on her hips and stared at Steve. Steve stared back, then down. Eleanor looked up, sighed, and then went back into her book.

Steve shuddered. He felt things going downhill in a hurry and Rosie was going to give him a very rough landing.

She poured herself a coffee, didn't stop glaring at Steve, who was slowly sinking in his chair. She came over, sat next to him. She put down her coffee, lit a cigarette. She took a puff, held it in while she stared at Steve, then blew the smoke in his face. She didn't speak hard or mean, or soft or sweet, just directly.

"What's the story on this guy that looks like you?"

"He's my Uncle Joe,"

She smiled, this time, warmly. "For real?"

"He's got pictures of me and him. When I was a baby,"

Rosie put her elbow on the table and rested her chin in her hand. She didn't stop smiling. "A brand new Uncle,"

"Well, I don't know about brand new. He's older than me. He gave me this." He took off his toque and showed it to her.

She took it, looked at the flag, and then gave it back. "What's with the flag,"

"Hungarian flag with no hammer and sickle, before the communists took over,"

"Far out, before the communists. What's that mean?"

Steve thought about that. "Hungarian revolution, 1956,"

"This new uncle of yours, he was in on that?"

"Ya, so were my folks,"

"So how come you never met him before?"

"Good question," sighed Steve.

"Told your folks about him?"

"Ya,"

"What'd they say?"

"Mom freaked. I haven't talked to my Dad yet,"

"I take it they have some kind of family feud going on?"

"Far as I can see,"

"So where do you fit in?"

"I don't know. I know that Mom wants to talk to him. She's going to talk to Dad. I was supposed to put them all on the phone at six tonight,"

"You left him behind?"

"Yes,"

Rosie took a puff on her cigarette again, blew the smoke in his face again. "Rolly'll have your balls for bookends if he finds out you left him behind. Leaving folks behind doesn't sit well with him,"

Steve shuddered at the thought of having to deal with a pissed-off Rolly.

"Well, what are you doing here then," Rosie said.

"I wanted to talk to Rolly. He knows about these things,"

"Right now, Rolly's got his plate full with his own family,"

"He's talked to them?"

"No. He got a letter from his kid brother,"

"I didn't know he had a kid brother,"

"You know that letter the bus driver gave to you, to give to Larry,"

"Yes,"

"That's the letter. We're going to Whitehorse to see him."

"What are you going to do about getting your uncle on the phone with your folks?"

"Ummm, I think I'll call home and tell them I'm a hundred miles away and have to do it later,"

"How much later,"

"I don't know,"

"You can't leave this one 'till later,"

Eleanor put her book down. "That's what I told him. Told him he wasn't paying attention,"

"That right, Steve? You not paying attention?"

Steve returned his gaze to the floor. "Yes,"

"Paying too much attention to yourself and forgot everybody else," Rosie said.

"He missed the main point," Eleanor said.

"What's the main point?" Steve said.

"It's your job to get your family together," Eleanor said.

"That's a big point,"

"It's a big job," Eleanor said. "Only you can do it. They need you to do it,"

"Where's Rolly?" Steve said.

"He's asleep in the truck. Leave him outta it. He's got enough on his mind,"

Steve looked up at Rosie. "If I pay for the gas, will you drive me back to Elsa? So I can put them on the phone,"

Rosie looked up to the ceiling. "Get in the truck. Now."

Rosie took the last sip of her coffee as Steve headed out the door. She paid for his sandwich and coffee. "Hey, Eleanor, you ever get tired of babysitting these white people?"

She chuckled. "I'm a bartender, it's my job. What's your excuse?"

"Gimme some time to think one up."

Eleanor smiled and went back into her book.

Steve cautiously approached Rolly's truck. He peered in the window and watched Rolly snore. He was happy to see both eyes closed. He quietly and firmly gripped the door handle, hoping to open the door without waking Rolly. He pressed down on the latch and it wouldn't open. He pulled gently, still didn't open. He pulled harder, still didn't open.

A little harder, harder, still harder yet, then it sprang open with the grating screech of rusty door hinges. Steve shuddered, thinking of maps. Rolly didn't move.

He lightly placed his bag on the floor, and even though it had only been a couple of days, he felt as if he was back home after a long absence. Dog lifted his head and yawned, showing his mouthful of long white teeth. Steve smiled at Dog, Dog smiled back.

Steve quietly pulled door shut. The latch wouldn't hold. He pulled again, still didn't hold. A little harder, still harder yet, then he pushed out a bit and gave it a good pull, the door slammed shut, and Steve felt the shock wave go back and forth across the cab. Still Rolly snored. He was wrapped up in his old sleeping bag, and it looked like he had pieces of pizza in his beard. Steve smiled, remembering a day in Whitehorse, how long ago was that?

Rosie yanked open the door. The squeaking and grating of the hinges made Steve jump up, he hit his head on the ceiling and the thump from the hit made the windows shake. Still Rolly snored.

She jumped in and slammed the door shut; hit the key, the engine coughed once, twice, then started purring. "How he ever keeps this bucket of bolts running is beyond me," Rosie yelled as she put the truck in gear and it bounced up and down in the potholes.

"I really appreciate this, Rosie,"

"You better."

"I don't," Rolly said, one eye open.

"Go back to sleep, you're still tired," Rosie said with a glare at Steve.

"Okay." Rolly went back to snoring.

On the way back to Elsa, Steve had a hard time trying to figure why he felt he had been gone for so long. Uncle Josef was a long lost relative, that much he knew, but why the sense of time loss? Why did he feel the way he did, when he couldn't explain it to himself, and when he asked other people they only answered him with more questions? No matter how hard he tried, he couldn't keep his mind focused on any one question. He'd get half way to an answer and then another question would push its way into his head and he would have to deal with that one. Half way through that one and another would push in and on and on it went.

He knew that what he was doing was right, but he couldn't escape the feeling that it was all going to come crashing down on him and the whole bloody world was going to take one big bite out of him.

Unless Rolly would wake up and explain it all to him, which he did with a growl. "What the hell are we doing back in Elsa?"

"Quiet, Rolly," Rosie said. "Steve has to make a phone call, then we're back to Whitehorse,"

"No phone at Pelly Crossing? Did Eleanor throw it out again?"

"No, Eleanor did not throw the phone out again. Steve has to get his Uncle Joe on the phone with his folks,"

"'Uncle Joe', who the fuck is Uncle Joe,"

"That Joe Smith guy, he's my uncle,"

"Your uncle? Is this family reunion week or what?"

Steve shrugged, "Seems so. Rosie tells me your kid brother is in Whitehorse,"

"That's what she tells me. How long's this phone call gonna take? You staying or coming back to Whitehorse or what,"

"I don't know,"

"Shit," Rolly gave Steve a nasty look. Steve didn't like getting nasty looks from Rolly, they scared him. He thought he'd change the topic; say something else, something to get him off his back. He remembered the front page from the newspaper the bartender was reading in the Elsa Bar. "Rolly, they called off the peace negotiations in Paris. The communists walked out again."

Rosie snapped her head around and gave Steve a look that said if she had a knife she'd cut his throat.

Her eyes burned as she slowly shook her head back and forth, telling Steve he'd done something terribly wrong.

"Steve," Rosie said sternly, barely keeping her anger in, breathing through her nose, talking through her teeth, "We don't talk about how the war is going. It's not good for Rolly,"

Rolly looked like he'd just been kicked in the balls and it knocked the wind out of him. He sighed, patted Rosie on the shoulder, "It's okay, Rosie. Steves' okay; he doesn't know he fucked up."

Steve began to wilt, felt like puking. Now Rolly was hurt and Steve had hurt him and that made Steve feel like absolute shit. After all they had been through the past few days, the miles they put down, not only on the truck, but on themselves. How much Steve felt like Rolly was an older brother, feeding him when Hank took all his money; giving him a job after he had turned him down to go gold mining in a job that wasn't there, taking the time to explain his father to him so he'd better understand him.

He'd saved him from falling off the cliff, held his head while he puked out his truck window. He'd even wiped his puke covered mouth on the sleeve of Rolly's coat that Rolly gave him in the cold to help him with his frostbite. Now he'd tried to change the topic so Rolly wouldn't stay pissed at him, and thinking only of himself, he had hurt Rolly.

"Man, you look like shit," Rolly quietly said. "It's an honest mistake, you thought I'd want to know about that, but I don't. I still have friends over there, and I don't want any of them to die for nothing. I just want the war to end so they can all come home,"

"I'm sorry, Rolly. I truly am, I thought you'd want to know," Steve felt himself getting smaller and smaller.

"Look at these, Steve," Rolly pointed to the two blast heaters stacked over his transmission. "Know what I tore out to make room for those,"

"No,"

"I tore out the radio. I don't like the news, don't like the cold either. So if you get some news out of the 'Nam, and it's anything but the troops are coming home, I don't want to hear about it. Got it?"

"Got it,"

"So now you owe me a beer. Do you want me to give you some more money so you can buy me a beer?"

"No, I haven't spent all the money you already gave me," Steve was choking on his sobs.

"Jesus Christ, Steve, don't break up on me, it's an honest mistake," Rolly put his arms around Steve and gave him a hug.

Steves' knees turned to rubber, his shoulders caved in, his head went down onto Rolly's shoulder.
"God damn it, Steve," Rolly stood back and hollered at Steve. "Stand up straight, suck in your gut, shoulders back, and stick out your tits. Now go get your Uncle Joe, meet me in the bar, and buy me a beer before you run out of my money."

Rosie put her knife away, patted Steve on the shoulder and quietly said, "Do what Rolly says."

Steve took another deep sigh, wiped his frostbitten cheeks dry, pulled down his toque and headed up the long slippery walkway to Uncle Joe's room.

"You are late," Uncle Joe sat quietly on his bed.

He inhaled deeply on his cigarette, pushed the butt out into his overflowing ashtray and motioned for Steve to sit down.

"You have talked to Janos and Tara,"

"Yes, no. Just to Mom,"

"And she says,"

"She wants to know how you are,"

Uncle Joe spread his arms. "This is how I am. You didn't talk to your father,"

"He wasn't home,"

"Does Tara say how he is?"

"Well, he's okay. She doesn't know how he's going to take it that you're here, I don't think they knew you were alive. What else don't I know?"

"About what,"

"Why didn't they even know if you're alive?"

Uncle Joe started rolling another cigarette. He looked up from his rolling to look at Steve with the deep eyes that had scared Steve before, and they scared him again.

"One of the last things I did, before I left Budapest, after you were safe in Austria, was burn some lists and make some new ones. Remember, the Russians didn't know I could read or write. One of these was a list of the dead,"

"The dead," Steve said.

"Yes, the dead," Uncle Joe took a match and lit it, turned it around in his hand and watched it burn almost to the end, then lit his cigarette.

He took a deep puff, held it in as he thought for a moment, then exhaled the blue smoke till it almost filled the room.

"Then I put your names on it,"

"Our names,"

"And mine,"

Steve waved his hand in front of his face to clear the cigarette smoke from his eyes.

Then he looked into Uncle Joes' eyes and they had changed again. Now they were soft and fearful.

"Why?" Steve said.

Uncle Joe took another deep puff on his cigarette, held it while he looked at Steve, then blew out the smoke. "I put the list in the office, with all the other lists, and left for the border. When the Russians got that list, they knew who to search for and who to forget.   That list, with your names on it, meant no more Kovacs in Hungary, and no Russians looking for any of you. Not even for me. In Hungary, or wherever the Russians look, we are all dead,"

"So the people who are dead on the list are really alive in another country?"

"Some of them,"

"You brought the dead back to life?"

"You could say that. I knew the Russians would use the lists for propaganda. The Red Cross got the lists, and published them. Anybody with family in Hungary could read them, so I suppose Janos got a copy, and thought I was killed in the fighting. I put many who escaped on the lists; maybe I put your Hungarians friends from the bar on the lists. The rest were really dead,"

Steve took off his toque and felt the flag.

"You like that toque?"

"Very much, yes."

"Good. So, by now, Janos knows I am here,"

"Yes,"

"This is also good. Tell me, what do you think your mother and father will think?"

"Well, Mom was kind of shook up, she was worried about Dad. She didn't know how he would take it,"

"Janos is strong. He has his fathers' heart. Do you think he will still… will you tell him what I told you? That I had to,"

"I'll tell him," Steve said. "One way or another, I'll get it straight between you two,"

"Good. You want a drink,"

"Palinka?"

"Yes,"

"No,"

"Your mother, she says 'don't drink Palinka'',"

"Yes,"

"I thought so. You like beer,"

"Yes,"

"I have some for you."

Uncle Joe opened his window. There was a space between the window and a sheet of plastic that was nailed to the outside frame, and lined up in the space were twelve bottles of beer. They were all covered in frost and Uncle Joe took one and popped off the cap. Frozen foam slowly pushed its' way out of the neck.

"If you were on time, they would be cold and not half frozen,"

"Sorry,"

"Tough shit, drink it anyways,"

"You know, I had quite a bit the other night," Steve said.

"I know. You puked on my floor. You better now,"

"Sure, thanks for cleaning up after me,"

"I told you, I have done it before, many times. When you were much younger,"

"A baby," smiled Steve.

"Yes, a baby. You are no longer a baby now, so you have your bee Little Stephan, and then we call Janos,"

"Are you nervous," Steve said.

"Are you?"

"Well, I don't know if 'nervous' is the right word to describe how I feel. I feel angry,"

Uncle Joe started rolling another cigarette, without ever taking his eyes off Steve. "Angry,"

"Yes,"

"What makes you angry?"

"What happened to you, why I don't know anything about it."

Uncle Joe lit his cigarette, inhaled deeply, held it in and stared at Steve.

Steve had learned this much so far about Uncle Joe; when he inhaled deeply, he was thinking deeply, and he should listen closely to what he was about to say. But he was still uneasy with the intensity of his eyes.

"I will ask Janos about that, for you, and for me. Finish your beer."

Steve's beer had thawed enough for him to drink it down quickly. He put his toque back on his head, and enjoyed the smile it brought out of Uncle Joe.

They went back out into the blowing snow and freezing wind, across to a pool hall, where a phone was nailed to a post on the front porch. Steve picked up the phone and turned to Uncle Joe.

"Ready,"

"I have spent many years wondering if this would ever happen. I am ready,"

Steve took a deep breath, held that in, and then dialed. The phone rang at his parents' home in Vancouver. Then it rang again, and again and again. He let it ring five more times until he was sure they weren't home.

"Maybe some other place?" Uncle Joe said.

"Not that I know of. I'm going to call Dad at work. Maybe he got stuck with more overtime,"

Uncle Joe shook his head. "No. Janos doesn't work overtime if he belongs at home,"

Steve looked at Uncle Joe and nodded. "You're right. Dad don't follow orders he don't like,"

"I know," Uncle Joe said.

"I'm going to call anyways,"

"You do that."

Steve called the machine shop and talked to Cathy, the afternoon shift secretary. Steve and Cathy's son, Ricky, played on the same soccer team. Janos was their coach. Cathy and Tara volunteered together at Vancouver General Hospital. They had all been close since the Kovacs' arrival in Vancouver.

"Listen Cathy, any idea if Dad is working tonight?"

"Where the hell have you been? You just disappeared and your folks have been worried sick. What kind of son are you,"

"What do you mean what kind of son? Listen, do you know if Dad is working tonight,"

Cathy stated to yell into the phone. "Where are you? This phone connection is the shits,"

"I'm in the Yukon,"

"Where's that? Is that part of Alaska?"

"No, it's part of Canada,"

"Which province is it in?"

"It's not a province, it's a territory,"

"There's a territory in a province in Canada? I never knew that,"

"It's not a territory in a province; it's a territory on its own,"

"On its own? And still in Canada,"

"Yes! Is Dad working tonight?"

Cathy was yelling even louder now. "What's that? This phone connection is the shits,"

Now Steve started to yell back at Cathy. "Is Dad working tonight?"

"Is your Dad working tonight? Is that what you said?"

"Yes,"

"No. Tara came and got him and they took off to the airport,"

"Airport? Where did they go?"

"Where did they what,"

"Go. Where did they go?"

"I don't know,"

"Do you know when they left?"

"When they what,"

"Left. When did they leave?"

"Oh, this afternoon,"

"Thank you, Cathy,"

"Are you coming home? Don't you have exams coming up?"

"No,"

"Well, you don't have to get nasty about it,"

"Goodbye, Cathy,"

"Bye, Stephan. See you when you get home. When's that going to be,"

"I don't know,"

"Okay. Bye."

Steve turned to Uncle Joe and was about to speak when Uncle Joe spoke first. "Airport,"

"Yes," Steve said.

"They are on their way," Uncle Joe said.

"On their way where?"

"You don't know," Uncle Joe said with that scary smile again.

"You think they're coming here,"

"Yes," Uncle Joe said.

"Well, now what," Steve said.

"We wait, or we go to meet them,"

"Meet them where,"

"Whitehorse, the nearest airport. Steve, do you know how to drive,"

"You don't,"

"Where would I drive to? I haven't driven for, well, since I left,"

"We've got a ride, come with me." Steve sprinted off the porch, down more slippery stairways and back to the Elsa Bar.

Steve walked into the bar, looked around, found Rosie sitting in a corner, Rolly sitting next to her, back to the wall.

"Where's your new Uncle Joe," Rolly said. Steve spun around. No Uncle Joe. He went to the door and looked through, looked in the bathroom.

"He's gone," Steve said.

"Steve," Rolly had that nasty look again, "Did you lose your new Uncle?"

Steve began to panic, he couldn't take upsetting Rolly twice in the same lifetime. Did the other Hungarians get to Uncle Joe? Did he fall off the stairway?

"Listen Rolly, can you wait here? He's probably gone back to his room,"

"Clock's ticking, Steve. Gotta make Whitehorse tonight,"

Steve ran back to Uncle Joes' room, found him sitting on the bed, rolling a cigarette. "Where'd you go?"

"I didn't go anywhere,"

"I've got a friend in the bar. He going to Whitehorse right now,"

"I don't know your friend,"

"So? You can meet him,"

"I don't meet people,"

"What?"

"I don't like them,"

"You don't like people?"

"No."

Steve sat down, then he stood up, went to the window, opened it and grabbed a beer.

He popped open the cap, watched the frozen foam slowly seep out the neck, then bit it off and chewed on it. He looked at Uncle Joe, waiting for an answer.

"Now you want me to go into the bar, where I never go, and talk to some people I don't know. I stay away from people,"

"Listen, you don't have to stay away from these people. They're good people,"

"How do you know?"

Steve took another bite of frozen beer. "I know because I know, that's how I know,"

"You're going in circles,"

"Where the hell else am I going to go,"

"You want me to go into the bar and talk with these people?"

"Yes,"

"There's going to be trouble,"

"Trouble? What kind of trouble,"

"You know the men we met in the cook shack? One of them you nearly got in a fight with,"

"I met them in the bar, they know Dad,"

"I know. Your father and I are different. They may like him, but they don't like me,"

Steve wanted to walk, to get up and move around, but he felt trapped on the bed. "Have you ever talked to them?"

"Once,"

"What happened?"

"How do you tell people that aren't listening, that they aren't listening?"

Steve thought about that. "Then I will,"

"And what will you say?"

"I don't know,"

"You weren't in Budapest during the revolt. You don't understand and they won't listen to you, no matter what you say,"

"Listen, Uncle Joe, if I talk to them and," Steve looked at Uncle Joe with the same eyes he saw in Uncle Joe. Steves' eyes got tight and narrow, his stomach settled and his jaw sat hard.

"I don't care what they say or think or believe. You say I wasn't there, well, you're right. So that's all there is to it,"

"There's a lot more to it,"

"How much more? Aren't you ever going to finish this war,"

"It will never finish," Uncle Joe said from behind a cloud of smoke.

"Then I'll finish it for you,"

"Ya, how you gonna do it?"

"Beats the shit outta me, but I'm gonna do it."

Uncle Joe took another deep puff on his cigarette. He held it in, blew it out, and stubbed the butt in his overflowing ashtray. "You think I smoke too much?"

"Yes,"

"So, let's go to the bar and you can finish my war for me."

Uncle Joe stood up, put on his coat and headed out the door as Steve stood there, once again, stunned by his Uncle Joe.

Uncle Joe did not hesitate at the door of the Elsa Bar; he walked right in like he owned the place and stood beside Steve, waiting for him to point out his friends.

"Rolly, Rosie, this is my Uncle Joe,"

Uncle Joe was a little nervous. Rosie saw this, stood up with a smile, and extended her hand. "Pleasure to meet you, Mr. Smith,"

"My name is, Josef Kovacs,"

Rolly nodded. "Pleasure to meet you, Josef Kovacs,"

Rosie pushed her chair away from the table and walked out from behind it. She came close to Uncle Joe, felt his shyness. He moved slightly back, then stopped.

Rosie stopped, then slowly stepped forward and put her arms out to Uncle Joe. He looked confused, then relaxed, and Rosie put her arms around him.

"I'm very happy to meet you. Please sit down with us. Do I call you Mr. Kovacs or Joe, or... Uncle Joe,"

Uncle Joe looked at Steve. Steve shrugged and said, "Well, so just what do they call you,"

Uncle Joe looked at Steve and smiled. "You can call me Uncle Joe. I am so much older than you, and,"

Rolly jumped in, "Uncle Joe, can I buy you a beer?"

"Yes, yes I would like a beer. But you have to let me buy them for you,"

Uncle Joe turned to Steve and whispered, "Do I go to the bar and ask her for beer, or does she bring it to us,"

"Gotta get it yourself. No table service," said a smiling Steve.

Uncle Joe stood up, eyed the waitress and walked directly to her. `

She smiled at him and said, "What would you like?"

"Four beers please,"

She reached into the cooler and brought out four beers. "That'll be four dollars,"

Uncle Joe looked at her. "Four dollars?"

"Yes, four dollars,"

"Price has gone up,"

"Taxes,"

"Yes, taxes. Always taxes," he smiled and she smiled as Steve watched closely, then jumped up and ran over to the bar, whispered into Uncle Joes' ear. "Got any cash, Uncle Joe,"

Uncle Joe turned to him, red in the face. "No,"

"It's okay, here," Steve slipped Uncle Joe some of the money Rolly lent him, then quickly returned to his seat. Uncle Joe followed, carrying the beers.

He placed one in front of Rolly, one in front of Rosie, and one in front of Steve. He kept the last close to his stomach. Then he lifted it.

"A toast," he said.

Rolly, Rosie and Steve all lifted their beers. Uncle Joe held his up high, and then paused. His lowered his beer, then raised it again."To my nephew, who found me."

Rosie leaned over and gave Steve a little kiss on the cheek.

Rolly looked at Steve. "I ain't kissing you."

The three Hungarians walked into the bar. Uncle Joe turned to look at them. They all stopped and stood still and looked back. "Well, I never think I live to see the day that you are in this bar," said John Wayne.

Uncle Joe turned to Steve. "You sit here and you stay here."

Rolly quietly moved the chair in front of him out of the way. It gave himself a straight line to John Wayne's head.

Steve watched Rolly and said, "This ain't your show,"

"You're my show," said Rolly

Uncle Joe walked over to John Wayne. Steve started to stand up, but Rolly quickly pulled him back into his chair.

"Leave 'em be. For now," Rolly said.

Rosie quietly removed her heavy coat, never taking her eyes off the three Hungarians and Uncle Joe.

"Easy, Rosie," Rolly said.

"There's three of them, three of us." she said.

Kendall walked in, stopped at the door. He watched Uncle Joe walk over to John Wayne. Then he walked over to the table next to Steve and sat down. "How ya' doin'?" he said.

"Fine, and you?" Steve said.

"I've been waiting a long time for this."

Peter and Henry took seats. John Wayne stayed standing to stare at Uncle Joe, and then he pointed at Steve. "That young man is your nephew,"

"Yes, he is," Uncle Joe said.

John looked over to Steve, who nodded slightly, then he turned back to Uncle Joe. He never took his eyes off Uncle Joe as he went to the bar and ordered three beers.

Uncle Joe never moved. Neither did Rolly or Rosie, or Kendall or Steve. The waitress was very quiet as she handed John Wayne his beers. The rest of the Elsa Bar, which was its' usual noisy self when Steve and Uncle Joe entered, went dead quiet.

John Wayne walked back to Uncle Joe. "Your name is not Smith,"

"No,"

"Your name is Kovacs,"

"Yes,"

"Brother of Janos Kovacs,"

"Yes,"

Wayne took a drink of his beer. Still his eyes never left Uncle Joes'. "Your brother will always be a hero of the revolution, but you shall go to your grave as a traitor,"

"You can make things simple so you can understand them; but for me, I brought the dead back to life. I made the lists,"

"I saw those lists, they were lies,"

"I made those lies. Maybe I put your names on the list, maybe I brought you back from the dead, and saved what was left of your families," Uncle Joe paused for a drink. "If I knew your real names," he said as he wiped his sleeve across his mouth.

John Wayne's head snapped back like he was slapped in the face, "You made those lists? You did these things for Hungary?"

He paused and drank his beer, never taking his eyes off Uncle Joe. "How do I know this is true? I can never believe you,"

"I don't need you to believe me," Uncle Joe pointed at Steve. "I only need that man to believe me,"

Steve jumped up, waved his hand in the air, and cried out, "I believe, I believe," like he was at a church revival. Everybody in the bar turned and stared at Steve.

Rolly lowered his head and covered his eyes with his hand, Rosie stared at the floor, Kendall's eyes went to the ceiling, and the whole bar started laughing at Steve, except the four Hungarians.

"Sit down, Steve," Rolly said. Steve looked around, he didn't get it. "Sit." Rolly ordered.

Uncle Joe turned his back on John Wayne and Peter and Henry, and started walking toward his table.

John Wayne held his beer high and called out loudly, so that everyone in the bar could hear.

"To your grave, Josef Kovacs. To your grave." He took another long drink and wiped his sleeve across his mouth.

Uncle Joe stopped walking and kept his back to John Wayne. He took one more step to the table, picked up his beer and turned around to face John Wayne. He held his beer high in the air and called out, "And to your grave, John Wayne, or whatever your real name is. I have a reason for my name, what is your reason?"

Uncle Joe never took his eyes off John Wayne, took a long drink of his beer, wiped his sleeve across his mouth, sat down and smiled at Steve. "You don't think that's his real name do you? John Wayne is an American cowboy movie star, even I know that. He's got more to hide than I do. But none of that matters anymore, you said you'd finish my war and you did, so it's over, let's drink."

He finished his beer, wiped his sleeve across his mouth again. "Memories don't die," he said, shaking his head. "And some wars will never end,"

Rolly leaned over to Uncle Joe, "We can wait them out,"

Uncle Joe stared at Rolly, "Our war will end when we are all dead,"

Rolly stared back, "So will mine."

Steve was again struggling to keep up, but he wanted to keep moving. "Rolly, can Uncle Joe and me catch a ride to Whitehorse with you,"

"Right fucken' now,"

"Uncle Joe, pack a bag," Steve said. "We're going to Whitehorse,"

"Now?" Uncle Joe said.

"Right fucken' now," Steve said.

"I'm gonna warm up the truck," Rolly said. "Steve, you help your Uncle get a bag and we're outta here,"

"What am I going to say to Klutzfuck?" Uncle Joe said.

"I don't know," Steve shrugged.

"I'll tell him I'm taking days off and," Uncle Joe broke into the widest grin Steve had seen so far, "I'll tell him how many days I am taking off, when I get back,"

Steve smiled, "You do that, Uncle Joe. You do that."

As they drove out of Elsa, Uncle Joe peered out the window. He watched the buildings go by, and smiled. "What is Whitehorse like?"

"Well," said Rolly, "consider yourself a tourist. We'll give you the tour. Takes five minutes,"

"Tell me, Rolly, have you ever had Palinka,"

"What's that?"

"National drink of Hungary," Uncle Joe chuckled.

"Mom says to leave it alone," Steve said. "Said its rotten plums,"

"Rotten plums?" Rolly said. "What kind of drink you make out of rotten plums,"

"You make Palinka," Uncle Joe said.

"Steve," said Rolly, "Your Mom in the truck,"

Steve groaned, "No,"

"Okay, Uncle Joe, let's give this 'Palinka' a run up the flag pole and see if anybody salutes it,"

"Rolly," Rosie said. "You get into this Palinka stuff and I get the wheel,"

Rolly shrugged, pulled the truck over to the side of the road and said, "Okay, Rosie, the wheel is yours."

Rolly slid over to the middle of the seat and Rosie jumped up on his lap and reached over for the wheel.Rolly gently massaged her breasts.

Rosie swung her elbow around and Rolly ducked.

"Pig," she cried out.

Rolly started to howl out his laughing. "Go on, swing again. It was worth it,"

"Pig! Get on your own side of the seat,"

"Give us a kiss; come on, just a little kiss,"

Rosie leaned against the window and glared at Rolly. "You don't deserve a kiss, and I don't give little kisses. So there,"

Rolly laughed the loudest Steve had ever heard. "You don't give little kisses, that's for sure," he looked at the Palinka, "Hey, Steve, you gonna try this stuff,"

"I already have, thank you very much,"

"Then you got the front seat, but you better watch out for Rosie, she's in a bad mood,"

"I am not in a bad mood,"   "Yes, you are,"

"You better get your sorry ass in the backseat, 'cause now I am in a bad mood and I'm going to take it out on you,"

"Well, Rosie my dear, you're right,"

Rosie looked very distrusting at Rolly. "Right about what,"

"I'm getting in the backseat,"

"Pig. Stay there,"

"Move over, Uncle Joe, let's try this Palinka,"

Rolly started climbing over the seat to the back, and Steve started climbing over the seat to the front. Steve's elbow hit Rolly in the chin, so Rolly elbowed Steve in the ribs.

Steve grabbed Rolly's leg and yanked it up, putting Rolly headfirst over the seat while his feet were firmly planted on the ceiling. He did a handstand on the back seat floor. Rolly twisted around and grabbed Steve's leg and gave it a twist, so Steve let out a yelp.

"Will you two behave like, just what the hell are you two doing," Rosie spun around and slapped Rolly hard on the butt. "Teach you to grab my boobs,"

Rolly started yelling, "Two on one, two on one, ain't fair, ain't fair. Help me, Uncle Joe, help me. They're ganging up on me,"

Uncle Joe sat up straight in his seat and in a clear and steady voice said, "I think Rosie is a very nice young lady and you shouldn't grab her by the…, you're on your own and good luck to you."

Rosie laughed so hard she fell over backward onto the steering wheel, and her butt slid down between the wheel and the seat, where she was stuck. "Rolly, Rolly, I'm stuck,"

"Tough shit. Slap my butt, you pay the price,"

Rolly and Steve exchanged a couple of slaps and Rolly spun around and fell ass first onto the back seat. Steve went face first onto the floor and squirmed around down there till he could stand up. He stood on the seat and pulled on Rosie's arms until she came unstuck.

"Well, at least there's one gentleman in the truck," Rosie said.

"She talking 'bout me again," Rolly said.

"I don't think so," Uncle Joe said. "Here, try some of this."

"I don't see any rotten plums," he said.

"Fermented," Uncle Joe said.

Rolly had a drink, gave it a good taste, then handed it back. "Another time, Uncle Joe. We got a long drive ahead of us, I got a kid brother to see and I ain't doing it half-pissed,"

"And I have a big brother to see," Uncle Joe said.

"And a sister, Uncle Joe," Steve said.

"And a sister." Uncle Joe said.

ESCAPE FROM BUDAPEST

Janos carefully lowered Stephan to the couch, then collapsed next to him. "Where's Tara," he said. He heard nothing in the flat. "Where's Little Stephan?"

Stephan looked at Janos, and they both froze - both thinking - the AVO have her and this time, they have Little Stephan. Stephan perked up his ears, cocked his head towards the door, "What's that," he whispered.

From the hallway they heard the thump of a footstep, the clump of a crutch, the pitter-patter of little feet. The door swung open, "Daddy, Daddy," followed by Tara.

Janos grabbed them both, pulled them onto the couch next to Uncle Stephan, hugged and hugged and started to breathe again. So did Uncle Stephan.

"Where have you been," they both said.

"In the cellar, under the table, we had a picnic."

Tara took the medic bag off Stephan's shoulder and started digging in it. Stephan put his hand inside the folds of his sweater, brought it out red and his face went white.

Janos went to his side, "Why didn't you tell me,"

"No point, only in the stomach, not much," Stephan said.

"It's not as bad as many others."

"Many others are dead, Stephan."

"What happened at the Kilian," Tara said.

Janos slowly shook his head, "Not good, but we beat them back again,"

"Stephan, let me see your stomach," Tara cut away Stephan's sweater, and let out a gasp. "I can do a few stitches, but this needs a doctor, we have to go to the hospital,"

"Can't. AVO has them all staked out, if we go in for wounds, they know where I got them. You gotta stitch me,"

"I'll do the best I can, but,"

"But nothing, you have to do it,"

"Janos, I'm going to need the fish line, lots of anti-septic. Jesus, Stephan,"

"You can do it,"

"It's deep, you've lost a lot of blood, lucky it didn't go deeper, you have to rest for a few days. You're going to have a nasty scar from the Kilian, we have to keep it clean, we have to watch for infections,"

Tara started cutting fish line for stitches while Stephan chuckled through the pain. "Not a scar from the Kilian, oh, no, not from the Kilian. Gotta be better than that, not this scar. How about I got it in a sword duel, let's say, how about this, I got it in a sword duel with a Nazi officer for the hand of a fair young..." Stephan gasped, "Jesus, Tara, take it easy will you."

"Be quiet, these stitches are going to take awhile,"

"How many," Stephan said.

"Twenty, maybe twenty-five. Deep through the flesh, it's long; this is going to hurt,"

"No kidding, it's going to hurt. Janos, get me the Palinka." Stephan gritted his teeth, then smiled at Tara.

"Rotten plums," she said. "Why do you drink rotten plums,"

"Because you get drunk quick. Finally got us a car,"

"What," she said.

"Not so new, but it runs. Got some holes in it, got some extra petrol hidden out back, too." Stephan took another deep breath, "One of the party bosses gave it to me,"

"Gave it to you, from the bottom of his heart, I suspect,"

"Talked him into it, yes, from the bottom of his heart."

Tara spent most of the evening stitching Stephan's stomach wound. She changed the bandages on Janos' leg, put Little Stephan to bed, then had a drink of Palinka herself. It was very quiet in the Kovacs home that night.

In the morning, when Janos rose from a sleepless night, there was a letter on the floor. He picked it up and read it. He felt a wave of hot sweat, then shivered.

"Where did you get that," Tara said.

"Slipped under the door,"

Janos felt his stomach rise to his throat. He thought he might vomit. He poured himself a glass of water and forced it down.

Stephan leaned up on his elbow and held his stomach. "What does it say?" He read the letter and sighed. "We should do as it says. Hungary is in worse shape than when the Nazis were here. What kind of life do you want for Little Stephan?"

"Let me read it." Tara said.

AVO COMING TONIGHT
NO GUARDS AT ANDAU
GET OUT OF HUNGARY

"Do you think it's from Josef?" Janos said.

"We should go to Andau," Stephan said. "I can walk. Tara stitched me well. We have to leave right now; we have to be through the forest and swamps before sunrise. I'll help you get to the border,"

"Aren't you coming with us," Janos said.

"I said, 'I'll get you to the border'. I have to get back to the Kilian, they need me there,"

"Stephan," Janos looked deeply into Stephan's eyes and was quiet as he said, "The Kilian can't hold on much longer. The tanks keep coming,"

"I know," Stephan said. "I know,"

"What can we take," Tara said. "Do we have to leave everything?"

"We can't carry anything, tanks are on the roads and the fields are mined; we have to cover fifteen miles of bush and swamp."

Stephan looked out the window and into the sky. Dark clouds were forming and a cold wind was blowing.

"Put on your work boots, warm socks, extra sweaters, a warm blanket for Little Stephan. Take some pictures of Mom and Dad out of their frames. Move now, we haven't much time, don't forget Dad's compass,"

Janos and Tara did as Stephan said. They had tears in their eyes as they put together their warm clothes.

"For Little Stephan, my baby Stephan," Tara said. "We leave Hungary so he won't grow up under Russian orders, where he can read and write what he wants. Janos, you talked about Canada, can we go there,"

"Canada, how do we get to Canada? We have to get to Andau first."

Janos reached up above their bed and took down a family picture from earlier, happier years. It was a family portrait, when the boys were children. Josef sat on his father's knee, next to Janos and Stephan.

"Josef is not going with you," Stephan said. "He will stay in Hungary with his Russian bosses,"

Stephan took the picture of him and his brothers as children, the one with Josef on his father's knee, and threw it to the floor. He reached up and took another, the last one taken of him, Janos and Josef before Josef was conscripted. He threw that one to the floor. Then he took a picture of his father in his Mokan Army uniform, before they drove the Nazis from Hungary. He stood proudly next to his wife, another of his parents at their wedding and one of Tara and Janos at their wedding, two more of him and Janos as young boys. He handed them to Tara.

Stephan didn't see Tara as she reached down behind him and picked up the pictures he had thrown to the floor. She took all the pictures out of their frames, put them in some waxed brown paper, and quietly slipped them into her pocket.

"Tara, I want you to wrap Little Stephan real tight," Janos said.

Then he turned to Tara, "Do you think Stephan's stitches will hold?"

"I'll wrap him tight," Tara sighed, "very tight." She tore their last bed sheet into strips. "Sit, Stephan. I want to wrap you more."

"I'm fine," Stephan said.

"Stephan, sit down and shut up. SIT!"

Stephan sat uncomfortably as Tara wrapped him more, then he was up and getting dressed.

He put on two pairs of socks, two pairs of pants, two undershirts, two shirts and his one warm sweater.

Tara reached to the bedside table and picked up the letter that had appeared on the floor. She put it in the waxed brown paper with the family pictures of Josef.

Stephan went to the cupboard, pulled out a small glass jar, opened it, shook out a few pills and handed one to Tara.

"Break that in half, give one half to Little Stephan now, the other when we leave the car,"

"Sleeping pills, Stephan?"

"We can't risk him crying, best he sleep through it all, we have a long night,"

Tara took the pill, broke it in half, went into the bedroom and fed one half to Little Stephan. She wrapped the other half in a piece of paper and put it in her coat pocket.

"Janos, carry the rifle. Got Dad's compass,"

"Yes."

"We go."

Stephan went to the window, slowly pulled back the curtains, and looked up and down the street. He went to the door, looked up and down the hallway, then went out and around to the back of the tenement building. He lifted the garbage can lids that hid the petrol can, then leaned in and pulled on the handle of the can. He felt his stomach stretching, the stitches pulling as he lifted out the petrol can. It was a full five-gallon can and weighed over forty-five pounds.

He carried the can to the car, struggled as he walked, then leaned over as he poured the petrol into the car's fuel tank, keeping as much pressure off his stitches as he could. He leaned against the car and put his hand on his stomach. He slipped a finger under the wrapping, pulled it out and saw blood. He pulled out his shirttail, wiped his finger clean, then tucked his shirt back in.

Janos and Tara came out with Little Stephan wrapped in blankets. "We're ready," Tara said. "How is your stomach?"

"It's fine. Janos, you drive, I'll take the rifle. Tara, you keep Little Stephan, and remember that we're doing this for him." They got in the car and started for the border.

"Listen Janos, when you cross at Andau," Stephan started.

"'When? " Janos said. "What about 'if'? If it gets too dangerous, we might have to turn back,"

"No, you won't turn back. You have nothing to 'turn back' to. If the AVO gets any of us, none of us will be coming back. They know whose side we're on. There is no 'if' here, only 'when'. Little Stephan needs both of you, both of you have to make it,"

Janos nodded, knowing full well what Stephan meant. "What about you, why aren't you coming with us,"

"Because they need me at the Kilian; Hungary needs me, Little Stephan needs you and Tara. After you cross at Andau, keep going to Vienna, make contact with the International Red Cross, they'll put you in touch with the right people, get to Canada, they don't have wars in Canada. I met some Canadians after the Nazis were gone, but those Russians made them leave Hungary, they were good people those Canadians, not like those crazy Yanks."

"You let the Red Cross know where you are in Canada, you can trust them. I'll track you down in Canada, I'll find you, it's not over for us, I'll find you and you have a room for me, and I want a room of my own,"

"Stephan, you'll have a room of your own," Tara said.

Stephan turned to smile Tara, "Do me a favor will you, Tara,"

"Anything, Stephan, anything,"

"When you get settled in Canada, do you think you can find me a Canadian wife?"

"Stephan, you'll get your own room, but you'll have to find your own Canadian wife,"

"Oh, come on Tara; find me a wife, will you? I'm a busy man, I don't have time for such things, and make her pretty, I don't want a wife I can't look at,"

"No Stephan, you'll find your own wife in Canada, and you can decide if she's pretty or not,"

"Don't want an ugly wife, Tara. You find me one, Janos. You got a pretty wife; find me one, will you?"

"Find your own wife; I got my hands full with the one I've got,"

"Shit, as if I don't have enough to do already, I've got to find my own wife,"

Tara reached over to pat Stephan on the back. "That's okay, Stephan, I'll find you a wife in Canada, but I can't promise she'll be pretty,"

"Oh no, she has to be pretty, don't want a wife I can't look at, can't have an ugly wife, oh no, she has to be pretty. And a nice lady, too, can't have a bad tempered ugly wife. Got to be good with kids, too,"

"Okay, Stephan. Let me get this straight, you want a pretty, not bad tempered wife who's good with kids. You want her to have kids already,"

"No, no. We're going to make our own kids, lots of kids. Little Stephan needs cousins, lots and lots of cousins, going to make lots of kids with this pretty not bad tempered Canadian wife you're going to find for me." Stephan laughed and felt the pull on his stitches.

It was a hundred miles and a three-hour bumpy ride to the western most point the back roads would take them. On every bump Stephan felt the pull on his stitches and he never said a thing. All the main roads, all the intersections and all the rail stations were in the hands of Russian tanks. Snow was beginning to fall as they drove the car as far as they could, out of sight, into the deep brush.

"The weathers' going to work against us, isn't it, Stephan?" Janos said.

"No, little brother," said Stephan, "it'll work for us. We can hide better in bad weather. Give the border guards less to shoot at. And remember, there are patrols out there. We don't want anybody seeing us. If we hear anybody, keep quiet. Get the compass out, and stay off the fields, they're mined."

Janos took the compass out of his pocket.

"Aim west, little brother, aim west," said Stephan. "Janos, I want you to carry Tara, I'll carry Little Stephan. Tara, give him the other half of the sleeping pill,"

Stephan went into the car and lifted out Little Stephan. He winced, with his back turned so Janos or Tara couldn't see.

Janos put his left arm around Tara and with his right hand aimed his father's compass west to Austria.

Stephan cradled Little Stephan in his arms and said, "Okay, little brother, lead us away from the Russians, and remember, just because the letter said 'no border guards', don't believe it."

They carefully stepped off the road and into the bushes. Tara limped, and leaned heavily on Janos. Stephan walked behind, both arms tightly holding Little Stephan. They walked easily for about two miles, and then the swamps began.

Quickly, they were up to their stomachs in icy water and their feet stuck in the deep sucking mud.

They had to turn south and north steadily to make their way through the impassable parts of the swamp as they wove their way west. The sun went down, it got colder, and the water started to freeze.

Stephan lifted Little Stephan up, placed him across his own shoulders, and kept him balanced there.

His right hand held the back of Little Stephan's head and shoulders, his left hand held the back of his knees, and he cradled Little Stephan around the back of his own head. He broke through the ice with his stomach. He kept his jaw clamped shut, and did not utter a sound as the pain shot through his stomach and the stitches slowly tore open with each ice-breaking lunge. Behind him, moving through the ice that Stephan had broken, Janos carried Tara.

On the top of a small hill, out of the icy water, Janos stopped and lay Tara down. Stephan lay Little Stephan down beside Tara. She picked him up and saw that he still warmly wrapped in dry blankets and was fast asleep. Janos had Tara's boots off, her feet were purple. He tried rubbing the blood back into them.

"We'd better stop a bit, warm up some," sputtered Janos.

"No," Stephan said. "There's nothing here to warm us; we can't risk a fire. We're too close to the border. Keep moving. That'll keep us warm,"

Tara mumbled, "Are we in Austria, yet?"

"Not yet. How are your feet," Stephan asked.

"They'll work," she said. She blinked her eyes, rubbed them, and then struggled to her feet. She put her arm around Janos.

"We have to be close now. Keep moving, keeps your blood flowing," Stephan said.

"You should take a break, Stephan," said Janos. "How's your stomach,"

"My stomach's fine. If we stop, we may not get started again. We can't stop, remember; the border before sunrise."

"Come on Janos," Tara said. "We'll carry each other. Little Stephan is safe with his uncle."

There was a heavy boom from far behind, then rifle fire.

Janos turned to look at Stephan.

"Back in the water." Stephan said.

They slid back into the swamp and Stephan looked down to the water and saw his blood rising. He felt its' warmth spread down to his hips and across his stomach. It was comforting, this warmth, it fought off the chill of the ice.

He felt the line between the warm blood and the cold water, felt the line move down to his thighs, felt how it insulated him against the cold, kept his thighs from cramping up, strong for pushing, breaking a trail for Janos and Tara.

With every push he saw his blood spread out in front of him in gentle ripples, mixing with the broken sheets of ice, flowing across those sheets, gentle ripples, quiet and steady, one step at a time. Holding Little Stephan, still tight to the back of his neck, gripped by both arms, to stay dry, to stay warm.

They crept up another little hill; Janos looked at his fathers' compass, "I can't read it,"

"Look there,"

Down the hill were guard towers, no searchlights, the barbed wire fences down. There was a small wooden bridge crossing a canal. Stephan put Little Stephan down, and then lay down on his stomach. "That's it, go there," he gasped.

"What?"

"Go," his blood was soaking into the frozen ground.

Tara lay down next to him and fell unconscious. Stephan sat up and looked at her. Her face was white, her lips, purple.

"Janos, get Tara, get across the bridge. I'll be behind you,"

Janos leaned over and fell down. Stephan looked at Janos. He was white with purple lips.

"Janos, get up, get up," Stephan was stern, was loud.

Janos sat up. He blinked, rubbed his eyes into focus."What,"

"Get Tara back on your shoulders, one more kilometer, Janos!"

Janos got up on his knees, leaned over, put his arms around Tara and hoisted her up to his shoulders, then wavered as he stood up.

Stephan sat up. He put Little Stephan across his shoulder, and then let out one muffled cry as he stood up. "One more kilometer, can you smell it?"

"Smell what?" Janos said.

"Freedom Janos, and wood smoke, someone has a fire."

They climbed down the hill and crossed the bridge. Stephan had Little Stephan over his shoulder with one hand, the other hand under Janos' arm. Tara was still over Janos' shoulder.

They started walking north on the west side of the canal, turned onto a small footpath and continued west

"Hey," someone called out in Hungarian.

"Over here," another voice called out.

Janos turned and squinted into the darkness. He couldn't focus his eyes to where the voice came from. He wavered with Tara on his shoulder, began to tip over, then someone ran out of the bush and grabbed him before he collapsed

"Who are you," Stephan asked.

"International Red Cross, welcome to Austria. We have a heated shack right here."

Two more people ran out from the bush. One of them lifted Tara from Janos' shoulders, and said, "I'm a doctor,"

Tara woke up, looked at the doctor and started to cry.

"Good to see you, Tara Kovacs," the doctor said.

Tara was pulling for air, trying to get her breath, "Janos," she mumbled between gasps, "Doctor Hadjok,"

"Thank you, Doctor," Janos said. "Thank you."

Doctor Hadjok cradled Tara in his arms, carried her into the bushes, into the heated shack. A Red Cross worker helped Janos; another took Little Stephan from Stephan's shoulders.

"Can you walk," the Red Cross worker asked Stephan.

Stephan nodded as the Red Cross took his family into the warmth of their shack.

Stephan turned to face east, blinked into the cold wind, looked back to the rising sun, and lifted his eyes to the few remaining stars. Their beauty put him in awe, and he couldn't believe that these same stars shone over Hungary. Reaching under his ice-soaked sweater, through the frozen folds, he put his hand on his stomach, on the bandages, all the while staring at the morning stars, then felt the warmth of the last bit of his blood. He looked down to his hands, white with bits of ice on them, streaked with red, tried to wiggle his fingers, but couldn't.

Its okay now, he thought, smelling the warmth of the wood smoke, knowing that Janos and Tara and Little Stephan were warm, were with doctors. He knew he'd done his job, now it was his turn to rest. The Red Cross would take care of his family. He felt a warm flush on his cheeks, looked up again and saw his mothers' smiling face spread across the starry heavens.

In the morning, Janos awoke in the shack still clutching his father's compass. He saw Tara and Little Stephan sleeping soundly together. The color was back in their faces. They were in dry clothes on soft beds, under warm blankets.

Doctors and nurses moved about quietly, tending to those that needed it. Others were heating soup on a wood stove, all quietly speaking in Hungarian. He sat up and his head ached. He looked around the room for Stephan.

One of the Red Cross workers said, "It's a long walk to Austria, isn't it,"

"Where's Stephan,"

"Was he the other man with you?"

"Yes, my brother. Where is he?"

"I'm sorry, he didn't make it."

REUNION AT THE MINER'S INN

Rippling blankets of blues and greens ebbed and flowed from horizon to horizon as a cold wind blew hard and steady under a clear black sky. A full moon was quickly climbing up in the southeast as the plane bounced lightly on the frozen tarmac and rolled up to the control tower at the Whitehorse Airport.

"Look at that," Janos said, in awe of the Northern Lights.

"Beautiful, absolutely beautiful," exclaimed Tara.

Peter shook his head back and forth, "Too much, way too much,"

"To think that Little Stephan and Josef see this as we see it," Tara said.

"This is not the sky we come from," Janos said.

Peter smiled at both of them, "But it is the sky we come to."

The other passengers put on their parkas and mitts and toques and filed down the aisle before Janos stood up and held out his hand to Tara.

"We always wait for everybody else to go by," Janos said. "Tara's leg slows them down,"

"I know what that's like," Peter said. "Except, they just leave me behind,"

Tara gripped her cane as Peter helped her to her feet, then took his own cane.

"It looks cold out there," Janos said.

"I hope Stephan is warm," Tara said.

"Does it get this cold in California," Janos said.

"No way," laughed Peter. "But Rolly can handle it."

There was a heavy curtain at the end of the aisle and as soon as they went through it, they felt the full force of the frozen wind.

"Jesus Christ Almighty," yelled Janos.

"Language," Tara said firmly.

"Well, he'd think it was cold, too," pleaded Janos.

"Shit, oh shit is it cold," yelled Peter. Tara turned to glare at Peter.

"Sorry," he said.

The stewardess stood by the door. She was fully covered in a parka, toque, mitts and snow pants. "Enjoy your stay in the Yukon," she said

"Is it always this cold," Janos said.

"No," the stewardess said with a smile, "only in the winter."

By now all the other passengers had sprinted down the stairway and across the tarmac to the control tower. Inside was a huge oil heater with a large summer fan behind it, blowing the heat towards the door. The other passengers ran in and slammed the door, which banged once, got caught in the wind, and then flew open again. Then they slammed it shut again and this time it stayed shut.

Janos and Peter helped Tara down the stairway and onto the tarmac, with Janos on her right arm and Peter on her left arm, the three of them leaned into the wind and quickly shuffled across the tarmac to the door.

Janos flung it open, and Tara staggered through the doorway, half pulling Peter. There the three of them fell onto benches and started laughing.

"Never before have I been in a freezer like that," Janos said.

"I thought for sure," Tara said, catching her breath, "that my cane was going to slip and I would fall down and freeze to the ice,"

Janos smiled at Tara. "I carried you once through the ice, I can do it again,"

Tara wiped a single frozen tear from her cheek. "Was it this cold,"

Janos smiled again and put his arm around Tara. "No, with you it is never cold."

Peter stared at his foot, then at Tara, then back to his foot, and then in a panic he spun around and started looking all around.

"Peter, where is your cane," Tara said.

"I don't know," he said. "I must have..." Peter looked under the bench, "dropped it or...," He looked behind the bench. "Well, how the hell did I get here without that damn thing,"

"You were holding me up," Tara said. "I wasn't holding you,"

Janos stood up and walked over to the window. There, out on the tarmac at the bottom of the steps, being quickly covered over by the blowing snow, was Peters' cane.

"I'll get it for you," Janos said.

"You sit down, Janos Kovacs," ordered Tara. She turned to Peter, put her hand on his hand, and firmly said, "Peter, go get your cane."Peters' face was not white from the cold, nor was it white with fear. Janos walked over to Peter and put out his hand. Peter took it and stood up uneasily. His throat choked and he felt like he was going to puke. The pain shot across his foot and up and down his leg.

He took a step forward on his good foot, and then his bad foot and the pain shot across his foot again. A few more steps, he took the pain, opened the door and limped out onto the tarmac, bent over and picked up his cane.

Standing still in the wind and gazing up into the sky, he watched the northern lights dance their way across the horizon. The colors, he thought. What makes them? How do they move that way and why do they move at all? Does Rolly lie up at night and watch this show? Does he know what these lights are all about? Are these northern lights any better than, the stars he told me about in Vietnam?

Peter remembered the cold and put his cane up across his shoulders. He gripped each end tightly and limped back to the control tower with the huge oil heater and Janos and Tara waiting.

Janos met Peter at the door, grabbed him under the arms and half carried him to the bench. The pain in Peters' foot built in waves until it choked him and pushed the tears out onto his cheeks.

He gagged back the urge to cry out, held his breath, felt himself relax, just a little, then puked all over the front of Janos' one warm coat.

Janos sighed, and wiped the front of his coat with his sleeve.

"Peter, it was important to you, that you get your cane," Tara said. "Someday you won't need it anymore,"

Peter wiped his face with his sleeve and shrugged, "If you say so."

Janos chuckled as Tara reached into her pocket and pulled out some paper napkins and handed them to Peter and Janos. Peter wiped his face clean and Janos wiped puke off his coat and smeared it all over his coat at the same time. Janos threw a small glare at Peter and chuckled again.

"Think I'll hang onto this for awhile, yet," Peter said as he leaned onto his cane to sit up on the bench.

"Might need some firewood in this territory," Janos said. "Best you hang onto it,"

Janos' eyes brightened and his smile stretched deep into his cheeks, and he started laughing, "For awhile yet, anyways."

Peter nodded. "Ya, Janos. Firewood's not a bad idea, not a bad idea at all."

After they had gathered up their bags and caught an old rusted and dented bus into Whitehorse, Janos turned to Tara and asked, "Where is our room,"

A slight shadow covered Tara's face. "Our room,"

"Our room, to sleep in, awful cold up here, hate to sleep outside,"

"I didn't get one,"

"No problem here," Peter said. "I have one. You can have it,"

"Then where will you sleep,"

"It'll be easier for me to get a single room. Old family friend runs a place in town here. Called the 'Miners' Inn',"

"Miners' Inn? Sounds nice enough, but we have to pay you for it,"

"No, you don't. I give it to you,"

"Oh, no," Tara said. "You can't do that,"

"What do you mean, 'I can't' do that," Peter said. "I've already done it. It's yours now,"

Janos chuckled. "Thank you, Peter. But you have to let us buy you dinner,"

"That's a good idea," said Peter looking at the smears on Janos' coat. "I'm ready to refill my stomach. But now, we meet an old friend of mine."

The bus dropped off all the other passengers and completed its rounds in front of the Miner's Inn.

Peter looked up and down Main Street in Whitehorse. "Funky," he said.

"Looks like... from an American western movie," Janos said.

"Don't forget your cane, Peter," Tara said.

Peter took Tara by the arm, and with each on their own cane, led her down the steps of the bus, over the slippery sidewalk, and up the steps and into the Miner's Inn.

Janos followed behind with their bags. They all gathered in the lobby and piled their bags on an old sagging couch. Peter sat on the arm at the end of the couch, then stood up and wiped the snow from his butt.

Tara looked at the picture hanging on the wall over the couch. Painted on crushed black velvet, showing a pack of wolves attacking a bull moose."I don't like that. The moose is in trouble," Tara said.

"Wolves gotta eat, too," Janos said.

Peter took a deep breath, then walked through the swinging doors and into the bar.

He saw an old man sitting at the bar. He had a wide fuzzy gray beard, black cowboy hat, and what looked like pieces of bed sheet wrapped scarf-like around his neck. He was haggling with the bartender over a set of old balance beam weigh scales.

The bartenders' sweater had a picture on it of two vultures sitting in a tree. "Listen, Sammy, I told you already," said the bartender. "One case of beer and ten dollars,"

"Two cases of beer and ten dollars," said Sammy.

Peter leaned on his cane and limped to the bar. "Hi, Larry," he said.

Larry looked up and his jaw dropped to this chest.

He vaulted over the bar and landed running to Peter. He picked him up in a bear hug and yelled out, "God damn it, Peter, it's good to see you,"

"Lemme go, lemme go,"

Larry put Peter down, held him tight by the shoulders, and then gave him another bear hug. "Damn, damn, damn. Welcome to draft-free Canada, home away from home for wandering Americans,"

"Good to see you, Larry. Real good,"

Larry looked over Peters' head to see Janos and Tara standing quietly behind Peter. "Whose grandma and grandpa?"

Peter turned around to Janos and Tara. "This is my friend Larry. He's from California, too,"

"It is very good to meet you Larry," Janos said, extending his hand.

Larry took Janos' hand and shook it up and down and Janos shook up and down.

Tara reached out for Larry's hand and said, "No shaking too much,"

Larry took her hand delicately in both of his, and Tara nodded her head lightly and smiled. "Come on and sit," said Larry. "Beers on me."

He led to them to a table by the bar, and as Janos and Peter sat, Larry held out a chair for Tara, and as she sat he slid the chair up to the table. "You folks hungry? Didn't eat on the plane did you? They didn't make you eat that slop did they,"

"You have food here," Peter said.

"Food? You might call it that, but I'm not going to let you eat it. I'll phone next door. They have a real cook who cooks real food. Even got a menu,"

Larry sat next to Peter and tugged firmly on his ponytail. "What's this? You a hippy now,"

Peter chuckled, then tugged, a little more firmly, on Larry's beard. "What's this? You a beatnik, now?"

Larry gripped Peters' arm, Peter swung up his other arm, Larry grabbed that, and they started pulling and pushing in a tight wrestling match. Larry tipped over backward and yanked Peter over and they both crashed to the floor.

Janos leaned slightly to one side to give them room to wrestle, while Tara let out a sigh, looked closely then jumped up, pointing at Larry. "You Larry! You watch his foot,"

Larry let go of Peter, sat up, and stared at Peters' foot. "How is it these days?"

"It's okay,"

"How okay,"

" 'Okay' okay. It works,"

"Walking on it much,"

"More every day, pain is, is getting less."

"Come on," Larry lifted Peter up and helped him back to his chair, then went to the bar for beer.

Tara leaned over to Peter and asked, "Do you think he's seen Stephan,"

"Yo, Larry, ever seen a Stephan Kovacs,"

"You mean Steve Kovacs? Was in here few days back, took off with your brother,"

"Stephan and your brother are together," Tara said.

Peter yelled at Larry, "Rolly and Stephan are together?"

"You deaf as well as stupid? What did I just say?"

Tara walked over to the bar and asked Larry, "You have seen my Stephan,"

"Steve's yours?"

"He calls himself 'Steve', " Tara said.

"That's what he told me. He's with Rolly, you don't have to worry, he's okay. Matter of fact, look for yourself," Larry said.

Tara looked for herself and saw Steve, Rolly, and Rosie walk into the bar. She turned to see her Little Stephan stop, his eyes lit up and he half laughed. "Mom! What are you doing here?"

Tara stood sternly, both hands gripping her cane, which she pointed out directly in front of her. "I have come to see you," she said lifting her cane even higher to point at Steve. "You left without saying good bye. You should have come home for dinner. You should have said goodbye." She lowered her cane.

"Mom," Steve put his arms around his mother and hugged her long and hard, and then he released her and leaned over to hug his father. "Dad, Dad, how are you?"

"I am better now that I see you. Your mother is right. Why did you leave without saying goodbye?"

"Well I... I was in a hurry, the plane was leaving,"

"Bullshit you were in a hurry. The Yukon Territory has been here a long time; it would have waited for you, and...

WHAT THE HELL IS THAT ON YOUR HEAD?

Steve took off his toque, smiled and said, "It was my grandfathers',"

"I know god damn well whose it was. How'd you get it?"

"Your brother gave it to me."

Janos stuck out his hand and Steve gently put the toque in it. Janos turned it over and over in his hands, looking closely at the threads and the wool. He massaged the flag with his thumbs, handed it back to Steve, then reached into his pocket.

"Something else from your grandfather." He handed Steve his grandfathers' compass. "This took all of us to Andau. If you're going to chart your own way from here, this might help."

Steve looked stunned. He looked up from his hand to his father

"Take good care of it," Janos said. "Someday you will give it to your own son."

Rolly watched as Steve hugged his family, and then turned to meet Peters' eyes. He walked directly across the floor to Peter, who stood up slowly, still wincing slightly with the pain.

Rolly stopped two feet short of Peter, reached over and picked up Peters' beer, had a good drink, wiped his mouth with his sleeve.

"Anybody shoot Nixon?" he said.

"Nope," Peter said.

"Anybody try?"

"Nope,"

"Too bad," Rolly said.

"Ya, too bad," Peter said. "Gimme back my beer."

Rolly took another long drink then handed the bottle back to Peter, who looked at it, then turned to Rolly."You asshole. You only left the backwash."

Rolly shrugged and stared at Peters' foot. He leaned over, picked up Peters' cane, swung it up high over his head, spun away from Peter, and slammed it down hard on the bar.

It exploded into pieces that flew in all directions. The handle shot straight forward, hit a whiskey bottle, the bottle bounced backward into the mirror, then flopped forward into midair. Larry dove and caught it just before it smashed on the floor. He rolled onto his back, held the whiskey bottle high in his hands, sprang up to his feet, lifted the bottle over his head and yelled out. "The McGarret boys are back in town."

Rosie walked over to Tara and gave her a hug. "I'm Rosie, a friend of Steves'. Welcome to the Yukon,"

"It's very nice to meet you Rosie. When did he become 'Steve',"

"I guess when you gave him birth,"

"Oh, no. He's always been my 'Little Stephan',"

Rosie shrugged. "Guess maybe he changed it for you,"

Tara shook her head. "No, he changed it for himself,"

"Come on Tara, let's sit,"

Janos leaned into Steve, "You scared your mother. You scared Sheila,"

"I know."

Rosie turned to Tara, "If Peter is anything like Rolly, well let's just see what he does."

Peter looked at Larry holding the bottle over his head, his ear-to-ear grin, the scattered pieces of his cane, than glared at Rolly. "You stupid asshole, now how the hell am I supposed to get around?"

"Time for a change." Rolly walked behind the bar and came back holding a carved, yellow hardwood cane. The handle was sanded smooth, flat and oval, with finger grooves on the bottom and a thumb grip on the top.

Braided with beadwork and leather fringe just below the handle, the entire length was carved with intricate figures and inlaid designs.

The tip was hardened black with a rubber tip and copper brace.

Rolly held it out in both hands, and gave it to Peter. "I cut it and carved it my first winter up here. Sat at the lake by myself and did it. Got an Indian friend to show me some of the tricky stuff, didn't know if I'd ever get the chance to give it to you. Happy birthday, Merry Christmas, a few times over."

Peter took it, leaned on it, walked back and forth a few times. "Seems to work, you got the length right, handle feels good."

He lifted it up like a baseball bat, and in one quick move, extended his arms, spun on his good foot, turned his shoulders towards Rolly and swung the cane full speed at his head, then stopped a half inch short of his ear. "Swings okay," he said.

"Good balance," Rolly said. He reached into his pocket and handed Peter a small cloth bag. "You want these,"

Peter looked inside. "You don't,"

"Nope,"

"Okay, fine. They're mine,"

"Give 'em to your kids," Rolly said.

"You give 'em to your kids," Peter said.

"Whoever's get's 'em first."

Tara looked like she was in shock, Janos shrugged, Rosie looked like she had seen it all before, Larry grinned, and Rolly and Peter leaned into each other and held on tight.

Janos looked around nervously. He leaned over to Steve, "Where is Josef,"

Now Steve looked around nervously. "Shit! He's gone again. Don't move,"

"Move," Janos said. "Where am I going to move to?"

Steve ran out into the lobby. There, sitting in the middle of the sagging couch, was Uncle Joe. "What are you doing here?" Steve said.

"Everybody was busy. I sat here to wait,"

"Well now, Uncle Joe, it's your turn,"

Uncle Joe stayed sitting. He looked very worried, his eyes ran about the lobby looking for a place to rest, his hands were locked between his knees. "I'm scared Little Stephan,"

"Its okay, Uncle Joe, you're home now,"

"Home? You help me up,"

Steve leaned over and put his arms around his Uncle Joe and lifted him up. "I'm home now? What does that mean?"

"You're with your family. Come on, your brother is waiting for you. Ready,"

"I've been ready for... let's go,"

Steve led the way to the door, but Uncle Joe reached out and put a hand on Steves' shoulder. "I go first,"

"You do that, Uncle Joe. You do that."

Joe walked in the door and across the floor. Rolly pointed at Larry and put his finger to his lips, then whispered to Peter, who nodded and smiled. Rosie held Tara's' hand.

"You look good, Janos,"

"And you look good, Joseph,"

Janos reached out with both hands and ran them through Josef's' hair. "It's thin,"

Josef reached out with both hands and ran them through Janos' hair. "And yours is gray,"

"And I have more,"

"Yes, you do."

For a very long few seconds, they just stood and held each other as their eyes buried into each other's and the tears leaked out and ran down their cheeks. Then their elbows bent, and they pulled each other close.

Janos stammered, "We didn't know,"

Josef nodded. "I know, Little Stephan told me,"

"How much did you tell him?"

"As much as I could remember, you tell him the rest,"

Tara came over and took Janos by the arm and said, "My turn,"

Josef put his arms around Tara as she hugged him close, and Josef said, "Hello, Little Sister,"

"Hello, Big Brother."

Larry came over and pulled together three tables and three more chairs. "Okay folks, reunion is on! Bring on the beer,"

Rolly took Rosie by the hand and sat next to Peter. "Peter, this is Rosie. Mind your manners, or she'll bite you,"

Rosie glared at Rolly, then kissed Peter on the cheek. "Thanks for coming,"

"Thanks for writing,"

"Mom sends her love," Peter said to Rolly. "She wants you to phone,"

"And Dad,"

"Him too, only he don't say it,"

"I been gone a long time," said Rolly.

"You never came home, you been gone since you left for Nam. This home now? Here in the Yukon?"

"No jungle, no rice paddies, no tunnels. You can walk through the bush without having' to take a machete to it. Locals ain't shooting' at me,"

"So what's with this Ethel Lake place?"

"Built a cabin there, cut wood; go hunting, fishing's' good. You wanna come out,"

"You built a cabin?"

"Ya,"

"I wanna see it,"

"Okay."

Tara sat between Janos and Josef and held both of their hands. "Tell me of our brother," Josef said.

"He got shot in the stomach by a..." Janos started.

"AVO," said Josef.

"Yes,"

"Did he shoot him back?"

"Yes,"

"Dead,"

"Yes."

Josef thought that over. "We weren't all bad, we were conscripted, we had no choice," he shook his head. "They made me... if I didn't; they would have taken you all,"

"Yes, we know. Josef, do you remember Georgi Kopaski?"

"An engineer, yes, I remember him,"

"He's head of the Hungarian Cultural Center in Vancouver, I see him every Saturday night. We fought together at the Kilian.

He speaks three languages, he was conscripted, they forced him to be an interpreter. Many were conscripted, not all were corrupted,"

"And don't forget my Doctor," Tara added.

"Your Doctor," Josef said. "Was that Doctor Hadjok?"

"Yes, you knew him," Tara was shocked.

"He took many risks; he was a very brave man, many nights I prayed for him,"

"Hadjok is in Ottawa," Tara said. "We write letters,"

Now Josef was shocked. "But his name was on the list, I saw it there when I...he's alive, you say,"

"I have pictures of his children. Canadian children,"

"Now that is good news. Do you remember that son-of-a-bitch Viknikov,"

"How can I forget?"

"He died on the front steps of AVO headquarters,"

"How," Tara felt a long time nightmare going away.

Josef took a drink of his beer, turned to Janos, "I'm happy the son-of-a-bitch is dead. I'm only sorry I didn't pull the trigger on him,"

"Tell me," Janos said.

"My pistol jammed," Josef smiled and turned to Tara, "It must have been made in Russia,"

Tara went cold on the inside, thinking of a joke that cost her time with the AVO.

Josef put his hand on her shoulder, "It's okay, we're in Canada now, you remember that Tara, they can't hurt us here in Canada,"

"Yes, Canada, no AVO, or anybody like them. What about Viknikov?"

"My one friend in the AVO, the only man I could ever trust, got him. Same fellow took the note to Viknikov, when they had you,"

"You got to Viknikov, Josef. How,"

"Blackmail, that's how everything is done in the AVO. You let my sister-in-law free or..."

"Or what," Janos and Tara said together. "Or what?"

Josef pulled out his tobacco and started rolling a cigarette. He looked over at Steve, who knew what his rolling a cigarette meant, then winked at him. When he finished rolling, his hands went up and they started to form the words right out of the air.

"The Russians were very afraid of every Hungarian, even those of us under their direct control. There were more afraid of us than of you. We had guns. Little ones mind you, but guns never-the-less and they could still put holes in people. The problem was that no Hungarian could threaten a Russian, in any way. A Hungarian could only threaten another Hungarian. Its how they took our country apart, it's how they took our families apart. So I threatened a senior AVO with exposure for sympathies with the nationalist resistance, if he didn't let you go. He was too dumb to have sympathies with anybody or anything other than himself, but he was easy to scare. He passed the word to my friend, who delivered the word to Viknikov. Remember, the Russians didn't know I could read or write. So I put a note in their correspondence saying you were loyal, and I knew they wouldn't believe it. Then I changed your address in the files. They wanted to follow you home, spy on you, and Janos and Stephan. So when you left Viknikov through the front door, I sent the AVO out the back, chasing ghosts,"

"That was the stampede in the front hallway, when I left," Tara remembered.

"Yes," Josef turned his head to the side, away from everybody else, and blew out a lungful of blue smoke. "They had the wrong address; most of the AVO couldn't read anyways. They get lost easy. That gave you enough time to get out of the country. It was the only way out; I knew Stephan could do it,"

"But, Josef how did you get out?"

Josef pulled heavily on his cigarette, let his eyes wander to the ceiling and his hands went back to forming words.

"I had to get back to the border, but I had to find a way to get the note to you, telling you it was time to go, and where to go. I was stationed across from Andau. I told my supervisor that I didn't trust the only man I ever trusted. I told him to station him with me, so I could watch him. He did the same thing with his supervisor, and next thing you know, we are stationed together by Andau, watching each other. Like I said, they weren't a very smart bunch. It was risky, but we knew it had to be, he had family, too. So on the way, I drove and he ran the note up to your flat. I had to watch that we weren't being followed. Then we went to his flat and he got us both a change of clothes, something for when we got out of uniform. If they caught us with civilian clothes we would have been gone," Uncle Joe snapped his fingers, "just like that. So we went back to our watchtower and spent the night shooting at stars. We knew the next watchtower down the line was doing the same."

"You went out the same night as us?"

"Oh no, we had too much to do. We spent a lot of time, out of uniform, we would have been shot for that, finding the escapers and guiding them to Andau. If we were in uniform, they would have run away from us. We waited for the Russians to come back, when we could do no more, then I went over,"

"What happened to your friend?"

"Like I said, he had family, if he left with me; they would have been rounded up and... I didn't have family in Budapest; I knew you were all safe across the border, so I left,"

"When was that?" Janos said.

"Late in November, '56. That's when I wrote all the lies on the lists. They are to protect the families still in Hungary. Families of known escapers were all rounded up. We told everyone we met 'make sure the Russians don't get your name.' Families of people on the list of the dead were safe, I saw to that before I left."

Uncle Joe paused for a puff on his cigarette, blew the smoke away, then went on.

"How did that night go for you, with Stephan and," Uncle Joe pointed at Steve, "this one here?"

"Stephan carried Little Stephan on his shoulders, he held him there with both arms, to keep him out of the water," Janos went on. "The water was frozen and it opened his wound. He got us to the border, then..."

"I knew he could do it. I didn't know he would die doing it. I didn't know about his wound,"

"Here," Tara said. She reached into her pocket and brought out a small piece of paper wrapped in brown wax paper, handed it to Josef.

He took it, opened it, read it, handed it back. "Why do you keep this,"

"To remind me of you and what you did,"

Tara handed the note to Janos. He looked at it, wiped the sweat from his forehead.

Josef tucked his hands between his knees, dropped his head down and quietly sobbed.

Tara put her arms around Josef, and whispered into his ear. "My Little Stephan is alive because of you,"

"Stephan carried him," Josef said.

"We all do our part. What you did, and what Stephan did. It's family,"

Josef looked into Tara's eyes. "Family."

Janos struggled to get to his feet. He picked up his beer, held it high and waited for the others to stand. Rosie helped Tara to her feet, Rolly yanked up Peter leaning on his new cane. Steve put his hand under Uncle Joes' elbow and helped him up, too.

"To my big brother Stephan, may he rest in peace, for bringing me and my family from hell to heaven." Steve tried to drink; Janos stopped him, "Not finished. And to my little brother Josef, who did everything a brother could ask of another." Steve tried to drink again and Janos stopped him again. "And," Janos glared at Steve, "to my son, who brought us the gold. Now will you go back to university?"

THE END

Proof